WOMEN AND CHRIST

Living the Abundant Life

Talks Selected from the
1992 Women's Conference
Sponsored by
Brigham Young University
and the Relief Society

Edited by
Dawn Hall Anderson,
Susette Fletcher Green,
and Marie Cornwall

Deseret Book Company
Salt Lake City, Utah

Library of Congress Cataloging-in-Publication Data

Women and Christ: living the abundant life / edited by Dawn Hall
    Anderson, Susette Fletcher Green, Marie Cornwall.
      p. cm.
    Papers from the 1992 BYU Women's Conference.
    Includes bibliographical references and index.
    ISBN 0–87579–700–8 (HB)
    1. Women, Mormon — Religious life — Congresses. 2. Church of Jesus
Christ of Latter-day Saints — Congresses. I. Anderson, Dawn Hall.
II. Green, Susette Fletcher. III. Cornwall, Marie, 1949–. IV. BYU
Women's Conference (1992)
BX8641.W656 1993
248.8'43 — dc20   92–46566
                                                 CIP

Printed in the United States of America

10   9   8   7   6   5   4   3   2   1

Contents

SISTER SCHOLARS
AND SCRIPTORIANS

WOMEN'S LIVES,
WOMEN'S STORIES

Contents
....

Preface

This book is the sixth in the series from the annual Women's Conference, sponsored by Brigham Young University and the Relief Society of The Church of Jesus Christ of Latter-day Saints. Selections in this volume were presented in the 1992 conference.

We thank Carol Lee Hawkins, chair of the conference, and her committee of BYU faculty and Relief Society representatives, who spent many hours planning and coordinating the conference presentations.

We thank the staff of the Women's Research Institute, who helped create this volume. Tracey Wilkinson Sparks, Dawnmarie Lunnen, and Elise Bair transcribed hours of audio tape and coordinated transcripts, manuscripts, and page proofs between the authors and the editors.

We are grateful to the authors, without whose willingness to prepare their conference presentations for publication this book would not have been possible.

We are also grateful to our faithful readers, who so kindly report to us that they look forward to each volume. Royalties from these books are contributed to an endowment fund for the Women's Research Institute.

Lighten Up!

CHIEKO N. OKAZAKI

May 21: Slipped quietly out of bed so as not to disturb husband at 4:30 A.M. for an hour of reading scriptures, meditating, and writing in journal.

Went jogging before breakfast. Took time to smell the roses.

Made delicious whole wheat pancakes for the family for breakfast. My six-year-old said, 'Yucko. It looks gross!' I smiled sweetly and played a little game of 'Here comes the choo-choo' with him while I kindly and patiently explained why the Lord has ordained wheat for man.

While I was getting dressed, I polished my shoes, sewed on a button, designated two outfits for Deseret Industries, dusted my dresser top, and memorized one of the shorter chapters of the Doctrine and Covenants.

Had evil thought about a driver who cut in front of me. Immediately banished it by singing, "Know This, That Every Soul Is Free."

Do you recognize these diary entries? Do false standards of perfection haunt you even when you see through their Patti Perfect absurdity?

As a Relief Society general presidency, Elaine Jack, Aileen Clyde, and I receive letters and calls from many wonderful, faithful, righteous LDS women whose lives are burdened and blackened by inappropriate guilt. This guilt is not caused by sins for which they need to repent but by unrealistically high expectations of themselves or by someone who does not understand their life circumstances but who is nonetheless making a judgment about them that is painful. And at times women hear messages from their own sisters in the gospel and from the Church

Chieko N. Okazaki, born into a Japanese Buddhist family in Hawaii, joined the Church at age fifteen. A schoolteacher and principal for many years, she serves as first counselor in the Relief Society General Presidency. Her husband, Edward Yushio Okazaki, died a few weeks before this address was given; they are the parents of two sons.

organization that reinforce feelings of sadness and inadequacy. This hurts me. This is not the gospel. It's not what the Church is for.

If we're doing the best we can, that's good enough. I see women who are doing their absolute level best in every way—but they keep track only of their mistakes. They make lists of things they haven't done instead of the phenomenal number of things they have accomplished. No matter what mountain of achievement they've just climbed, they stumble over molehills, saying things like, "But it's not enough" or "I didn't do it well enough." So before we go any further, I want you to learn my favorite Japanese proverb. It's very short, so I know you can memorize it. It is from the ancient book of Okazaki, chapter 1, verse 1: "Lighten up!" Say it to yourself—or even out loud. "Lighten up!"

Now, "Lighten up" doesn't mean "Be irresponsible." It's a message for women who are already taking their responsibilities so seriously that they feel burdened and weighed down by them. Remember that lovely promise from the Savior in Matthew 11:28–30: "Come unto me, all ye that labour and are heavy laden, and I will give you rest. Take my yoke upon you, and learn of me; for I am meek and lowly in heart: and ye shall find rest unto your souls. For my yoke is easy, and my burden is light."

How can the burden be light? Because the yoke is a double one, designed for two. Jesus wants to be our yoke-fellow; but instead we struggle on, insisting on pulling the whole load ourselves, never realizing why it feels so lopsided. The Savior wants to share that burden, and we need to let him.

Lighten up! Let the sunshine into your lives. Don't be hard on yourself, and don't let other people be hard on you either. Give yourself credit for the good things you do. If you make a mistake, give yourself credit for trying. Laugh a lot. Catch yourself singing. Whistle or hum as you go about your duties. If you do only half of what you wanted to do, or do it only half as well as you'd like, pat yourself on half your back. But lighten up! Be light-hearted enough to float above the dark clouds and see the rainbows in your life.

The good news of the gospel is that who we are is okay. Our best is good enough. The Savior came for us—just as we are. If we were perfect, we wouldn't need a Savior. And heaven knows we do.

Guilt happens when we let things get out of control, when we get knocked off balance, and when we lose our sense of perspective. We start taking ourselves and our troubles too seriously. One of the best remedies I know is prayer. These are precious moments that help us see things from God's perspective and put everything back into focus.

I love the honesty and candor of children's faith, and one of my favorite books is *Children's Letters to God.* If you could write a letter to God, if you could ask him any question at all you had on your mind, what would it be? Here are some of my favorites:

"Dear God," writes a little girl named Martha, "I lost my glove again and I'm going to get heck unless somebody sticks up for me. Will you?"

Sherry writes: "Dear God, My father can never get a fire started. Could you make a burning bush in our yard?"

From Bert: "Dear God, O.K. I kept my half of the deal. Where's the bike?"

"Dear God," writes a young boy named Ward. "Where does everybody come from? I hope you explain it better than my father."

And this one may be my all-time favorite, from a little girl named Sylvia: "Dear God, Are boys better than girls? I know you are one but try to be fair."

And this one touches me: "Dear God, I want to be just like you when I am your age. OK? Tommy."[1]

Well, don't you suppose God loved those prayers? I certainly would have, if I were God. How do we feel about our own prayers? Are there times when we could learn a lesson from these children about being straightforward about our hopes and needs?

I have a testimony that revelation is waiting to happen, that the Lord is eager and anxious to reveal himself to us if we only have eyes to see. There's a great deal I don't understand in the book of Daniel, but one thing is really clear to me: how hard Daniel worked to understand the revelation he received and how willingly and graciously God worked to clarify his understanding. For example, Daniel prayed a very intelligent and humble prayer: "O my God, incline thine ear, and hear; open thine eyes, and behold our desolations, and the city which is called by thy name: for we do not present our supplications before thee for our righteousnesses, but for thy great mercies." (Daniel 9:18.)

Daniel reports that he continued "speaking, and praying, and confessing my sin and the sin of my people Israel, and presenting my supplication before the Lord." (V. 20.) While he was struggling thus in prayer, the Lord sent an angelic messenger to him. This messenger touched him to attract his attention. Daniel says, "And he informed me, and talked with me, and said, O Daniel, I am now come forth to give thee skill and understanding . . . for thou art greatly beloved: therefore understand the matter, and consider the vision." (Vv. 22–23.)

How would you like to have an angel touch you gently and say, "O Chieko—or O Maryanne, or O Janet—I am now come to give thee skill and understanding . . . for thou art greatly beloved: therefore understand the matter, and consider the vision."

We say that we believe that God "will yet reveal many great and important things pertaining to the kingdom of Heaven." (Articles of Faith 9.) Doesn't that article of faith make you start to ask questions? What are these great and important things? And who will he reveal them to? Could you be one of those who is struggling to "understand the matter and consider the vision"? If you are, then you're one of those who is worthy to receive an angelic visitor.

Furthermore, the promise of Joseph Smith to the Nauvoo Relief Society on 28 April 1842 was that, "angels cannot be restrained from being your associates."[2] Has this promise come true for you? Both Joseph Smith and Alma promise the ministration of angels to women. Yet such is the respect of our Heavenly Father for our agency that he will very rarely give us something for which we have not asked. What would happen, do you think, if we prayed for revelation, for knowledge, for the comfort of the ministration of angels?

But maybe there's another question rising up to loom over you. Is it a question something like this? "Oh, isn't it wrong to pray for such things, or even to think of such things? Aren't these things just for the prophets? Aren't we likely to go astray out of pride or ignorance?" Listen to the words of Moses, when Joshua heard that two men were prophesying in the camp of Israel and cried out to Moses to forbid them. Moses answered, "Would God that all the Lord's people were prophets, and that the Lord would put his spirit upon them!" (Numbers 11:29.)

Is it possible that we're asking the wrong questions and limiting the operation of the Holy Ghost, cutting off the spiritual gifts that the Father wants to bestow upon us, and feeling fear rather than faith? Here's what the Lord himself says: "For my thoughts are not your thoughts, neither are your ways my ways, saith the Lord. For as the heavens are higher than the earth, so are my ways higher than your ways, and my thoughts than your thoughts. For as the rain cometh down, and the snow from heaven, and returneth not thither, but watereth the earth, and maketh it bring forth and bud, that it may give seed to the sower, and bread to the eater: So shall my word be that goeth forth out of my mouth: it shall not return unto me void, but it shall accomplish that which I please, and it shall prosper in the thing whereto I sent it. For ye shall go out with joy, and be led forth with peace: the mountains and the hills shall break forth before you into singing, and all the trees of the field shall clap their hands." (Isaiah 55:8–12.)

Have you ever heard the hills break into song or the trees clap their hands? To me, this scripture says that the Lord has miracles prepared for us, miracles that we simply can't imagine, marvels that we will never be able to figure out if we try to think of God's thoughts as just simple variations of our own thoughts. And prayer is the channel for that communication of marvels, for ways of thought which are beyond our imagining.

When I think about what I would wish for every sister in the Church, I wish for a gift so powerful that it will sustain us into the eternities, so personal that only you can understand how completely it matches who you are and what you need, so joy-producing that you will feel like shouting hallelujah. That gift is a true knowledge of our Savior, Jesus Christ. He is the light of the world. That's what will really bring light into our lives. We need to know him. Not just concepts about him. Not just lists of things he wants us to do. Not just stories from the scriptures or from other people's testimonies, but our very own stories.

Our spirituality will increase, I believe, not necessarily as we spend more time with Jesus but as we let him spend more time with us, in our daily activities. We tend to compartmentalize our lives, or divide them up, into separate little cubbyholes labeled "family," "church," "gardening," and so on. I think we sometimes have the mistaken notion that religion is like a special room in our house. We go into this room when we need to "do" religion. After all, we cook in the kitchen, we entertain in the living room, we wash in the bathroom, we sleep in the bedroom, and we "do" religion in this spiritual room. You know what's wrong with that view of the religious life? It means that we can walk out of that room and close the door behind us. It means that we have compartmentalized our lives so that religious experience is just one cubbyhole out of many. It also means that we spend most of our time in other rooms. And we feel guilty because we keep hearing that it should be the most important room in the house and we should spend most of our time there. Does this sound just the tiniest bit familiar?

Instead, perhaps we should think of our spiritual lives, not as a separate room, but as the paint on the walls of all the rooms, or maybe a scent in the air that drifts through all the rooms – the way the fragrance of spaghetti sauce or baking bread has a way of drifting through all the rooms of the house, becoming part of the very air we breathe. Our spiritual lives should *be* our lives, not just a separate compartment in our lives.

Let me put it another way: suppose the Savior comes to visit you. You've rushed around and vacuumed the guest room, put the best sheets on the bed, even got some tulips in a vase on the dresser. Jesus looks around the room, then says, "Oh, thank you for inviting me into your home. Please tell me about your life."

You say, "I will in just a minute, but something's boiling over on the stove, and I need to let the cat out."

Jesus says, "I know a lot about cats and stoves. I'll come with you."

"Oh, no," you say. "I couldn't let you do that." And you rush out, carefully closing the door behind you.

And while you're turning down the stove, the phone rings, and then Jason comes in with a scrape on his elbow, and the visiting teacher supervisor calls for your report, and then it's suppertime, and you couldn't possibly have Jesus see that you don't even have placemats, for Pete's sake, and someone forgot to turn on the dishwasher so that you're eating off paper plates, and then you have to drive Lynne to her basketball game. So by the time you get back to the room where Jesus is still patiently waiting for you, you're so tired that you can barely keep your eyes open – let alone sit worshipfully at Jesus' feet to wait for those words of profound wisdom and spiritual power to wash over you, to make you different, to make everything else different – and you fall asleep whispering, "I'm sorry. I'll try to do better. I'm so sorry."

Well, my dear sisters, the gospel is the good news that can free us from guilt. We know that Jesus experienced the totality of mortal existence in Gethsemane. It's our faith that he experienced everything – absolutely everything. Sometimes we don't think through the implications of that belief. We talk in great generalities about the sins of all humankind, about the suffering of the entire human family. But we don't experience pain in generalities. We experience it individually. That means he knows what it felt like when your mother died of cancer – how it was for your mother, how it still is for you. He knows what it felt like to lose the student body election. He knows that moment when the brakes locked and the car started to skid. He experienced the slave ship sailing from Ghana toward Virginia. He experienced the gas chambers at Dachau. He experienced napalm in Vietnam. He knows about drug addiction and alcoholism.

Let me go further. There is nothing you have experienced *as a woman* that he does not also know and recognize. On a profound level, he understands about the hunger to hold your baby that sustains you through pregnancy. He understands both the physical pain of giving birth and the immense joy. He knows about PMS and cramps and menopause. He understands about rape and infertility and abortion. His last recorded words to his disciples were, "And, lo, I am with you alway, even unto the end of the world." (Matthew 28:20.) He understands your mother-pain when your five-year-old leaves for kindergarten, when a bully picks on your fifth-grader, when your daughter calls to say that the new baby has Down's syndrome. He knows your mother-rage when a trusted babysitter sexually abuses your two-year-old, when someone gives your thirteen-year-old drugs, when someone seduces your seventeen-year-old. He knows the pain you live with when you come home to a quiet apartment where the only children are visitors, when you hear that your former husband and his new wife were sealed in the temple last week, when your fiftieth wedding anniversary rolls around and your husband has been dead for two years. He knows all that. He's been there. He's been lower than all that.

So do you really think you're shielding him by keeping the door closed while you're throwing paper plates on the table and sending Chrissie off to wash her hands for the second time? Do you really think he doesn't know? doesn't understand? wouldn't laugh and help?

But he'll stay in that room if you put him there. Do you know why? Because if one great constant in the universe is the unfailing love of the Savior, the other great constant is his unfailing respect for human agency. He will not override your will, even for your own good. He will not compel you to accept his help. He will not force you to accept his companionship. He leaves you free to choose.

I beg you to open the door and let him out of that room. Give him your whole heart, all the pieces, and let him heal you. He promises us, "And ye shall seek me, and find me, when ye shall search for me with all your heart." (Jeremiah 29:13.) "With all [our] hearts." That means we don't have pieces of our hearts that he doesn't touch or that aren't relevant to him. That means we must live our lives as Savior-focused individuals. Jesus doesn't call you to abandon Jason's scraped elbow when you come unto him. He calls you to bandage Jason's scraped elbow as a Savior-focused mother. Let him be with you as you bandage Jason's scrape. Let him join in the conversation over those soggy paper plates. Let him carpool with you, fill out the quarterly budget with you, attend that sales seminar with you, talk over that Young Women's lesson with your daughter, try out for the wrestling team with your son, be with your mother when the doctor tells her the diagnosis.

He's not waiting for us to be perfect. Perfect people don't need a Savior. He came to save his people in their imperfections. He is the Lord of the living, and the living make mistakes. He's not embarrassed by us, angry at us, or shocked. He wants us in our brokenness, in our unhappiness, in our guilt and our grief.

You know that people who live above a certain latitude and experience very long winter nights can become depressed and even suicidal, because something in our bodies requires whole spectrum light for a certain number of hours a day. Our spiritual requirement for light is just as desperate and as deep as our physical need for light. Jesus is the light of the world. We know that this world is a dark place sometimes, but we need not walk in darkness. The people who sit in darkness have seen a great light, and the people who walk in darkness can have a bright companion. We need him, and he is ready to come to us, if we'll open the door and let him.

NOTES

1. Eric Marshall and Stuart Hample, comps., *Children's Letters to God,* enl. ed. (New York: Pocket Books, 1975).

2. Joseph Smith, *History of the Church of Jesus Christ of Latter-day Saints,* 7 vols., 2d ed. rev., edited by B. H. Roberts (Salt Lake City: Deseret Book Co., 1978), 4:605.

Love in Abundance: The Disadvantaged Children of India and Nepal

CÉCILE PELOUS

Introduction by Michael J. Call

Cécile Pelous first learned about the Latter-day Saint faith when, as a student recently graduated from high school in France, she toured America and visited several large cities, among which was Salt Lake City. There her tour group attended the play Promised Valley, *and by the end, Cécile found herself standing and singing with audience and cast, tears streaming down her face. When asked at the end of the tour which city had been the highlight of her trip, Cécile shocked her French friends by naming Salt Lake City. She told them she had felt something there unlike anything she had felt in other places they had visited.*

Three years later, two missionaries doing their daily tracting knocked on the door of her family's home in Paris. Cécile, noticing their American accent, asked if they were from Salt Lake City in Utah. When Elder Ed Borrell from Price, Utah, claimed to be from somewhere close by, Cécile consented to talk to them. (She has since learned just how far Elder Borrell was stretching the truth.) Cécile listened to the discussions, believed, and was baptized sometime later by Elder Borrell. Since joining the Church, Cécile has served in all the auxiliaries, at both ward and stake levels. She is currently a member of the Cergy-Pontoise Ward in the Paris Stake and has recently been called to serve as stake Relief Society president.

Professionally, Cécile has worked as a modelist for the best fashion houses in Paris, such as Christian Dior and Pierre Cardin, and is presently employed with Nina Ricci. Her job as a modelist is to take the dress designs created on paper by the designers and translate them into the full-sized prototypes from which the seamstresses will then produce the dress in the fabrics chosen by the designers. Her work is so valued by her employers at Nina Ricci that they are willing to give her three months' paid vacation every year to allow her to pursue her projects in India and Nepal. It is this very important part of her life, thousands of miles away from the fashion houses of Paris and the Cergy-Pontoise Ward, that she will describe to us.

I am not a heroine. My experience serving the children in India is a story of love and friendship.

A few years ago, I took stock of my blessings: I had been reared by loving parents, in a land of abundance; I was educated, had learned and was practicing a profession which I love; I was healthy, thanks to an abundance of nourishing food; and I knew the gospel. I also knew that many people in the world could only dream about such a life. I felt an intense need to share some of these same possibilities with those most deprived of them.

In July 1986, I boarded a plane for Calcutta, India, for my annual vacation. Armed with a first-aid certificate, suitcases full of medicine and my good will, I got off the plane determined to help my neighbor. I had read Dominique Lapierre's best-seller, *City of Joy*,[1] and had attended one of his lectures describing the situation in India; I knew there was plenty to do.

I worked first with Mother Theresa's missionaries and then with other groups, especially with old people, babies, and handicapped children. There was dirty laundry to boil and wash, meals to prepare and serve. In the hospitals, there were the sick to feed and to give medical care to; there were the dying to bathe and to help leave this world surrounded by warmth and tenderness; there were babies to change and feed, babies so weak I wished I could somehow give them my own strength.

During this trip, I discovered a home for about a hundred aged people, most of them bedridden. The home was run by only two Catholic missionaries, one of whom had been sick for three days. With the help of another volunteer worker, I set to work. Sister Theresina, one of the missionaries, who had single-handedly been taking care of all the needs, kissed me and said, "The Lord has sent you to us." And I believed it.

That same summer in Pilkana, a slum in the outskirts of Calcutta, I was confronted by scorching heat, flooding that lasts the entire monsoon season, and people living in extreme deprivation. I also found much hope, for the children still know how to laugh and have fun with nothing, like all children in the world. That helps their parents endure their misery. I also met a European couple, the Jallais family, who had lived in India for twenty years, helping the most disadvantaged Indians become self-reliant. I also witnessed the creation of a soup kitchen and a dispensary where medical treatment was given without charge. There, those who have little give to those who have nothing. I also came across a school where young women from ages fourteen to seventeen learn to do batik paintings on cloth, a skill that one day will help them meet the needs of their families. In that school I taught the girls to make patterns, to cut out and to sew their own clothing. These girls now make clothing for other orphan children.

Finally, I discovered the *ashrams*, orphanages run by religious organizations. Each ashram houses about one hundred children, ranging from five to twelve years old. Malnutrition and poor living conditions have claimed many of their parents; wild animals have killed others. The children arriving at the ashram are near starvation; it takes them three months to get used to the idea that there will be rice for them to eat each day. Many suffer from skin diseases, fever, intestinal disorders, and rickets. Presently, the Indian welfare system has created eight such orphanages in Bengal, one of which is the Dayal Ashram, or "House of Happiness," in Banipur.

That particular orphanage is very dear to me; it was there that I discovered the "heart" of the people of India. I felt at home there; I taught the children to play, to sing, and to laugh. They taught me to sleep on the floor, to eat with my fingers, to remove my shoes before entering houses or sacred places, and to appreciate the main thing in life – love.

The children and I bonded very quickly. They call me Cécile Didi (Big Sister Cécile). During my first trip there in 1986, when I became very ill from paratyphoid, my little friends took care of me and watched over me like true little mothers. They massaged my arms and legs to relieve the cramps caused by the sickness. They watched over me as I slept, and when I awakened, I would find little flower bracelets around my wrists.

Before my first visit to Banipur in 1986, the local welfare agency had built a chicken coop to provide one egg per week to each of the eight hundred children in the city's orphanages, a precious addition of protein to a diet consisting otherwise exclusively of rice and lentils.

Unfortunately, a disease had wiped out the chickens in August of that year.

When I returned to France, I said to myself, If I return to India, it will be to rebuild a chicken coop in Banipur. I went back to work at Nina Ricci and started to save my money. It did not take me long to realize that my money would not be enough. I prayed, and then I told my friends and the Paris Stake president of my plans. Three days later, I received a check from the stake, the result of a project named "Drop of Water," which the stake had organized several months previously to help relieve hunger in the world. The stake leaders had decided to donate the money raised to build the chicken coop in Banipur. Friends also contributed to the cause.

Because I knew absolutely nothing about running a chicken coop, I talked to chicken farmers in France to educate myself. I was so naive, I thought you had to have one rooster per hen to make things work!

Donations in hand, in September 1987, I returned to Banipur. I bought 120 laying hens and 120 chicks (which began to lay eggs five months later), thirty laying ducks, and enough grain to feed the birds for a whole year. I also bought materials to build a chicken coop (which the villagers built) and six months' worth of powdered milk for the children.

All the while I was giving this emergency food assistance, I insisted on reinforcing the goal of self-reliance for the ashrams; even the littlest child had certain duties in the running of the coop. In this way they learned to feel responsible for one another's well-being. As a matter of fact, each orphanage has only two adult leaders and three handicapped cooks to supervise the one hundred children.

Since 1987, I have been going to Bengal twice a year. During the first years, I had to quit my job each time I left, without any guarantee of getting it back again. But the Lord has blessed me: my current employers (who are not LDS) have granted me two paid vacations a year of six weeks each to allow me to pursue my projects. I am convinced that when we undertake to do our share on the first mile, as proposed by the Lord, the second mile is given to us.

I notice progress from one visit to the next. In Banipur, uncultivated land has been transformed into a vegetable garden for the orphanage. At first, the children, who had no tools, worked in the garden with wooden sticks. Now they have shovels and picks. Fish have been planted in the orphanage's little pond. Almost six hundred pounds of fish are regularly harvested each year from the pond. Each child can eat vegetables and eggs regularly and fish now and again.

Gaston Grandjean, a Catholic priest who has chosen to live among the poor of India, talked to me about another project, the dispensary in the village of Belari. The dispensary had been constructed through the efforts of Sorit Kumar Da, a local civic leader who gave up a life of ease to help the "untouchables," the lowest social caste in India, and the villagers after a road had been opened to the village in September 1986. Formerly serving three thousand patients per month, the dispensary now serves nine thousand, who are coming from farther and farther away for treatment. We have established a nursery, which cares for twenty-five babies suffering from malnutrition. Mothers receive 250 grams of powdered milk each week for their babies and a free checkup by a nurse. Young lives are being saved.

Also at Belari, villagers have constructed a school for forty-five children. Men, women, and children each brought bricks made in the rice fields and baked in the sun. I too made and donated my bricks. Contributions help pay the costs of construction, the teaching personnel, and the cooks at the school. As a result, while helping their neighbors, some villagers are also earning a salary.

A well has been sunk by the villagers and equipped with a pump purchased with money donated by the youth of a ward in the Paris Stake. A second well with potable water is now in operation. Infectious diseases have been reduced.

After the typhoon of November 1988, which caused widespread destruction, we established family chicken coops, selecting thirty-five families in Belari to learn how to run a coop. We gave each of them two hens and a rooster. At the end of six months, the families who hadn't eaten their capital immediately had more than thirty chickens each. These chickens became for them a means of exchange to buy rice, medicine, books, and clothing. It was a start towards autonomy.

At the beginning of 1988, the Paris Stake ordered one thousand batik greeting cards from the girls in the school at Pilkana. The girls benefitted from this opportunity to work for pay. The stake repeated the order in 1990. The Primary children of the Paris Stake donated toys, and the youth of the stake exchanged letters with the children of the orphanage. This interaction allowed the French young people to better appreciate their own blessings and to see that one can accomplish much with little.

In 1989, a friend of mine, Father François Laborde, contacted me, telling me that he felt inspired to ask me to help a teacher in Nepalgang, Nepal, named Parijat Gosh. Gosh was supporting fifty homeless children on his teacher's salary and wanted to establish a home for them. He hoped also to build a dispensary and eventually a small farm, which would permit him to feed them. I traveled to Nepalgang and evaluated the needs. When I returned to Paris, I tried unsuccessfully to raise the necessary money. Fortunately, some real estate investors gave me a great offer on my home. I accepted, feeling that the Lord was offering me a solution. I purchased a less expensive home, and with the money left over, I financed the construction of the home in Nepalgang, which was completed in 1991. The children now have a place to sleep, but they also need to be fed, clothed, and educated. Thus, my next project will be the dispensary and the farm. Once everything is built, the daily cost for food, health care, and schooling will be seventy-five cents per child — the cost of two doughnuts.

I know that when people have food to eat and clothes to wear, they can then become interested in the gospel. I try to follow Church welfare principles. I obey Indian law, and I work through Indian organizations. I am learning Bengali and Nepali. I hope to represent the Church in a good light. I give copies of excerpts of the Book of Mormon in Bengali to those who ask me questions about the Church. Each time I travel to India or Nepal, I ask for a priesthood blessing, which guides me during my entire stay. The Lord opens doors for me. Once, customs officials in Calcutta allowed me to bring in twice the amount of medicine usually allowed other volunteers who have been working in India for more than twenty years. Once, at the very last minute, I secured a seat on an already full plane headed for Nepal because I absolutely needed to go. Often, I am granted authorization from officials who are not known for their helpfulness. When the Lord wishes something, I need only to do my part for him to do his.

Of course, I realize that the needs are immense. Hundreds of schools, pumps, nurseries, chicken coops, dispensaries, and health instructors are needed to relieve the current level of deprivation in India and to prepare a better, more humane future. What I have seen accomplished is little and yet a lot. Hope has been reborn. My friends in Banipur and Belari now know that the vicious cycle of hunger and sickness can be overcome. They have found new courage and are beginning to take charge of their lives.

What prompts my actions? I cannot forget the look on the face of a grandmother, bringing her dehydrated and anemic granddaughter to the Belari dispensary, and pleading: "Save my grandchild." I also remember the image of groups of young Hindu children in the ashram of Banipur, saying their prayers, alone, without adults, with the utmost reverence. What spiritual treasures in these impoverished children! But for me, it is, above all, people, faces, smiles: those of the children — Milli, Ranu, Tulu, Sima, Boula, Aouti, and many others — and the adult leaders — Sukeshi, Shonda, Lucy, Minoti. This work has a soul.

The first time I went to India, I wanted to give a little of what I had to disadvantaged children. And I realize that in giving a little, it is I who have received much. I have cared for sick children, and they have cared for me. I wanted to be a mother for them, and I have found a family in them. I want to bring them the spirituality the gospel offers us, and I see them already living the gospel daily in their spontaneous way of helping one another and of being responsible for one another, in their disregard of material things, in their family relationships formed out of respect and love. When I think of the children of Banipur, I see them playing with little or nothing at all. They carefully place in their little treasure boxes the toys they receive from their French friends. They keep the candy wrappers which I give them and from which they will make flower garlands to welcome me back next time I visit. I see them proud of their harvests from the vegetable garden and the chicken coop. I see them, reverent in worshipping God.

For them, I discover in myself talents and energy that I never would have sought for myself. Without previous training but with the sincere desire to serve, I have been able to do much more than I thought possible. I see that what I accomplish is a part of the work of the Lord and that I am his instrument. He guides me and opens doors for me, sometimes in unforeseen ways.

Each of us has work to do on this earth and responsibilities for our neighbor, far or near. We cannot and must not remain indifferent. We are blessed because we have knowledge and a marvelous personal relationship with our Heavenly Father. For me, that is my greatest capital. The surest way to make it bear fruit is to place it in the service of others. This is a chain of unending love. Let's not wait for the Church to instruct us how to do good. If we forget ourselves in helping others, we will be blessed above and beyond what we can imagine. That has been true for me. We read in Mosiah 4:26: "I would that ye should impart of your substance to the poor, every man according to that which he hath, such as feeding the hungry, clothing the naked, visiting the sick and administering to their relief, both spiritually and temporally, according to their wants."

Doctrine and Covenants 35:14 says: "Their arm shall be my arm." This is one of the most sacred and most personal responsibilities I read in the scriptures. The Lord says that this arm that belongs to me is his arm. This mind, this tongue, these hands, these feet, this heart, this wallet—all these are the only tools he has to work with, at least as far as I am concerned. And I feel good, because I am where I should be, and the children know it. They love me, and I love them. Through love we learn to create together the conditions of their self-reliance. There is so much to do for them. Let us love them.

My friends in Nepal laughingly tell me: "You are a V.I.P., not for the world but for God." And I believe them. And that gives me the desire to move mountains for our Lord, Jesus Christ.

NOTE

1. Dominique Lapierre, *La Cité de la Joie* (Paris: Editions Robert Laffont, 1985); *The City of Joy*, trans. Kathryn Spink (New York: Warner Books, 1986).

The Abundant Life
Is the Teachable Life

KAREN LYNN DAVIDSON

"I am come that they might have life, and that they might have it more abundantly." (John 10:10.) This beautiful and powerful statement of our Savior is the focus of my remarks. An abundant life can be so many things, and President Harold B. Lee pointed out one of the most important: "The abundant life is the teachable life."

Being teachable is an indispensable key to an abundant life. When we use the word *abundant* in a phrase such as "abundant harvest" or "abundant resources," we think of growth, luxuriance, and fullness. Someone who is teachable is always growing, always becoming more, always inviting and fostering a truly abundant life. Being teachable is not necessarily the same as being educated. Being educated is wonderful, of course. I've spent much of my life in the academic world, giving it some of my best energies, and I truly love the world of formal schooling. For me, the start of the year has always been September, not January. Formal schooling is a goal to be pursued, even at great sacrifice.

Nonetheless, being teachable doesn't necessarily correspond to learning or formal degrees. A degree shows that a woman is diligent but not necessarily that she is teachable. It's possible, in fact, for a diploma to symbolize just the opposite. Some graduates, unfortunately, think that a diploma certifies that their learning is now finished; they now know everything they need to know. A diploma can add an extra layer of arrogance that makes someone less teachable than ever. Some students go all the way through school raising their hands and asking, "Will we be held responsible for this on a test?" By this method they

Karen Lynn Davidson has been a member of the English faculty and director of the honors program at Brigham Young University. She is the author of Our Latter-day Hymns *and* Thriving on Our Differences. *She and her husband, David A. Davidson, reside in California, where she serves as a stake Relief Society president.*

keep their education to the necessary minimum and their teachability at zero.

So being educated is not necessarily the same as being teachable. Being teachable is something very different: it is an attitude that leaves us open to new information, open not only to new ways of thinking but to new ways of feeling and valuing.

Though it's possible to be educated without being teachable, I don't think the reverse is true. Especially in our day, with resources all around us, someone who is teachable and alert will end up knowing a lot, with or without a degree. We all are acquainted with women—perhaps a grandmother, or a friend who grew up with few advantages—who in spite of minimal schooling are so alive, so perceptive, and so eager that they have become very knowledgeable.

In some editing work I've been doing recently, I've become well acquainted with Effie Marquess Carmack, a wonderful example of a teachable woman. She is the grandmother of Elder John Carmack of the First Quorum of the Seventy. Although I didn't meet Sister Carmack before she passed away, her vast, colorful, and very literate journal gives a wonderful picture of a seeking mind, alive and thoughtful every minute, ready to respond to every opportunity.

Effie Marquess Carmack was born in rural Kentucky in 1885. Opportunities for school were few, and although she would have dearly loved to pursue an education, she had to leave school after the eighth grade to care for her ailing father. No matter—she didn't need a classroom. From childhood she was in the habit of teaching herself. She and her brothers and sisters played spelling and geography games. When someone made her a present of the first roll of toilet paper she had ever seen, she used the precious little sheets to practice drawing, and she kept this roll of drawings for a long time. Every outsider who visited was a source of information. It's the old story—the opportunities to learn were so scarce that they became very precious, and ordinary situations became learning opportunities.

Effie was so accustomed to finding a way to learn and do what she wished to in any area that as an adult she went ahead to a whole list of diverse accomplishments. With her own hands she built a large room to use as an art studio and meeting room, she won second prize at the New York World's Fair in 1939 for a painting of Indian life in Mexico, she published many stories and poems in magazines, she wrote a novel, she wrote two autobiographies (one in prose and one in verse), she was such a collector of musical folklore that today some of her materials are in the archives of the Smithsonian Institution, and she was asked to make recordings for the folklore archives of Occidental College.

Effie's open, teachable spirit shines most brightly in the response of Effie and her family to the missionaries of The Church of Jesus Christ of Latter-day Saints. Now I would guess, realistically, that this family's initial willingness to listen to the missionaries was motivated as much by boredom as anything else. It's clear from her journal that for the people of this area, any outsider, Mormon missionary included, who promised an event of any kind to break the monotony of the hard work, was a welcome attraction. The townspeople craved something new to do and talk about. Effie was an eleven-year-old girl, eager and teachable, and the elders were young, handsome, and charismatic. She wrote of the experience:

"One day, when Mammy was scrubbing the kitchen floor, I was in there with her. I happened to look through the window up towards the Big Road. I saw two men in long frock-tailed coats, with derby hats on, each carrying a small grip.

"Mammy said, 'Mercy, I'll bet that's them Mormon preachers, hand me my clean apron right quick.' She pulled her dirty apron off, dried her hands on it, and by the time she had the clean one tied on they were knocking. They walked fast.

"They wanted to see the husband, they said, as they were told that he was a school trustee, and they wanted permission to preach in the schoolhouse. Mammy told them where he was, they got his permission, and then invited us to come to services that night.

"Our dad hitched the mules to the wagon and we all went. That night marked the beginning of a new life for us. No more groping around in the dark in search of truth. No more trying to fit manmade doctrines with the teachings of the Savior.

"The school house was small, and of course was poorly lighted. All the lights to be had at that time, in the country, were coal oil lamps, but as I remember the songs, the prayer, the sermon, our conversation after the meeting, and the buying of a little red-backed book, *The Voice of Warning,* it seems to me that we all walked in a halo of beautiful light.

"They sang 'Oh Ye Mountains High,' also 'Praise to the Man Who Communed With Jehovah,' and 'Truth Reflects Upon Our Senses.'

"The senior elder was Alvin Ipsen, a little Danishman from Bear

River City, Box Elder County, Utah. He had a mop of yellow curly hair, was a grand singer, with a wonderful personality, and a power of persuasion that was almost irresistible. I think that the secret of his power for good was in his humility, which gave him an extra portion of the spirit of the Lord, and his intense love and understanding of all kinds of human beings. His companion was a local missionary, Wister G. Wallace, from Center, Metcalf County, Kentucky; a handsome dark-haired young fellow who fitted in perfectly with his companion.

"The first night we went to hear them Elder Ipsen preached on the scattering of Israel. A rather deep subject for a child of eleven to understand, especially when I had never even *heard* of the scattering of Israel.

"I had no idea what my parents or brothers and sisters were thinking of it, but I was so thrilled that I could hardly contain my feelings. I was sitting about halfway back, with a group of my schoolmates, who kept trying to whisper to me, but I had no time for foolishness that night. Something great and wonderful had come, something we had dreamed of and waited for for years. I'm sure it was the spirit of it, and not the letter, that whispered to my spirit, and filled me with such joy.

"As soon as the meeting was dismissed I hurried up to the front to see my mother and father, and to see what they had thought of it. They were complimenting the young missionaries, and inviting them to go home with us. Others were crowding up, wanting tracts and books to read. *Many* people invited them to go and spend the night with them. It just seemed perfectly natural that they should go home with *us*.

"I can't remember just what month it was, but it was cold enough that we had a fire in the fireplace, for I remember distinctly that long conversation after we reached home. The eager questions; the logical answers. The growing wonder that they were teaching *exactly* what we had always believed, and the complete agreement between their teachings and those of the Savior in the New Testament.

"About one o'clock my mother suddenly remembered that I should have been in bed hours before, but I could not be shaken till the conversation was ended. I was afraid that I might miss something.

"The hours at home were spent in hunting out the passages of scripture they quoted in their sermons. I went upstairs and lay flat on my stomach by the long low window and searched through the little old dog-eared Bible. They were hard to find, and I soon learned to listen when they told where the passages were to be found.

"The first time our father went to town he bought a new Bible, and I remember with what pride I stacked our newly acquired bunch of religious books. The new Bible, a copy of the Book of Mormon, *The Voice of Warning*, several tracts, and the little song books. Not a very expensive set of books, but wonderfully precious to us.

"One evening as we sat around the fire, one of the missionaries spied the end of Pappy's violin case sticking out from under the old walnut dresser, and asked who played it. Soon they were tuning the fiddle and guitar together for the first time in a long while, and again the music came streaming from the old violin in sweet harmony. The missionaries were charmed, and kept their feet going in time with the music.

" 'So you folks are not opposed to violin music?' my father asked, at the end of a lively tune, at which they plainly showed their pleasure.

" 'No indeed. Music, and dancing also, has given me lots of happy hours in my short life,' Elder Ipsen declared.

"*There* was another very important thing we agreed on. The preachers of the different denominations around us were bitterly opposed to both violin music and dancing. They often told their congregations that the devil was in the fiddle, though they had never succeeded in making us believe it.

"Well, this newfound religion had measured up to our every idea so far, and tonight's discovery was another step in favor of it. A happy people, with a happy religion."[1]

Effie was ready to be taught, ready to grow in a whole new direction.

The responsibility for self-education is not just part of our pioneer past. When I moved to La Canada Second Ward in California about ten years ago, I met a young wife and mother named Christie Frandsen. She was lovely and talented—a wonderful contralto and flute player—and the word that describes Christie most completely is "refined." She has every refinement, a wonderful background in literature as well as music. She's an excellent writer and has published in the *Ensign*. I assumed that she had grown up in a fairly large city, surrounded not only by educational opportunities but by every courtesy and social grace.

Then I got to know something about her background. Until she graduated from high school, Christie lived in just one kind of community—an Indian reservation. She says about her circumstances:

"Until the time I left for BYU, I spent my entire life on Indian reservations where my father worked as a range conservationist with six different tribes in Montana, North Dakota, Nevada, and Arizona. The eight children in my family were among only two or three non-Indians in our school classes. It was a 'bare-bones' education to say the least! My teachers had all they could handle teaching the Indian children the fundamentals of English and other basics. There were no enriched or accelerated classes of any kind for us. Extracurricular opportunities were also very limited — no gymnastics, ballet, violin or flute lessons, not even Girl Scouts.

"But I never felt deprived. My remarkable mother was determined that her children would not feel disadvantaged because of our circumstances. Instead of bemoaning what wasn't available, she made sure we took full advantage of what was. She took us regularly to the nearest library or bookmobile, then supplemented their meager offerings with memberships in mail-order book clubs. We lived in government housing and never owned any furniture, except our cherished piano, which we carefully packed and moved wherever we went. Money was never plentiful, but Mama and Daddy set aside enough for piano lessons for all of us, and then searched until they found a teacher. Several of us attended summer music camps at BYU and other university campuses. And we had plentiful opportunities to develop our musical abilities in the small branches of the Church that we attended. As a ten-year-old I served as branch chorister!

"Another thing my parents did was to show us the world beyond the reservation. We couldn't afford deluxe travel arrangements, but that didn't stop my father. He took us camping across America and into Canada and Mexico during our summer vacations. It's not easy taking eight children camping (now I know!), but Mama and Daddy realized how important it was to expand our cultural horizons. Through the windows of our well-traveled VW bus, we saw New York City, Chicago, Washington, D.C., and Vancouver, learning more than was ever possible in even the most advanced classrooms.

"It wasn't until I reached BYU that I realized just how unique my childhood experiences were, and appreciated how blessed I was. My only regret in growing up on Indian reservations is that I didn't learn more of the Indian culture. We were so busy trying to teach them our ways, we didn't take the time to let them teach us theirs.

"I have come to understand that much of my self-esteem and confidence comes from the chance I had to teach and serve at such an early age. The message I was given at home, school, and church was, 'You are so smart and so talented, you can help all these other children around you.' By the time I realized that I am no smarter or talented than most, and less so than many, my self-image was too ingrained to change! And now as I raise my own nine children in metropolitan Los Angeles, ironically I find myself working very hard to find the opportunities for them that I had on the reservation!'"

Christie noted that in the first grade, she was the only non-Indian student in the class. The teacher, who was working hard to teach the other students English, gave Christie a stack of books to read on her own. She says, "That taught me a love of reading, and besides that, the teacher was so grateful that I wasn't causing any trouble that I got all kinds of positive reinforcement for what a good reader and a good student I was. It was the best thing that could have happened for me." Christie is so teachable and so positive that she thinks of her background as more than just okay—it was actually an advantage!

Today Christie and her brothers and sisters are accomplished and well rounded, full of skills and talents that they share with others. Christie and her family remind us that truly teachable people will find a way to learn and grow under virtually any circumstances.

For a teachable person, the surrounding opportunities, or lack of them, need not be an insurmountable difficulty. A much more serious barrier to teachability is likely to come from within. Pride can stop up our ears and stand in the way of change and growth. A constant theme of the Book of Mormon is that a godly people is a teachable people and a wicked people is a proud people. Nations fall because of pride, stiff-neckedness, and unwillingness to hear. Alma admonishes the unbelieving Zeezrom with the reminder, "He that will harden his heart, the same receiveth the lesser portion of the word; and he that will not harden his heart, to him is given the greater portion of the word." (Alma 12:10.) In his great sermon on faith, how does Alma tell us we can prepare ourselves so that the seed of faith may grow? "If ye will awake and arouse your faculties; . . . if ye give place, that a seed may be planted in your heart"—that's the beginning. (Alma 32:27–28.) The beginning is in the attitude we adopt, not the knowledge we garner. Just give a place in your heart.

The opposite of teachability is probably pride, yet as Church members we tend not to worry enough about the sin of pride. I well remember when I taught classes in medieval literature at Brigham Young University. I would discuss the Seven Deadly Sins so important in medieval Christianity, and I would comment that it was interesting to me that pride, which in Catholic doctrine is the greatest sin of all, was something Latter-day Saints usually mentioned only in passing.

But on the morning of April 1, 1989, President Ezra Taft Benson chose "Beware of Pride" as his general conference topic. I listened with intense interest as he warned us of "the severe consequences of the sin of pride to individuals, groups, cities, and nations." He declared, "This message has been weighing heavily on my soul for some time. I know the Lord wants this message delivered now."[2]

Perhaps the greatest test of teachability is how we handle a major change in our lives. What if we are happy in our lives and our routines, and suddenly it becomes our challenge to find pleasure and meaning in a whole new set of circumstances, to relate to our Father in Heaven through a different kind of activity and service? If life calls us to a new path, or our Father in Heaven calls us to a new path, are we open enough to say, "All right, others have lived such a life and been happy. I can too. For this season of my life, or perhaps for the rest of my life, a different set of priorities will absorb my thinking."

Changes may come about for many reasons. A woman who has found great self-esteem from a paycheck may find that the birth of a child calls upon her to find satisfaction in a different kind of payday. A family's finances may take a turn for the worse and require a complete reorientation in thinking and life-style on the part of all family members. A woman may lose a family member and be required to make a new life without that person, or a geographical uprooting may change a life completely. Illness or old age may bring inevitable and unwelcome changes.

Three years ago I was cast into a different world. This wasn't one of those major changes affecting every aspect of one's life, but it was quite a change, nonetheless. I took a teaching job at a very Catholic girls' high school, a high school owned and run by an order of nuns, the Sisters of the Holy Child Jesus. I had taught at BYU, so church-related education was not new to me, but this time it was not my church.

At Mayfield Senior School of the Holy Child Jesus, I've learned to use *reverence* as a verb and *faith* as an adjective, as in "We must reverence the faith life of others." And I've tried to reverence the faith life of others. I've tried to be open and teachable in this opportunity. I am still who I am — my beliefs and my identity grow from deep Latter-day Saint roots — but at the same time I find much to learn and appreciate among the Catholics. The motto of this particular order of nuns is "Actions, Not Words." So far so good!

I already respected the Catholic Church as the preserver of Western culture through the Middle Ages, and now I've come to admire the dedication of so many Catholics to service and to social issues.

I was especially impressed by the life of the woman who founded this order of nuns, called the Order of the Holy Child Jesus. Cornelia Connelly represents one of the most amazing examples I know of someone who made the best of things — the very best of things — when life handed her a turn of events she couldn't possibly have prepared for. She was born in 1809 into Philadelphia society, and it was assumed that the beautiful and accomplished Cornelia would make a brilliant match. She had attended both the Presbyterian and the Episcopalian churches. Then as a young woman she met and married an ambitious Episcopalian clergyman named Pierce Connelly. They had a reputation as one of the happiest couples anyone knew, and she willingly went with him when his ministry took him to Mississippi.

Then Cornelia's husband began an intense study of Catholicism, and, after much introspection, he decided to become a Catholic. Cornelia followed him in this step and was also received into the Catholic faith. Pierce continued his work as an educator, though, of course, he was no longer a clergyman of the Episcopalian faith.

When Cornelia was pregnant with their fifth child, her husband dropped the bombshell: he had been discussing with the Catholic authorities his desire to be accepted into the Catholic priesthood. The Catholic priesthood is, of course, an unmarried priesthood. At that time, such a decision on the part of a married man meant asking for a special dispensation from the pope, and it meant that the man and his wife must mutually agree to a life of permanent separation and celibacy.

After much agony and prayer, Cornelia agreed to go along with her husband's decision, and the family traveled to Rome to make arrangements. She summoned up all her faith and all her willpower and decided that if God required her to give up the husband she loved for the sake of his own divine purposes, she would do so.

Cornelia was never to return to the United States to live, for it did not take her long to decide that she, too, was called to the Catholic religious life. She wished to enter holy orders. She made special arrangements to keep her youngest children near her side, and thus we have the unusual picture of a nun caring for her own little children.

The pope asked her to establish a new religious order with the special mission of Catholic girls' education in England. To this work she devoted her whole heart and soul, and soon many young women were joining her order and eagerly learning her very advanced teaching methods and views on women's education.

This by itself would make quite a story, but another amazing set of happenings was still to occur. To phrase it in the briefest way possible, Pierce changed his mind. Several years after his ordination, he renounced his vows and became rabidly anti-Catholic. He began to spread vicious rumors about Catholics, and he decided, furthermore, that he would just like to pick up family life where he left off. The only picture harder to imagine than a Catholic sister caring for her own babies is the picture of a Catholic sister being sued by her husband in court for the restitution of his conjugal rights. Yet that is exactly what happened. The trial in the English court dragged on for two and a half years. The verdict at first went to Pierce Connelly but was overturned on appeal.

Cornelia was originally at the mercy of her husband's decision to become a Catholic priest. But instead of just living the life she was handed by default, she created a new life. Today the Order of the Holy Child Jesus continues its work of education, missionary work, and work with the poor all around the globe.

I tell this story because Cornelia Connelly is an irresistible example of someone so teachable that she could explore new ideals and take risks and make sacrifices on behalf of those new ideals. She accepted a changed life, found beauty and meaning in those altered circumstances, and went forth with courage and energy. I should mention, too, that in the spring of 1992, Pope John Paul II declared her to be The Venerable Cornelia Connelly. That is an important step toward canonization as a saint, and the order hopes that one day it will be able to refer to its foundress as Saint Cornelia.[3]

Who in our Church would I compare with Cornelia Connelly in her ability to be totally teachable, to have such openness, such a seeking, pioneering spirit? The answer is easy. I would compare her with missionaries, especially those missionaries who accept assignments that put them in worlds where the old pleasures are not available and most of the time the old answers do not work. I think of my friends Jan and Vern Hill, who have just been called to Czechoslovakia; Marshall and Ruth Craig, who have been English teachers in mainland China in an area that someone described as "a primitive mud village of four million people"; Joyce and Joe Grigg, who have just been called to open the missionary work in New Guinea. New Guinea! That's National Geographic country. I try to picture Joyce and Joe Grigg in New Guinea; all I can picture is Margaret Mead.

What distinguishes all these couples? Why are they able to be successful in these assignments? They have a sense of adventure, a sense of questing, a sense of seeking. They do not think they have all the answers. They are not smug. Even at retirement age, they don't begin to think they have already learned and done everything in the world that is worthwhile. That attitude is completely foreign to them. Of course, they miss their grandchildren, their friends, their lovely homes; now the meaning of their lives must rest on other things. They are so teachable they can change the way they look at and appreciate the world.

It's hard not to be smug when we have the fullness of restored truth. Why should we be teachable if we have it all?

Once I met an attorney, a man not a member of our church, who was pursuing a second graduate program with plans to become an ordained Protestant minister. Without thinking how foolish I sounded, I blurted out, "But what are you going to do with a degree in law *and* a degree in divinity?" Without a second's hesitation he replied simply, "God never wastes education."

And I think that's the key. We should never be so proud, so smug, that we think we have learned enough. God never wastes education. When we are teachable, we are always learning—from books, from experiences, from observation. This education is never wasted on us individually; we become more appreciative, more alive. And as we can do more and share more, this education blesses others, in every interaction, every day of our lives.

NOTES

1. Effie Marquess Carmack, *Down Memory Lane: The Autobiography of Effie Marquess Carmack* (Atascadero, Calif.: Atascadero News Press, 1973), pp. 77–79; slightly edited.

2. Ezra Taft Benson, "Beware of Pride," *Ensign*, May 1989, pp. 5, 4.

3. For further information, see Mary Andrew Armour, *Cornelia* (Pompano Beach, Fla.: Exposition Press, 1984); and Radegunde Flaxman, *A Woman Styled Bold: The Life of Cornelia Connelly, 1809–1879* (London: Darton, Longman and Todd, 1991).

There's a Horse in the House

MAREN M. MOURITSEN

Those of you who read biographical notes in printed programs may be thinking, "Oh, another Ph.D., another single woman, another professional devoted to the world of work." All of that is true. By way of reconciliation, however, I simply take a line from Moroni: "Condemn me not because of mine imperfection." (Mormon 9:31.) Life brings challenges as well as opportunities. I have simply tried to do my best with both. As Mame Dennis of *Auntie Mame* fame said, "Life is a banquet, and most poor suckers are starving to death." Life *is* a banquet, and it has been wonderful to me. Yet, somehow I want you to know that in many respects life has not been easy for me. I never planned not to have a husband and not to be married. I always planned on having a family. Those blessings never came for me. I really never planned to get a doctorate. That blessing I worked for. All of these things came as my life unfolded, and each and every one of these developments has brought challenge and opportunity and abundance to my life.

A line from Martin Luther applies here: "The kingdom of God is like a besieged city surrounded on all sides. . . . Each man has his place on the wall to defend and no one can stand where another stands, but nothing prevents us from calling encouragement to one another."[1] It is in that spirit that I'd like to share some thoughts about the abundant life.

Recently, a friend showed me a copy of the *San Francisco Chronicle* published during the recent riots in Los Angeles. What struck me about this particular newspaper was not the main headline about the riots but a headline just above it, which read, "Study Finds No Return to Traditional Values." I thought to myself, how ironic and how connected these

Maren M. Mouritsen serves as dean of student life and as assistant executive vice president at Brigham Young University. She has been a missionary in Japan and a member of the Young Women General Board.

two headlines are. The Savior's words "I am come that they might have life . . . more abundantly" (John 10:10) help bring clearly into focus the issues of avarice versus abundance.

For a moment, I would like to talk about context. We often slice the scriptures so thin that we but thinly know them. We find a line here or a word there that touches our heart, or our mind, or our circumstance. But the context is often everything. We cannot truly understand this scripture about abundance until we put it in its full context. Just before those words, the Savior had been at the marriage at Cana. He had been with Nicodemus. He had been with the adulterers and had healed the nobleman's son. He had been with the woman of Samaria at the well. He had walked on the waters and spoken of coming to do his Father's will. He had all of these experiences and more, and then come his words in John 10:10 about abundance. Soon after this verse, the Savior raises Lazarus from the dead. I don't think the sequence of those experiences or verses is accidental. Verses 10 and 11 read: "The thief cometh not, but for to steal, and to kill, and to destroy: I am come, that they might have life, and that they might have it more abundantly. I am the good shepherd: the good shepherd giveth his life for the sheep."

Just recently, I read in *Time* magazine about a woman who was suing her veterinarian for more than a million dollars for malpractice because of the bereavement she experienced over the death of her pet iguana. As one of my students says, "That's just about half a bubble off level." In builder's parlance, when the bubble in the window of the spirit level is not lined up exactly, things are not square. If you are constructing a building, that means the walls could end up on the ceiling!

Avarice and abundance. These are the bookends that provide John 10:10 a context — greed, stealing, killing, and destroying are contrasted with the Shepherd's life, which gives the abundance of eternity to each of us. Given that context, let me challenge you to think differently with me about abundance.

I grew up on a ranch in Arizona with my family — Mom, Dad, Grandmother, my older sister, the hired hands, and animals galore. We had sacrificed often in our household for a good animal. But our newest purchase was very special. We had been looking for the right mare, and we had found her. She was about fifteen hands high at the withers, strong in the flank, well appointed, and came from a line of strong quarter horse stock. I will never forget the day we brought her home. Over the ensuing months we loved her, cared for her, and prepared her to bear a foal. We figured the foal would be a good one because she had borne two before, and they were exceptional. We were all excited. I was particularly excited because this new pony was to be my pony. We'd had a lot of other ponies. I had cared for them, and groomed them, and dressed them, but this pony was to be mine. Mine to care for, mine to love, mine to raise.

One afternoon we were in the main corral when suddenly the jarring snap of a support cable sent a nearby holding gate smashing to the ground. Like an electrically charged eel, the cable sliced uncontrolled through the air, striking the mare in the face. Though unforeseen and tragic, the accident was not as bad as it might have been: the pregnant mare survived, only losing the sight in her right eye. It was unlikely that we could use her for work again, but she could certainly produce a fine foal.

Time passed, and we began to make the necessary preparations for the birth of my pony. I cleaned and scrubbed the stall and filled it with fresh, sweet straw. We brought in a couple of large sterile buckets, lots of white towels, salves, and the instruments that we might need. My dad was good at this. He'd done it before.

I went every day to check the mare and sometimes more than once, reluctant even to go to school. Dad promised that if anything happened, he'd come and get me, and my father always kept his promises. The day the word came, I hurried home. Toward late evening the turmoil and promise of new life began. It was a struggle. I brought boiled water and stood by as my dad gently worked with the mare. In one brilliant instant with a heave of that great equine body, out came a head — it was the most beautiful thing I'd ever seen — then a leg, and a back, and a rump, and a tail. I knelt beside my father and watched in amazement. My pony was there, wet and warm and wonderful.

Almost immediately the mare began to lick and to clean her foal. (Nature is wonderful. As soon as a child arrives, it finds a mother ready to care for it.) As this mother cared for my little one, I watched every movement. I had watched this ritual before, but this was my pony. I remember my Dad saying, "Fine animal, fine pony!" Assuming that all was well, he left for a moment, to do what, I can't remember. I looked at my pony and thought, "Fine animal, fine pony!" Then, suddenly and without warning, that large body heaved to her blind side onto that tiny, tiny new thing, and onto me. My leg was caught under the back of her hind quarter. I could not move. I could see the pony struggling with everything it had to free itself, and I could see it wasn't going to be possible. I was frantic. The pony was such a tiny thing. I managed to free my leg and braced myself against the stall wall. With one foot and both my hands, I pushed and pushed and pushed as hard as I could. I pounded on the mare's flank, but it was no use. I was just too small, and the little colt was even tinier.

Soon my father returned, and when he saw what had happened, he ran to us and began to push and pull in an effort to maneuver the mare. Finally, she freed herself and rolled onto her left side. Exhausted, I took a deep breath, but there in the new straw lay a little withered body, almost as withered as my heart. Stumbling toward the colt, I remember taking it into my arms. Still moist from birth, it was limp and lifeless. For how long I am not sure, but I rocked and rocked and rocked. Back and forth, back and forth. But there just wasn't any movement, any life. I continued to rock anyway. Soon my father, with his arm around my shoulder, said, "It's over, sweetheart. It's over. I'll care for the mare. I'll give you a few more minutes. We'll have another foal."

I was used to the ebb and flow of life on the ranch, but I don't remember a time when I've ever been sadder. This was to have been my pony. As I held that little thing in my arms, those childhood promises were echoing in my mind: "If you have faith, anything can happen. If you just ask, you can receive." I probably didn't do it consciously, but with the simple faith that only a child can have, I thought, "It's time to try. I've got to try." With every ounce of my being, I prayed that it wasn't so. It just couldn't be so. Then suddenly those little eyes, with the longest eyelashes I had ever seen, fluttered and opened. There was tension in the body, there was warmth. The next thing I knew the pony was standing. When my father came back, he was amazed. I was amazed. My pony was standing, my pony was alive, and he was mine.

That night, when my father asked if I'd like to sleep in the barn, you know what the answer was. (I slept in the barn a lot because we often had visitors in our home. You see, my dad picked up more stray people than he did animals. It was a welcome thing, because if there was somebody in my bed, I could be in the barn with my pony.) That night, I slept in a little tiny nook by the mare and my pony. As my father lifted me into the manger, he whispered in my ear, "When you are good, and you have done all you can do, and you have faith, and you ask for help, then miracles can happen." This had been, for me, a miracle.

How do we seek miracles? How do we find the abundant life as opposed to the avaricious life? Miracles are hints of the abundance of eternity. Possessions are mere substitutes, which never fill our real needs. So where do we begin? In the Book of Mormon, I find a verse that offers insight: "And because of the redemption of man, which came by Jesus Christ, they are brought back into the presence of the Lord; yea, this is wherein all men are redeemed because the death of Christ bringeth to pass the resurrection, which bringeth to pass a redemption from an endless sleep, from which sleep all men shall be awakened by the power of God." (Mormon 9:13.)

That is the abundant life. It isn't related to things; it isn't related to possessions; it is related to a promise.

In sometimes overwhelming circumstances, you may lose your health, your home, your family, or your business — even your pony. But the promise of the abundant life is that every single thing will be restored. It is a very personal promise of hope. It is a plea from the Lord that you not be overwhelmed. It might have been that very promise which kept Moroni from despair — the promise that someday, somewhere, everything would be restored. That is the abundant life.

Several months after my pony was born, I came home from school one day to be greeted by my mother, who was waiting for me on the porch, looking very concerned. She said, "Maren, there's a horse in the house." "There is?" I replied to what I thought was wonderful news, although I dared not seem overjoyed. She said again, gently but firmly, as only she could, "Maren Mathilda, there is a horse in your bedroom!" It happened that my bedroom had French doors and was located just off the main yard. My pony, Tepee, had butted through those French doors and, sure enough, there he was, right in the middle of my bed.

Now, my mother had put up with a lot, but you have to admit this would strain any child-parent relationship, no matter how good. My dad was in the background, and I could see him turning around to flee this situation. My grandmother, the most influential person in my life, was smiling. Now, every child needs a grandmother who thinks the child can do no wrong, but Mother was right. Now that I have my own home and watch my nieces and nephews pass through, leaving little handprints all over newly painted walls, I have come to appreciate her position.

My message is quite simple and not very profound. It is this: There will always be a horse in the house. Expect the unexpected. Whenever life is darker than I would like it to be, I recall that little piece of family wisdom: "There will always be a horse in the house." You can see that horse as either a challenge or an opportunity. Pain is inevitable, but we may choose whether or not to be miserable. The choice is ours.

The real abundance is within us. And when you are good, and you have done all you can do, and you have faith, and you ask for help, then miracles can happen. Because, you see, we're not talking about salvation. That is a given. We're talking about exaltation. It's one thing to call upon the throne, but quite another thing to approach the throne.

"Wherefore, whoso believeth in God might with surety hope for a better world" — Los Angeles or Phoenix; Nagoya or Nairobi — "yea, even a place at the right hand of God" — we are talking about standing on God's right hand; we are talking about approaching the throne — "which hope cometh of faith, maketh an anchor to the souls of men" — in a rudderless world, if there's anything we need, it is an anchor — "which would make them sure and steadfast, always abounding in good works, being led to glorify God." (Ether 12:4.) When we choose to glorify God, we choose the abundant life. That is what is meant by breaking the bands of death: every single thing will be redeemed and restored — every hope, every wish, every dream.

That night, that miracle night when my pony was restored, I listened from my loft as my father returned to the house. My father often hummed or whistled and tonight he whistled, "Have I Done Any Good in the World Today?" That hymn says more than I possibly could about who we have to be, about what we have to do, and about how we can obtain the abundant life. Most of us will never do great things. But we can do small things in a great way. And I promise, if you are good, and you do all you can do, and you have faith, and you ask for help, then miracles can happen. They've happened for me.

NOTE

1. Lewis W. Spitz, *The Renaissance and Reformation Movements* (Chicago: Rand McNally and Co., 1971), p. 335.

Honoring Our God-given Gifts

MARGARET J. WHEATLEY

Two years ago I began reading the scriptures with a specific intent: to see if I could understand better who God is. In his sermon at the funeral of a friend, Joseph Smith told the Saints that it was essential "to comprehend the character of God" in order to comprehend ourselves and our relation to Him. He invited the congregation to "answer the question in their own hearts what kind of being God is?"[1] I invite you also to consider this question as you read the following scriptures. Who is this Creator? Who is the great intelligence who speaks these words?

"I, the Lord, stretched out the heavens and built the earth, my very handiwork; and all things therein are mine. And it is my purpose to provide for my saints for all things are mine. . . . For the earth is full, and there is enough and to spare, and I have prepared all things, and have given unto the children of men to be agents unto themselves." (D&C 104:14–16.)

From Doctrine and Covenants 59:16–20: "The fulness of the earth is yours, the beasts of the field and the fowls of the air, and that which climbeth upon the trees and walketh upon the earth; Yea, and the herb and the good things which come of the earth, whether for food or for raiment, or for houses, or for barns, or for orchards, or for gardens or for vineyards; Yea, all things which come of the earth, in the season thereof, are made for the benefit and the use of man, both to please the eye and to gladden the heart; . . . to strengthen the body and to enliven the soul. And it pleaseth God that he hath given all these things unto man."

Margaret J. Wheatley, an associate professor of management at Brigham Young University, has been a management consultant to several Fortune 500 clients and educational, nonprofit, and health care organizations. She and her husband, Nello-John Pesci, have a combined family of seven children.

If you reread the first book of Genesis, what you can discover in those familiar words is a revelation about God as a wonderful, creative, artistic, loving presence. But we need not look only to scriptures for an awareness of who God is. We know God by looking at his creation. He went to considerable effort to make things incredibly beautiful and varied, detailed and diversified. I assume that he didn't have to do that. I think God could have mass-produced nature. Or he could have thought four types of flowers sufficient. Instead, the world confronts us with breathtaking variety, beauty upon beauty, joy upon joy. And the same principle of variety is true of each of us. We are each unique and different—not to make life difficult, but to make life joyful.

Two further insights into the character of God are to be found in Nephi's writings. The first is "men are, that they might have joy." (2 Nephi 2:25.) Some Latter-day Saints believe that "might have" is conditional: we might have joy if we meet certain requirements. I believe, however, that the statement is not conditional but a present tense description of why we're here. We are here to experience joy. The scripture lends itself to being interpreted either way. But I want to focus on the second meaning: we're here to experience joy—not in a future life, but here and now.

This past Sunday I found the second passage from Nephi on my kitchen counter in pieces, a take-home puzzle project from Primary. My eleven-year-old was supposed to put it back together. I began to play with it, to see if I could do it. The wonderful message that emerged was that the Lord giveth no commandment save he prepare a way for it to be accomplished. (1 Nephi 3:7.) Although I love this scriptural promise, I have one concern about it. God relates to us in many different ways. He is life-giver, spiritual parent, creator, law-giver, to mention only a few. Out of all these roles, I worry that we are too good at accepting God primarily as the order-giver. Most of us believe that God has the right to command us to do very difficult things, things that, as the scripture says, he will prepare a way for us to do. We speak frequently about the refiner's fire, about growing through trials, tribulations, and sufferings. We even say how we are blessed by our sufferings, and a few people courageously pray that their sufferings may be increased. I've never understood this train of thought myself; but it is true that when we suffer, we very often draw closer to the Lord. One path to the Lord is through trials and tribulations. But I think we dwell too much and too exclusively on that path to God. There are other ways God will participate in our lives if we invite him. I believe we spend far too much time appreciating the difficulties by which God tests us and not nearly enough time celebrating how easy life can be in the hands of this loving, creative, and artistic being who is our Father in Heaven.

Richard Bach, author of *Illusions: The Adventures of a Reluctant Messiah,* tells a parable of a master to whom the masses gathered seeking instruction and healing from their woes. "And he said unto them, 'If a man told God that he wanted most of all to help the suffering world, no matter the price to himself, and God answered and told him what he must do, should the man do as he is told?'

" 'Of course, Master!' cried the many. 'It should be pleasure for him to suffer the tortures of hell itself, should God ask it!'

" 'No matter what those tortures, nor how difficult the task?'

" 'Honor to be hanged, glory to be nailed to a tree and burned, if it so be that God has asked,' said they.

" 'And what would you do,' the Master said unto the multitude, 'if God spoke directly to your face and said, "I COMMAND THAT YOU BE HAPPY IN THE WORLD, AS LONG AS YOU LIVE." What would you do then?'

"And the multitude was silent, not a voice, not a sound was heard upon the hillsides, across the valleys where they stood.

"And the Master said unto the silence, 'In the path of our happiness shall we find the learning for which we have chosen this lifetime.' "[2]

I don't know whether they were unwilling, or just by long social conditioning unable, to be joyful. I find that I have been stunted in my capacity to be joyful, primarily from misunderstanding what God wants of us. We don't comprehend that we are here to experience joy. Our real purpose is to understand that not only is life joyful but also in fact God designed it to be easy, although I am not discounting the role of suffering. Clearly, we all will continue to have trials. But I think we persistently overlook the other side of this equation, which is that we might just have joy while we're here. Why not let our lives celebrate God?

It's very difficult to trust that life can be easy, however, unless we have a very clear sense of God as generous and loving. If we think he is a God of judgment, then we clearly cannot relax into life and look for the joy. If we think God stages true/false or multiple-choice tests throughout life, then that's going to interfere with our ability to dwell within life's joyfulness. If we think God is a punishing father, we're going to have trouble trusting him.

The easiest way to determine your own preconceptions of the Father is to notice how you feel as you say, as we have all been taught to say, "Thy will be done." When you finally surrender your will to God, what do you really expect to happen? What I discovered inside of me was, "Watch it, Meg, you're really going to catch it now!" Nor was this fear unreasonable. The statement, "Thy will be done," immediately calls to mind Christ's prayer to the Father in the Garden of Gethsemane. He said, "Nevertheless not my will, but thine, be done" and was crucified. (Luke 22:42.) Somewhere in us, holding us back from placing our lives in God's hands are deep levels of fear and trepidation. How many of us can say those words, knowing that in that surrender we will find ultimate peace and sweetness and joy? It takes a lot of undoing of our conditioning to be able to say "Thy will be done" and feel that we have just opened the door to moving in concert with a wonderful, loving Deity rather than feel that we have surrendered ourselves to be cast into the fiery pit as a test of faith.

When I was taking the missionary discussions as a thirty-four-year-old — and using up a lot of missionaries with my questions — I was struck by how often in the New Testament the message was repeated, "Knock and it shall be opened unto you, Seek and ye shall find, Ask and ye shall receive." That invitation appears over and over again in Christ's counsel to us. This fundamental teaching points us toward a different relationship with the Lord. I visualize the meaning of the scripture in this way: God is standing at the door, just waiting to be asked, just waiting for us to notice another way of doing things, another way of viewing a situation. He is waiting to be a companion to us — not a multiple-choice test-giver, not a father of stern judgment, but a loving companion who will not interfere without being asked but who is eager to be asked.

Although my views keep changing as I keep seeking to know God, my view of my Father in Heaven right now is that he is a lavish, gentle, loving, supportive, constant companion. Yet I complicate the relationship far beyond what it needs to be. God is much closer, and there are far fewer tests of my righteousness, than I had thought. What I primarily need to bring to God is simply my willingness to listen. What stops my open willingness to listen is the same thing that stops my saying "Thy will be done" with any sense of joyfulness. That is fear of who God is and what he will require of me. But what I found in the scriptures two years ago was a wonderful God of abundance, a God of great generosity.

Two phrases I love to remind myself of are "The fullness of the earth is yours" and "There is enough and to spare." We have become obsessed in our society with the belief that scarcity is the rule of the globe. There's not enough food, there's not enough water, there's not enough air, there's not enough land, and there are too many people. We have also developed over the years a mentality that we each need to grab a piece of the earth's bounty, because the pieces are shrinking and pretty soon there's not going to be enough. Several years ago, however, the World Hunger Project stunned the world by announcing that there was enough food on the planet to feed everybody. The problem is not scarcity but politics that prevent distribution. Grain rots in Ohio while children starve in Somalia. We have now come to recognize the truth that there's plenty of food on this planet — that the earth is full and there is enough to spare.

We're also beginning to understand that the whole planet acts as an organism, a living breathing entity. It's not just an inert lump of rock. The earth is alive and has the capacity to heal itself, even to regulate its atmosphere and temperature so that life is well supported. British scientist James Lovelock has formulated this view as "the Gaia hypothesis" (named after Gaia, the ancient Greek earthmother). His theory, which is gaining steadily in credibility, postulates that the earth is one unified organism, a living entity in which all parts cooperate to create the conditions that support life.[3] Minuscule ocean algae play a role in regulating the temperature of the atmosphere, changing in number to help maintain a stable climate. Similarly, the dramatic eruption of Mount Pinatubo in the Philippines last year may have created enough atmospheric ash to counter the effects of global warming for a few years.

Ours is a planet of abundance and a life of abundance because it was formed by a Creator who could not think in terms of scarcity but could think only in terms of diversity and a wonderful fullness. Robinson Jeffers, an early twentieth-century American poet and son of a theology professor, found his own path to God in his studies of science and forestry. He wrote this poem, entitled "The Excesses of God."

> Is it not by his high superfluousness we know
> Our God? For to be equal a need
> Is natural, animal, mineral: but to fling

Rainbows over the rain
And beauty above the moon, and secret rainbows
On the domes of deep sea-shells,
And make the necessary embrace of breeding
Beautiful also as fire,
Not even the weeds to multiply without blossom
Nor the birds without music:
There is the great humaneness at the heart of things,
The extravagant kindness, the fountain
Humanity can understand, and would flow likewise
If power and desire were perch-mates.[4]

We need to recognize the abundance of God within our own lives as well. I am talking not about material abundance but about the great diversity of gifts that each of us is. Internally, we are each as varied and rich as any of God's creations, wonderful beings with multiple talents and perspectives. Every relationship we engage in brings forth different aspects of ourselves. We are different with our children than with our mate, than with each friend, than with each neighbor. Every relationship calls forth certain aspects of ourselves and leaves others hidden. The more relationships we engage in, the more we learn about our own diversity. We may have been taught that we should be consistent, the same yesterday, today, and tomorrow; but I believe consistency is best left to God as one of his attributes. We are here to discover ourselves, to discover the richness that God created in us, and we can do this only by seeking out new and different relationships — relationships not only with people but with places and ideas. As we expand into these new relationships, we will always be surprised to discover things we didn't know we could do, or things we didn't know we had thoughts about. This process of discovering who we are, once engaged in, always yields up a rich and varied portrait of ourselves.

Another way we discover our real gifts is to notice the things that are easiest for us to do in life. This advice challenges every good Christian hard-work tradition that ever was. All of us were raised on adages about the value of hard work, such as, "Good things don't come easy," "Hard work never killed anyone," and "If a thing's worth doing, it's worth doing well." Most of us have also been taught to believe that hard work actually creates value. We feel that the things that are time-consuming and that require self-discipline to accomplish are the most valuable. We build more value in an activity if it requires hard work. For me, a C in math meant more than any A because it was so hard. Most of the MBA students I work with don't study advanced business management practice because it's joyful. They study it because it's hard—and because they hope it will lead to a very good paycheck.

In our desire to value that which is difficult, I believe we turn away from God. I think God designed us so that our gifts and talents would be easily recognizable, arising almost effortlessly from who we are because "men are that they might have joy." We can create joy through the relatively effortless expression of our best gifts, those self-expressions which are most essentially and easily ourselves. I believe God in his creative intelligence intended us to find joy, to find ease-fulness, through the exercise of our gifts. Instead, we ascribe far too much value to struggle, making struggle almost the primary spiritual value by which we measure ourselves, making the refiner's fire our access point to divinity.

I cannot experience life that way any more. I have found that my life and accomplishments become effortless, full of grace and a peaceful ease, when I am doing what feels consonant with the Father's will for me. It isn't easy to stay on that joyful path, though, because when life gets easy, a strong puritan voice in my head pipes up, "You're having too much of a good time here. Let's get serious. This isn't a free lunch. This isn't a joy ride. This is life." So then I go back to exertions; I look for tasks that are difficult, I push and push and reorganize my life—creating struggle as a measure of my righteousness.

When I am in harmony with God, and not creating struggle to prove my worth, people seem to coalesce around me, the support I need arrives the minute I need it, and inspiration comes when I ask for it. It can be trivial things as well—finding a pen that I have lost or getting a phone call with the information I need. There is a definite feeling I have at times of moving with the flow rather than struggling against my life's natural, God-intended currents. At these moments in my life, I feel there is no need to worry because there is a movement that I am a part of. When I am in that place in my life, enjoying the natural flow of things, the hard part is to relax and enjoy it. It is very hard to relinquish the model that through struggle we are most sanctified.

If our gifts are those things that come easiest to us, one way to discover them is to notice what you do well without much effort, what you have fun doing, and what other people say you are good at that you never noticed. Think about the times someone has said, "You know, I just love being with you. You are so comfortable to be around," or "It's amazing how people open up to you," or "You get things done so quickly," or "You have such a wonderful relationship with your children." When those comments surprise us, they are often the gifts we have overlooked, gifts which come so naturally that we fail to notice them. Other people can help us notice what is easy for us, which might be difficult for them.

We need to learn to value the things that come easily to us and not dismiss them as unimportant. These are our unique gifts. In Doctrine and Covenants 88:33 Christ said, "For what doth it profit a man if a gift is bestowed upon him, and he receive not the gift? Behold, he rejoices not in that which is given unto him, neither rejoices in him who is the giver of the gift." I believe that every time we turn away from, deny, or fail to look for our gifts, we are failing to honor God. One Christmas, I thought I had found a very special gift for a child. But Christmas morning, she opened it, looked at it, said, "Oh, thanks," and put it aside. That hurt. A lot of us do that with our lives. We decide that a certain gift is not of value, or that it won't work in our lives right now, or that it isn't really a gift because everyone can do it. I have imagined the Lord's disappointment at the rejection of these wonderful gifts that were so carefully given. We say by our choices, "Oh thanks, but I don't have time for this right now because I need to make money," or "I have a family, so I will get to it later." I think we offend God greatly when we fail to celebrate our own uniqueness, our own gifts.

God not only provides a way for us to fulfill his commandments but also provides a way for us to exercise our gifts. We need to trust in his words, "Draw near unto me and I will draw near unto you; seek me diligently and ye shall find me; ask, and ye shall receive; knock, and it shall be opened unto you." (D&C 88:63.) Exercising our gifts brings forth an abundance of resources and supports that will help us celebrate who we are as we participate in the divine plan of creation. Our lives will become easy. I know that saying that life is *meant* to be easy is a foreign idea. But I urge you to reread the four Gospels, as I did, to see how Christ describes life. There is suffering, but there is also joy. Joy is not found only after suffering, but joy can be found through easefulness, through simply surrendering one's life and one's talents to God and being courageous enough to express them. The courage for expressing one's gifts doesn't mean, "Thy will be done; watch out." Rather it means, "If I am willing to dare to trust God, then he provides a way for the expression of my gifts. In fact, the way is made clear for me, and suffering is not part of the price I must pay."

We needlessly create too much suffering. Read Christ's teachings. They are not about suffering. He teaches about a Father who loves us so deeply that he never leaves our side. "Behold the fowls of the air: for they sow not, neither do they reap, nor gather into barns; yet your heavenly Father feedeth them. Are ye not much better than they? . . . And why take ye thought for raiment? Consider the lilies of the field, how they grow; they toil not, neither do they spin: And yet I say unto you, That even Solomon in all his glory was not arrayed like one of these. Wherefore, if God so clothe the grass of the field, which to day is, and to morrow is cast into the oven, shall he not much more clothe you, O ye of little faith? . . . Seek ye first the kingdom of God, and his righteousness; and all these things shall be added unto you." (Matthew 6:26, 28–30, 33.) Are we not of little faith to turn away from a God who waits behind every door just waiting for us to knock? Are we not of little faith when we believe that we can only cry out to God from the depths of our despair? Life is so much nicer, so much easier, so much more fun when we call upon the Lord in our moments of pleasure, when we call upon the Lord for companionship, for enjoyment, when we call upon the Lord for every little need, not just the big ones.

I find enlightening a concept in Eastern spiritual traditions of flowing with the movement of God. Fritz Perls, the founder of Gestalt therapy, said, "Don't push the river. It flows by itself." Too often we are pushing and bending and folding and cramping ourselves into some box that we've decided is us. We envision our lives as something we will suffer our way through, and, at the end, like a jack-in-the-box, we will pop up perfected and say, "Here I am!" What if we thought of ourselves instead as rivers that have a natural flow to them, that have a natural sense of direction? Every ounce of water on the planet knows where it's headed — to the ocean. We know where we're headed — to God — so that flow is already established for us. Once we are in the current, if we would only relax more, enjoy ourselves more, celebrate ourselves and one another more, I believe that we could find a wonderful easefulness to our lives. But we have to avoid grabbing onto a branch that's overhanging the stream and saying, "Uh-oh! That was too much fun. Let's get back to work here on the shore — let's dig out another riverbed here. This one is going along too smoothly."

As I have tried to practice these beliefs, I have found they require much self-discipline. To trust the Lord, to surrender each day to him and believe that that day will be more joyful as a result is not the norm in Western culture. In an attempt to develop trust, last year I did something almost heretical: I gave up my Franklin planner. But, I must tell you, I ended up taking it back. I gave it up as an experiment and because I hate what all these planners represent about our culture. Four years ago, when I first came to BYU, I was asked to speak to the management faculty. Eighty faculty members, assembled in amphitheater rows and many with planners open, were my first introduction to the new faculty I was to join. "Thank you," I said to them, "for letting me come to the land of Franklin planners."

Franklin planners are omnipresent in Utah, partly because they are a home-grown product but mostly because we Latter-day Saints believe that we need to exert a level of control over our lives to make everything happen that should happen. Furthermore, we are activity oriented. Life not only is hard but also has to be busy. We feel we are defining our worth by being busy. Our planners help us organize our activities, and therefore, in some sense, they make us feel productive, busy, and in control. Control, however, is not a spiritual virtue. Control makes us feel safe. Control makes us feel powerful, but control is the opposite of surrendering one's will to God. A very dear friend of mine, the one who encouraged me to give up my planner for six months, said, "Planning is a defense against God. You decide what you need to do that day, and you don't have to consult God at all." After six months, I went back to my planner because Little League baseball games, piano lessons, faculty meetings, student appointments — all still needed to be scheduled. But the experiment has changed my attitude. I realize that even though I'm in the world and need to be responsible, plan things out ahead, and show up at the right time, I no longer think that I have to control my time so carefully that there is no time to let God in, no time for serendipitous spiritual happenings, no time to be drawn off-track to talk to one student for three hours instead of efficiently scheduling six students for half an hour each.

Even though we live in a highly structured, controlled, activity-oriented culture that is becoming more so, as Latter-day Saints we need to resist that trend. We need to hold ourselves personally responsible for not becoming so activity-oriented that we forget that we are here to be instruments of God. When we act as instruments of God, the number of activities fades out, but our effectiveness grows enormously. You will be in the right place at the right time saying the right things to the person who needs it. Mother Theresa said, "Let God work through you without consulting you." When God is working through me, it is such a wonderful feeling that I wonder why I don't allow it to happen more often. I would suggest that everything in our society, and much in our church culture, pushes us away from moving into an easeful, happy, joyful life. Suffering, hardship, control, self-discipline — not God-discipline — have become our virtues. Activities are our days. Planning is an important Church leadership skill. But activities and planning are administrative, not spiritual, skills. In my personal life, I have found that I cannot commune with God and I cannot experience joy if I am planning, doing, suffering.

So what will we do with our lives? How do we give up our planners? How do we give up the belief that life is hard and hard work never killed anyone? The key to living life joyfully is to examine your views of God and the characteristics you are attributing to him. I would urge you to move away from suffering into an appreciation of the joyful, generous, expressive character of the Father. As you do that, you will grow in trust. He is a loving God, and therefore we *can* trust our whole lives in his hands. After changing your notions of who the Father is, experiment with turning over an hour, then a day. Then try committing a week to expressing your gifts. You don't have to know how. You just have to express your desire to the Lord, and he will make the way clear. Experiment. Notice how your life feels, and compare it to how it feels when you are busy planning, controlling, holding on, and being fearful. Your own experience will show you that a delightful opportunity exists to experience life joyfully — but it requires a different relationship with the Father. Remember, "For the earth is full and there is enough to spare." We are all wonderful, exquisite beings created by a wonderful, joyful, generous Father. It's time to start celebrating the Creator and celebrating each other in very new and different ways.

NOTES

1. Joseph Smith, Jr., *History of the Church of Jesus Christ of Latter-day Saints,* 7 vols. 2d ed. rev., edited by B. H. Roberts (Salt Lake City: Deseret Book Co., 1978), 6:303.

2. Richard Bach, *Illusions: The Adventures of a Reluctant Messiah* (New York: Dell Publishing Co., 1977).

3. See J. F. Lovelock, *Gaia* (New York: Oxford University Press, 1987).

4. Robinson Jeffers, *Selected Poems* (New York: Random House, 1965), p. 72.

Must We Always Run Faster Than We Have Strength?

KATHLEEN BUSHNELL JENSEN

*And see that all these things are done in wisdom and order; for it
is not requisite that a [woman] should run faster than [she] has strength.
And again, it is expedient that [she] should be diligent, that thereby [she]
might win the prize; therefore, all things must be done in order. (Mosiah
4:27.)*

One night last spring I remember sitting at my kitchen table thinking
in frustration, "I have not accomplished a thing this whole week." My
windows still needed washing, and there were a dozen other things
that I had not gotten to. I wondered why I felt so tired for not having
accomplished much. I got out a pencil and paper, but, on impulse,
instead of writing a to-do list, I began jotting down some of the things
that had gone on that week. I was surprised. I had been to two soccer
games, two soccer practices, two piano lessons, one gymnastics lesson,
and one doctor's appointment. I had made a fairy costume for the
Shakespeare festival for our fifth grader, gone on five one-hour exercise
walks with my husband, made a poster for the first-grade teacher for
teacher appreciation week, attended the ground breaking for the Bountiful temple, spent one-half day helping the fifth grade with the rain
forest unit, attended two tennis matches for our senior son, prepared
and served Sunday dinner for fourteen people, gone on a picnic, and
hiked around Causey Dam for family home evening. I was exhausted
even remembering! I had called people to serve and bring food for the
grade school Shakespeare festival feast, washed and dried at least twelve

*Kathleen Bushnell Jensen has taught first grade and served as PTA president. She and
her husband, Marlin K. Jensen, a member of the First Quorum of the Seventy, are
the parents of eight children. She teaches the marriage and family relations class in Sunday
School.*

batches of laundry, sobbed with my husband and our children when our dog got run over, attended a college football game, given my Primary inservice lesson, completed the cancer drive for my daughter who couldn't get it finished, lived through numerous teenager ups and downs, wrote to our missionary daughter in Germany, took our baby bunnies for first grade show and tell, planted pansies, watched a Jazz game. The list went on and on. I looked at it and thought, "Well, maybe I did accomplish something!"

I concluded that often we sell ourselves short. Maybe we're not so different from those hard-working pioneer women who were busy from sunup to sundown. Our days are every bit as challenging. We may not card wool, hoe beets, or slop hogs, but we need to give ourselves credit for what we do.

In fact, perhaps a more pressing question for us is, "Are we running faster than we have strength?" The role of women has changed dramatically in my lifetime. When I was a child, my mom was always home, and that was wonderfully gratifying for me, good for my self-esteem. My mother let me know somehow that when I came home, I lighted up her day. Many times I'm not home when my children come home, though I try to be. I try to do a lot of the worthwhile things for my children that my mother did for me, but it's difficult with our smorgasbord of options. When I attended college some twenty years ago, most women trained as either teachers or nurses. Any other career seemed almost eccentric. In contrast, my daughters and their friends have the world open to them. They can go into any of the professions, a wonderful change for women. But one thing hasn't changed: a day is still twenty-four hours. We still have our agency to choose what we want to do in those twenty-four hours. Therein lies the dilemma. I don't struggle so much with good and bad choices; rather, I have ten *good* choices, all worthwhile pursuits, vying for my time. It's often difficult to prioritize, to judge which things are really important and which to put on hold.

Anne Morrow Lindbergh wrote of this dilemma almost forty years ago in *Gift from the Sea*. Her words still ring true. She observes that in the modern world the women's movement has gained for women more privileges and opportunities. But "the exploration of their use, as in all pioneer movements, was left open to the women who would follow. And woman today is still searching. We are aware of our hunger and needs, but still ignorant of what will satisfy them. With our garnered free time, we are more apt to drain our creative springs than to refill them. With our pitchers, we attempt sometimes to water a field, not a garden. We throw ourselves indiscriminately into committees and causes. Not knowing how to feed the spirit, we try to muffle its demands in distractions. Instead of stilling the center, the axis of the wheel, we add more centrifugal activities to our lives—which tend to throw us off balance."[1]

How true! A few years ago I served in my ward Relief Society presidency. I was surprised to find that the problems women were having were not so much economic as spiritual and emotional. I had not known that so many women are unhappy and frustrated. This experience prompted me to think about why that is, and I have identified several possible reasons and solutions.

For one thing, we demand so much of ourselves. Most of us have a hard time saying no in this day and age. For another, it is too easy to forget to be grateful. The other day I went out to my garage, pushed the garage door opener, and was dismayed when the door wouldn't go up. I was full of exasperation and in a hurry. As I unplugged the opener and lifted the door manually, I was thinking, "I have got to get that fixed tomorrow, because I cannot manage without that garage door opener." And then I thought to myself, How odd. We've lived in our home for eighteen years, but before that we lived in a home with no garage at all. I had four small children, and I'd come home from grocery shopping and park in front. If it was raining, I'd be drenched by the time I carried in the baby, then the two-year-old, then the four-year-old, then the stroller, and finally the groceries. I'd think, "If I had a garage, life would be wonderful!" I used to envision life with a garage. I'd see garages, and I'd think, "Those people have got it made!" That day, after fuming about the defective garage door opener, I remembered what it used to be like with no garage at all and wondered, What's happened to me in eighteen years of living in this house? I never thank the Lord for my garage. I just go out and use it.

Apparently, I'm not the only one who forgets to be grateful for our many blessings. At a regional conference this year, Bonnie Pinegar spoke on this topic. She confessed that one of her self-assigned tasks is to be the worrier of the family. While her husband, Rex, is across the bed from her sleeping soundly, she is fretting about everything—all the problems of her married children, illnesses, money, anything. Finally, one morning after another restless night, she asked him, "How can you sleep with all the problems we have?" He answered, "One way, Bonnie. I count my blessings."

I don't know why that story brings tears to my eyes. I guess because I'm so lousy at counting mine. I'm the one who wants the garage door opener to be working all the time, and I forget that I'm awfully lucky to have a garage. I think we get spoiled; we want it all, and we want it now. Many times we're just not willing to wait. All that wanting makes us really unhappy.

Envy can also cause pointless frustrations. A friend of mine had needlepoint seats on all her dining room chairs. I love needlepoint. One day I looked at those chairs and thought, I'll never have that. I'll always have the kind you have to wash off real fast. I'll just never have pretty needlepoint chairs. And it's true. Maybe I won't ever have them. Needlepoint is a hobby my friend loves doing. Someday I may take up needlepoint, but perhaps I'll be too busy with grandchildren to make it a priority.

Still another reason we are needlessly unhappy is that we lose our spiritual perspective. Sometimes we forget that the Lord is aware of our presence, that he knows and cares about what we're doing. We can draw great strength from that knowledge. A notable example is early Church pioneer Joseph Millet, who recorded in his journal his experiences of homesteading in Nevada:

"One of my children came in, said that Brother Newton Hall's folks were out of bread. Had none that day. I put . . . our flour in sack to send up to Brother Hall's. Just then Brother Hall came in. Says I, 'Brother Hall, how are you out for flour.' 'Brother Millett, we have none.' 'Well, Brother Hall, there is some in that sack. I have divided and was going to send it to you. Your children told mine that you were out.' Brother Hall began to cry. Said he had tried others. Could not get any. Went to the cedars and prayed to the Lord and the Lord told him to go to Joseph Millett. 'Well, Brother Hall, you needn't bring this back if the Lord sent you for it. You don't owe me for it.' You can't tell how good it made me feel to know that the Lord knew that there was such a person as Joseph Millett."[2]

Sometimes we think we are all alone in our day-to-day struggles. We feel no one is really aware of our lives as they unfold. But the Lord is aware. He knows all; he has experienced all. The Lord knew that there was such a person as Joseph Millet. He knows there is such a person as Kathy Jensen. And he knows of you and your life.

Also, we mustn't forget "it must needs be, that there is an opposition in all things." (2 Nephi 2:11.) Note that the scripture doesn't say that there's opposition in some things, but in all things, in everything. I don't know why it has to be that way. Opposition makes life a lot more difficult, but then it also makes us appreciate what we have. People who lived through the Depression appreciate money differently from the rest of us. It is often difficult for them to spend money. Some die with huge savings accounts, certain the next economic catastrophe looms on the horizon. They never give anything to Deseret Industries. They recycle, mend, patch, redesign, and reuse. My husband's father always said to him, "You need to live through a depression. You'd be a lot more careful." And maybe it's true. Experiencing opposition does give one a perspective.

When our last baby was born, I was a basket case. I was forty-two years old. No one was telling me how smart I was for having a baby at that age. After her birth, I continued to worry. At about six weeks old, she still wasn't smiling. Was she all right? Would she be autistic? This fear ballooned into a real trauma to me. Every day I'd tell the other children to interact with her, smile at her, get her to look at them, get her to smile. But she didn't smile. I'd had enough children to know that by that age babies are ready to respond, and she just wasn't responding. I became distraught and sank into worse than usual postpartum blues. I felt overwhelmed as I worried that I might have to raise a child with imperfections. I know that many others have been asked to do so, but as I asked myself if I could do what they do, or handle it, I was in turmoil for a while. I prayed and pleaded with the Lord, promising that I would appreciate everything about her — every normal annoying little thing would be a gift to me. She did finally smile and is a very normal, active little girl. A year later, when I was out in the hall during sacrament meeting trying to settle her down, I tried to remember my promise. I've tried to keep my perspective. I watch her with gratitude for her active mind and energetic body. Maybe I wouldn't have been so grateful if I hadn't experienced fear that she might not be normal.

Another way to keep perspective is to remember that "to every thing there is a season." (Ecclesiastes 3:1.) When I had several small children, I tended to look at women who were out doing things — taking institute classes, tole painting, skiing — and I would think, "How do they do it? I'm so unorganized." As I look back, my advice is be content where you are. If you have young children, enjoy them! I'm old enough to know that you don't have young children very long. Those moments are fleeting. Don't wish away your toddlers and bright-eyed preschoolers. They will never be yours at that age again. Don't rush your seasons. I feel the most off balance when I'm trying to run faster than I have strength, when I'm trying to keep up with people who are single or who maybe don't have as many children at home. Our needs are different. When you have small children, you don't need to have a totally spotless home. When I go into a home that is full of young children and yet is totally spotless, I think, "What do the kids do all day? Live outdoors?" Be realistic; let your kids have some fun. Let them make messes. Don't worry about what everyone might be thinking. And don't compare your home to anyone else's.

One day several years ago, I had been harping at my children to clean their rooms and get the house looking nice. I assigned them several jobs and then left, telling them I expected to return to find everything perfect. When I got back, I found a sign on the refrigerator that our junior-high–aged daughter Julie had made. She had written, "Better to be happy and messy than clean and mean. If you agree, please sign here so we can show Mom." The missionaries had dropped by that day, and they'd signed it, all the kids' friends had signed it, everybody who had come by had signed it. It made me stop and think, What message am I sending my children? Is it more important to have a clean house or a happy house?

Sometimes we simply fail to communicate clearly by words or actions our real priorities. Many of us say, "My family is the most important thing." But do our lives show that? Every so often, we need to rethink our activities. Are the things we spend our time with really the things that are important to us? It's easy to get sidetracked when we have so many interests and opportunities.

Sometimes our seasons don't always include what we thought they would. We expect to have children and find we can't. We expect to be married and are single. We expect to raise our children a certain way and find we can't afford to be at home. We expect our children will always choose the right in the important things and they don't. And we feel guilty or ashamed that our lives don't match our ideal expectations and perhaps confused about what we should be doing now. Often we forget that we're entitled to inspiration in our lives, if we just ask for it. If we are being led by the Spirit, we don't have to feel guilty or ashamed of our choices and circumstances. We can feel secure in our own decisions. Many, many women, for example, have to work outside the home. If you and your husband have prayerfully decided that's what you need to do in your family, then do it. Feel good about your decision, and don't apologize for it. Church members often apologize for how few children they have. They'll say, "Oh, we just have two." And I want to say, "Well, that's great! What a joy to have those two!" We should never equate righteousness with numbers of children or judge what is appropriate for anyone else. A woman in our ward has eleven children. She's a wonderful mother. She comes to church with a smile on her face and even looks sane. I suspect that I am at least two children beyond my max, but clearly she is not. She's thrilled to have her eleven children. That was the right choice for her. Our place is to support and enjoy one another, not judge or compare.

I also feel that we really need to take care of ourselves. So many women give their all to their children or husband and have nothing left for themselves. We can become "depleted women," as Jo Ann Larson says in her book *I'm a Day Late and a Dollar Short . . . and It's Okay!*[3] We're always the ones who get the burnt toast or the spoon that's been caught in the disposal. It is important for our families that we value and spend some time caring for ourselves. President Marion G. Romney said: "How can we give if there is nothing there? Food for the hungry cannot come from empty shelves. Money to assist the needy cannot come from an empty purse. Support and understanding cannot come from the emotionally starved. Teaching cannot come from the un-learned. And most important of all, spiritual guidance cannot come from the spiritually weak."[4]

Neither can we afford to ignore our physical health. We owe it to ourselves and to our families to keep physically strong. Last year my husband and I agreed to start walking together in the mornings. It's been very good for both of us. It's fun, and I can tell him everything I want and he doesn't fall asleep. I have a captive audience for one hour, and so does he. Our walks have been good for our marriage, for our health, and for our mental outlook.

I recommend spending some time alone each day to think and be who you are. If you have small children, a moment alone is precious. It's easy to forget who you really are. Too often we become what we are needed for—the Cub Scout den mother, the soccer carpool driver, the PTA commissioner, the team mother—instead of who we are. Solitude is one way to not get lost in doing. Making sure you are having fun doing what you are doing is another way. Sometimes that is difficult in your own family. You may prepare a new recipe, knock yourself out working all afternoon, and then you can sit down to the meal and the kids pick out all the green things and say they'd rather have macaroni and cheese. When we're feeling that kind of discouragement, the world outside our homes seems pretty enticing. It's more gratifying to cook for a Relief Society luncheon. The other sisters rave and ask for the recipe. We get a lot of strokes that way. It's easy to be nice to people you see at a PTA meeting or in the church foyer or even at an office. It's much harder to work out a relationship with a teenaged son who's giving you a hard time. It becomes very enticing to spend your time away from home. But ultimately that is a counterfeit source of satisfaction. We need to build our family relationships, and that is all the more reason to build in fun times with the family.

Last Mother's Day I read an article about a woman who had been selected as Utah's Mother of the Year a few years ago. Her husband died when she had eight very young children, including an infant, and she raised an outstanding family in near poverty. Her son Monroe McKay said: "I tell people that she was not perfect; she simply did the best she could in that day. She didn't do the best that you wanted her to do or that she wanted to do, but she did the best she could; and that was good enough. She didn't raise perfect children either; we had our share of problems."[5]

Many times we think we have to be perfect instantly and perfect in everything: that's what causes us to run faster than we have strength. But God knew that we were all human and imperfect. He knew that we needed a Savior. If we had been capable of perfection on our own, we wouldn't need a Savior. Jesus came to help us make up the difference between what we can do at our best and what we aspire to become.

That is the comforting, good news of the gospel. If we're doing all we can do, and we keep trying, then our inevitable shortcomings and mistakes are not going to bar us from being Christ's. "See that all these things are done in wisdom and order; for it is not requisite that a [woman] should run faster than [she] has strength."

NOTES

1. Anne Morrow Lindbergh, *Gift from the Sea* (New York: Random House, 1955), p. 52.

2. Joseph Millett Journal, as quoted in Eugene England, "Without Purse or Scrip: A 19-Year-Old Missionary in 1853," *New Era*, July 1975, p. 28; reprinted as " 'The Lord Knew That There Was Such a Person': Joseph Millett's Journal, 1853," in Eugene England, *Why the Church Is As True As the Gospel* (Salt Lake City: Bookcraft, 1986), pp. 17–30.

3. Jo Ann Larson, *I'm a Day Late and a Dollar Short . . . and It's Okay!* (Salt Lake City: Deseret Book Co., 1991), pp. 150–76.

4. Marion G. Romney, "The Celestial Nature of Self-Reliance," *Ensign*, Nov. 1982, p. 93.

5. Carri P. Jenkins, "Judge Monroe McKay: Creating a Commotion," *BYU Today*, May 1992, p. 28.

Joseph Smith and the Prophetic Voice

KATHRYN H. SHIRTS

What does it mean to speak prophetically? For many Jewish and Christian scholars, a prophet is someone who calls people to a heightened awareness of their obligations to God and to their neighbors. The Hebrew prophets, for example, challenged the Israelites to understand that the essence of religion is justice and mercy, not ritual for the sake of obedience alone. Other students of the scriptures see prophecy primarily as inspired speech predicting future world events. From their perspective, the true test of a prophet is the ability to make accurate predictions. The book of Revelation, which is itself filled with projections of future events, offers yet another definition: "the testimony of Jesus is the spirit of prophecy." (Revelation 19:10.)

It is interesting to me that Joseph Smith relied on Revelation 19:10 to define his own prophetic role. In a sermon recorded by Willard Richards in the summer of 1839, Joseph declared: "No man is a minister for Jesus Christ, without being a Prophet. No man can be the minister of Jesus Christ, except he has the testimony of Jesus & this is the Spirit of Prophecy."[1] Joseph Smith's awareness of a prophet's calling to testify of Christ is reflected in the Book of Mormon. Book of Mormon prophets were vitally concerned about the role of the Holy One of Israel. Going beyond the Hebrew prophets, they saw the primary obligation to God as repentance, or turning to Christ to be filled with his power to love and to serve others. They were concerned with the future, but their predictions of future events revolved around the anticipated visits of the atoning Messiah to the earth.

Kathryn H. Shirts received her master's degree in American church history from Harvard Divinity School. A homemaker, she and her husband, Randall Shirts, are the parents of six children. She has taught high school history part time, and she serves in her ward's Relief Society.

Joseph Smith's personal revelations, the fruits of his willingness to enter into his own dialogue with God, are even bolder than the Book of Mormon witness of Christ. Not only do they testify of the mission of the Savior but they convey the very words, mind, and personality of the Lord. In the revelations recorded in the Doctrine and Covenants, Joseph speaks for the Lord, in the name of the Lord, and even as the Lord. Joseph's revelatory voice was prophetic not only because of what he said but because of how he said it. Form and content combined as dual witnesses of Christ.

Was Joseph Smith's prophetic voice unique? To address this question, we need to reflect on the United States of the early 1800s. At that time, salvation was a matter of public importance. Because most Americans were Protestants, they looked to the Bible as the focus of religious authority and the arbiter of all doctrinal disputes. The King James Bible was the standard text—in fact, the text from which almost everyone learned to read. The era of established, state-sponsored religion was coming to a close. In most states churches co-existed with one another and there was a heady feeling that individuals could consult the precious Bible and come to their own conclusions.

Most people, however, even those whose lives revolved around God's revealed word as contained in the Bible, believed revelation came only from a distant time and place—a New Testament era of gifts and miracles and immediate access to Christ and his apostles. Americans of the early nineteenth century generally felt that the light given to mankind during that extraordinary period of the Savior's appearance on earth would never be equaled. Cautious churchmen such as Congregational minister Joseph Lathrop of Massachusetts warned: "If one pretends to . . . special divine direction, as his warrant to preach, let him manifest it by miracles, as the apostles manifested their commission." Of course, that would be impossible, he continued, for "miracles have ceased and so have all immediate revelations."[2]

Even thinkers who were less established and more independent deferred to the common wisdom. Ozias Hart of Connecticut wrote a pamphlet in 1816 correcting the errors of contemporary religious denominations but did not actually claim inspiration. "We do not expect miracles or inspiration . . . but we do expect greater degrees of light."[3] The followers of Alexander Campbell sought to re-create the primitive church, focusing on Peter's speech in Acts 2, which outlined faith, repentance, baptism, and the gift of the Holy Ghost as the fundamentals of the gospel. Campbellites believed the fruits of the Spirit to be peace, joy, and love; however, they rejected the more dramatic spiritual gifts of the New Testament church. They felt those gifts had been given only once in history, as a special witness to the unique mission of the Savior.[4]

So much focus on the Bible and so much caution about modern miracles created a certain amount of psychological tension for Joseph Smith's contemporaries. Many felt that if miracles did not occur in their own time, it was highly unlikely that they ever did. A famous American deist, Thomas Jefferson, edited his own version of the Bible to exclude any reference to the miraculous. Such a Bible, he thought, would have greater appeal to moral, reasonable people. On the other hand, groups such as the Quakers resolved the tension by taking personal inspiration more seriously than the mainstream denominations. Quaker Samuel Hussey wrote in 1821: "It is consistent to believe that inspiration, or the teaching of the Holy Spirit, is yet the privilege of all that will attend to it, so far as to show them their particular duty.... Therefore none have a right to say this influence has ceased, merely because they have it not."[5]

The open atmosphere of Quaker meetings encouraged some to go beyond recognition of their own inner light and to speak for God. Joseph Hoag, an itinerant Quaker preacher, felt inspired by a heavenly voice in 1803 to declare that pride and a dividing spirit would cause calamities in the nation unless Americans returned to the faith and humility of their forefathers.[6] In England, Ann Lee affiliated with a group which had recently separated from the Quakers. After a disastrous marriage and a traumatic imprisonment for preaching, Ann felt herself transformed as the embodiment of Christ. "It is not I that speak, it is Christ who dwells in me," she told her followers. "I am Ann the Word."[7] In 1774 she brought her small band, known as Shakers for their exuberant forms of worship, to America. Just as she claimed to be Christ's Second Appearing, after her death a series of spiritual manifestations among the Shakers became known as "Mother Ann's Second Appearing." In a very diffuse sense of revelation, messages came to Shaker members from angels, the spirits of departed Shakers, the apostles, prophets, and famous persons in history.[8]

Although he had no Quaker background, young Joseph Smith's strong sense that he had received personal guidance parallels the Quaker assurance that God's "unspeakable gift," "the teachings of the Holy Ghost," would provide inner direction. Joseph's grandfather Asael Smith was associated with the Universalists, a loosely organized group that believed that the atonement of Christ was sufficient to save all humankind. The family of Joseph Smith, Sr., while deeply religious, was outside the mainstream of structured religion and was less susceptible to the mainstream cautions about taking personal inspiration too seriously. Historians are now aware that the Smiths had some involvement with folk beliefs that individuals could contact spirits for help and guidance. Some researchers have suggested that this belief was a kind of "schoolmaster to Christ," giving Joseph increased confidence that it was possible to communicate with heaven.

A perceptive biographer of Joseph Smith's early years is Richard Bushman. He points out that the revelation now printed as Doctrine and Covenants 3, received in July 1828 at Harmony, Pennsylvania, was Joseph's first revelation to be written down and the first indication of how he would speak as a prophet. In the revelation, Joseph was chastised for yielding the first 116 pages of the Book of Mormon manuscript to Martin Harris and was held responsible for their loss. "The works and designs, and the purposes of God cannot be frustrated, neither can they come to naught," the revelation begins. (V.1.) Bushman observes: "The speaker stands above and outside Joseph, sharply separated emotionally and intellectually, talking to the prophet or his associates. The rebuke of Joseph in the revelation of July, 1828, is as forthright as the denunciation of Martin Harris. There is no effort to conceal or rationalize, no sign of Joseph justifying himself to prospective followers. The words flow directly from the messenger to Joseph and have the single purpose of setting Joseph straight. . . . At age twenty-two Joseph knew how to speak prophetically."[9]

It is significant that in Joseph's first recorded use of his prophetic voice, he displayed his own mistakes so prominently. Joseph's sense of his larger-than-life role in God's plan was tempered by a profound awareness of his human weaknesses. Although he spoke in the name of God, unlike Ann Lee, he was careful to distinguish between himself and the Lord. He spoke the language of Jesus Christ but made no claim to be the Word. He received messages from angelic visitors, but he never spoke in behalf of angels or departed spirits, like the Shakers, only in behalf of God. Whereas the itinerant preacher Joseph Hoag gained his reputation as a prophet on the basis of a single vision, Joseph Smith claimed the ability to ask and receive God's inspiration according to the continuing needs of the infant Church.

Joseph's early confidence in his prophetic voice did not preclude him from understanding that it could be expanded or developed. An important element of the Restoration was Joseph's realization that spiritual knowledge is acquired line upon line and precept upon precept. (D&C 98:11–12.) Part of Joseph Smith's divine tutorial was an increasing awareness of the source of his inspiration. If we look carefully at Joseph's first revelations, we see the way in which his understanding of the reality behind his prophetic voice unfolded.[10]

Although the first written revelation, Doctrine and Covenants 3, was clearly given as the word of the Lord, we notice that God is never explicitly identified as the speaker. No other revelation was recorded for seven months, giving Joseph time to ponder, repent of his involvement in the loss of the 116 pages, and regain confidence in his special gifts. By February 1829, Joseph again felt secure in his ability to ask and to receive answers, now not only for himself but in behalf of another person, his father. Wanting to know his role in the kingdom, Joseph Smith, Sr., was invited through the mediating voice of his prophet-son to join in missionary work and was told, "Behold, the field is white already to harvest." (D&C 4:4.) As in Doctrine and Covenants 3, the words were delivered as if from God, but God was not specifically identified as the speaker.

In March 1829, in response to the desire of Martin Harris to know that Joseph had indeed received the plates from God, for the first time in the written revelations of Joseph Smith, God himself was explicitly introduced as speaker. Joseph was instructed to tell Martin Harris that the One for whom he, Joseph, was speaking had said: "I, the Lord, am God, and have given these things unto you, my servant Joseph Smith, Jun., and have commanded you that you should stand as a witness of these things." (D&C 5:2.)

The revelation continues, emphasizing that it is to be understood as God's words, not Joseph's. "Behold, if they will not believe my words, they would not believe you, my servant Joseph, if it were possible that you should show them all these things which I have committed unto you." (D&C 5:7.) The revelation given through Joseph Smith to Oliver Cowdery on April 7, 1829, one month later, is particularly significant, for it is the first to specify that Joseph's revelatory voice was the voice of Jesus Christ. The second verse of the revelation, which we know as Doctrine and Covenants 6, emphasizes the theme of previous revelations, that God himself is speaking and that this is his world: "Behold,

I am God; give heed unto my word, which is quick and powerful, sharper than a two-edged sword." (D&C 6:2.) Midway through the section, however, something remarkable happens, reminiscent of a tender interchange between Peter and the Lord. As recorded in Matthew 16, Jesus asks his disciples, "Whom say ye that I am?" and Simon Peter responds, "Thou art the Christ, the Son of the Living God." Recognizing that Peter has been blessed by revelation from the Father, Jesus in turn acknowledges Peter: "And I say also unto thee, that thou art Peter." (Matthew 16:13–18.)

Similarly, in Doctrine and Covenants 6:20, the speaker, who had been talking through Joseph to Oliver Cowdery, becomes more direct and personal: "Behold, thou art Oliver, and I have spoken unto thee because of thy desires." Completing the interchange, the Lord—for the first time in the written revelations of Joseph Smith—reveals his own identity: "Behold, I am Jesus Christ, the Son of God. I am the same that came unto mine own, and mine own received me not. I am the light which shineth in darkness, and the darkness comprehendeth it not." (D&C 6:20–21.) Heightening the sense of intimacy in the conversation, Oliver is asked to reflect back on a night when he cried unto the Savior in his heart to know the truth and was given peace, a moment known only to himself and God. As if to affirm the significance of what has just occurred, the section which first introduces Jesus Christ as the source of Joseph's revelation concludes by admonishing Oliver to see with his spiritual eyes the identifying marks of the Savior: "Behold the wounds which pierced my side, and also the prints of the nails in my hands and feet; be faithful, keep my commandments, and ye shall inherit the kingdom of heaven." (D&C 6:37.)

Subsequent revelations add even more richness and detail to the image of Jesus Christ as revealed through Joseph's prophetic voice, often in introductory or concluding statements. In Doctrine and Covenants 11:28–30, Jesus Christ proclaims himself as the preeminent Son of God who empowers as many as will receive him to become the sons of God. In Doctrine and Covenants 14:9 Christ declares that he is the creator of the heavens and the earth. Doctrine and Covenants 19:1–4, an exquisite portrayal of the sufferings of the atoning Savior, describes Jesus Christ as "Alpha and Omega" who retains all power "even to the destroying of Satan and his works at the end of the world" and who passes judgment on all men. In Doctrine and Covenants 29:5, the supreme Judge also becomes "your advocate with the Father." Revelation by revelation, Joseph's prophetic voice introduced a Savior of cosmic influence yet intimate caring.

In October 1830, nineteen-year-old Orson Pratt traveled two hundred miles to see Joseph Smith the Prophet and was given Doctrine and Covenants 34, which illustrates the extent to which the revelations were becoming totally immersed in the persona of Christ. Every instruction and explanation to Orson was given with reference to the Savior. Orson was told to listen to the Lord, called to preach the gospel of Christ in preparation for the coming of Christ in power and great glory, and promised that if he was faithful, Christ himself would be with him.

As the identity of the speaker behind Joseph's prophetic voice unfolded, the involvement of those who heard the word increased. At first listeners were admonished to believe the words of the Lord and then to testify of them. In June 1829, David Whitmer and Oliver Cowdery were told that because Joseph's revelations were given by the Spirit and would not be possible without Christ's power, they could testify that they had heard the voice of the Savior and knew his word. (D&C 18:34–36.)

Seventeen months later, in November 1831, permission to testify became an obligation. A conference was called during that month to discuss plans to publish the revelations in book form. Joseph received a preface to the Book of Commandments, now known as Doctrine and Covenants 1, during an intermission between the November 1 morning and afternoon sessions. In the afternoon meeting Joseph acknowledged God's blessings in giving the revelations and asked "what testimony they were willing to attach to these commandments which should shortly be sent to the world."[11] Several brethren were willing to testify that they were of the Lord, but others expressed reservations.

Addressing this dilemma, Joseph appealed to the Lord and received section 67. Joseph was instructed to take the least among the revelations that were to be published in the Book of Commandments and ask the wisest man at the conference to try to duplicate it. If anyone succeeded, the doubters would be justified in questioning the source of the revelations. If no one could produce a similar revelation, they would be under condemnation if they did not bear witness that Joseph's revelations were true. William McLellin accepted the challenge and tried to write a revelation before the next session of conference. His failure, as Joseph termed it, to "imitate the language of Jesus Christ," won over all the brethren, and they prepared a formal statement witnessing that the commandments were written by God's inspiration.[12]

Joseph's confidence in his own ability to act as mouthpiece for Jesus Christ could have given him reason to claim exclusive access to spiritual gifts and powers in the Church. In actuality, his confidence in his calling enabled him to be generous in his desire to enlighten and empower fellow Saints. Because he knew that his authority derived from the Spirit, not from himself, he showed a remarkable willingness to encourage others to seek guidance and support from the same source.

The preface to the Book of Commandments received in November 1831 forcefully stated that the very reason Joseph was given his prophetic calling was to enable others to speak and act for the Savior as well. Remember, the preface was given at the same conference where William McLellin had tried to imitate divine speech and failed, yet the preface insisted that the Lord called Joseph and spoke to him from heaven so "that man should not counsel his fellow man, neither trust in the arm of flesh—But that every man might speak in the name of God the Lord, even the Savior of the world." (D&C 1:19–20.)

Joseph was called to speak in the name of the Lord so that everyone who believed in his prophetic voice and obeyed the gospel could speak in the name of the Lord. How could they do this? Not by trying to imitate the form of Joseph's language but by learning to rely on the same Spirit that had inspired Joseph Smith. Defining the gospel as faith, repentance, and baptism for the gift of the Holy Ghost, Joseph's revelations insisted that an important part of entering into the fold of God was gaining access to spiritual powers. Thomas Marsh was called to preach and told, "It shall be given you by the Comforter what you shall do and whither you shall go." (D&C 31:11.) Ezra Thayre and Northrop Sweet were promised, "Open your mouths and they shall be filled." (D&C 33:8–9.) Orson Pratt was encouraged to "prophesy, and it shall be given by the power of the Holy Ghost." (D&C 34:10.) Emma Smith was ordained to "expound the scriptures, and to exhort the church, according as it shall be given thee by my Spirit." (D&C 25:7.) Indeed, as Joseph Smith noted, no one "is a minister of Jesus Christ, without being a Prophet."[13]

Gerard Manley Hopkins, the Catholic poet-priest born in 1844, the year that Joseph Smith died, expressed poetically what Doctrine and Covenants 1 asserts theologically. While almost everything in the world calls attention to itself, a true disciple of the Savior, "the just man," acts as Christ's witness and in his behalf:

[T]he just man . . .
Acts in God's eye what in God's eye he is —
Christ — for Christ plays in ten thousand places,
Lovely in limbs, and lovely in eyes not his
To the Father through the features of men's faces.[14]

Often historians explain that Joseph Smith's claims were appealing because he brought an authoritarian voice to a world that was becoming increasingly diverse and chaotic. The real appeal of the restored Church of Jesus Christ, however, was that it provided a dynamic balance between central authority and individual empowerment. Joseph offered seekers after the kingdom of God both clear direction and a sense of personal involvement in accomplishing God's purposes. The strength of Joseph's testimony of his own mission enabled others to understand their own. While insisting on Joseph's central prophetic role, the revelations extended a remarkable trust to early missionaries without manuals and leaders without handbooks. Given the difficult task of establishing authority where none was recognized before, no prophet has trusted his followers more and received in return a greater measure of love and loyalty. By speaking with the voice of authority and at the same time inspiring individual initiative, Joseph acted for the Lord in establishing a church of unique strength and energy.

NOTES

1. Andrew F. Ehat and Lyndon W. Cook, eds., *The Words of Joseph Smith* (Provo, Utah: Religious Studies Center, Brigham Young University, 1980), p. 10.

2. Joseph Lathrop, *Christ's Warning to the Churches, To Beware of False Prophets, Who Come as Wolves in Sheep's Clothing: And the Marks by Which They are Known: Illustrated in Two Discourses* (Boston: Printed by Samuel Hill, in Cornhill, 1793), p. 13.

3. Ozias Hart, *The Christian System, in Its Native Simplicity, or, the Errors of the Different Religious Denominations Corrected* (Hartford, Conn.: B.& J. Russell, Printers, 1816), p. vii.

4. Letter from Thomas Campbell to Sidney Rigdon, quoted in E. D. Howe, *Mormonism Unvailed* (Painesville, Ohio: By the author, 1834), pp. 116–23.

5. Samuel F. Hussey, *A Brief Examination of Asa Rand's Book, Called a "Word in Season;" with a Refutation of Some of His Erroneous Statements and Charges Against the People Called Quakers; Whereby His Work Will Appear Out of Season* (Salem, Mass.: Thomas C. Cushing, 1821), pp. 163–64, 123.

6. Joseph Hoag, "Vision of Joseph Hoag, — an eminent minister of the Society of

Friends ... Taken from Fred. Douglas's Paper. Vol. Vii — No. 29." n.p., n.d., c. 1857–58.

7. Edward Demming Andrews, *The People Called Shakers* (New York: Dover Publications, 1953), pp. 11–12.

8. Ibid., pp. 152–55.

9. Richard L. Bushman, *Joseph Smith and the Beginnings of Mormonism* (Urbana and Chicago: University of Illinois Press, 1984), pp. 93–94.

10. In analyzing the early revelations recorded in the Doctrine and Covenants, I use Orson Pratt's chronology, not B. H. Roberts's, following the Doctrine and Covenants sections in the order they appear rather than by the dates in the section headings. Robert J. Woodford in his Ph.D. dissertation, "The Historical Development of the Doctrine and Covenants," 1:200–205, suggests that Orson Pratt was correct regarding the disputed placement of section 10.

11. Quoted in Woodford, 1:22.

12. Joseph Smith, *History of the Church of Jesus Christ of Latter-day Saints,* 7 vols., 2d ed. rev., edited by B. H. Roberts (Salt Lake City: Deseret Book Co., 1978), 1:226.

13. Ehat and Cook, p. 10.

14. Gerard Manley Hopkins, "As Kingfishers Catch Fire, Dragonflies Draw Flame," in Oscar Williams, ed., *A Little Treasury of Modern Poetry* (New York: Charles Scribner's Sons, 1952), p. 21.

Searching the Scriptures

SANDRA BRADFORD PACKARD

An influential movement in twentieth-century philosophy has been hermeneutics. The name of this movement comes from the older discipline of hermeneutics, which was the art or science of interpretation, especially of scripture. The term derives from Hermes, who was the mythical Greek messenger of the gods. Hermeneutic philosophers believe that questions of how to interpret a text are central to philosophy; and, because of the influence of those philosophers, a central question of contemporary philosophy and literary criticism has come to be the hermeneutical question: How can we understand a text, particularly a text that is removed from our contemporary culture but that still has some authoritative claim on us? I would like to organize my comments here around some answers to this question given by a French Jewish philosopher by the name of Emmanuel Levinas. He exemplified his interpretive approach in his commentary on the Talmud, which is rabbinic commentary on the Torah, or the first five books of the Old Testament.

Before I do that, however, I want to talk about why interpretation has come to be so important to philosophy. Ancient Greek philosophers such as Plato believed that to find truth, a person had to somehow get beyond his culture and traditions, which, they believed, put blinders on his mind. For them, truth was an abstract, unembodied ideal best apprehended by an unembodied and unfettered mind. This Greek notion of truth influenced the early Christian conception of God, fostering the idea of an abstract, unembodied, and impersonal God.

Modern philosophy, which began in the Renaissance and continued

....

Sandra Bradford Packard holds a master's degree from Brigham Young University in child development. She and her husband, Dennis Packard, coauthored the book Feasting upon the Word. *They are the parents of six children. Sandra serves as her ward Primary secretary.*

through the Enlightenment, or Age of Reason, was also based on Greek philosophy and stressed the superiority of human reason to religious traditions. But contemporary philosophy—or postmodern, as it is called—has broken away from the rationalist trend that began with Plato. It has rejected the belief that the human mind can perceive truth independent of the culture and traditions that have nurtured it; and it has declared the unembodied "God of the philosophers" inaccessible and hence dead.

Postmodern philosophers believe that to discover truth, one must understand the limits of reason; and that to understand the limits of reason, one must understand the cultural contexts in which it operates. Since a crucial means of understanding any culture is understanding its significant literature, how best to interpret that literature has become an important problem for philosophers.

Postmodern philosophy may have more to say to Latter-day Saints than does ancient philosophy. We believe that God and truth are both embodied. Jesus Christ taught that he, a person, was the way, the truth, and the life. We believe that spirit is matter, that there is no such thing as immaterial matter. We believe that as man is, God once was, and that as God is, man may become. We link closely God, truth, and human life; and our guide to that truth is the scriptures in their fullness, not an abstract set of propositions, doctrines, or principles.

A spin-off of some postmodern philosophy has been moral relativism, the view that each particular culture determines what is right and what is wrong and that there are no broader standards of right and wrong that apply to all cultures. As Latter-day Saints, we, of course, reject moral relativism, as Levinas himself and most serious postmodern philosophers do. But that does not mean that we embrace an abstract view of morality. The law of Moses may have been, or approached, an abstract set of rules; but the higher law gave us a living example of right and wrong, Jesus Christ, whose perfection could not have been defined by an abstract set of laws. We discover how to live by studying how he lived, by observing the lives of those who follow him, and by coming to understand his influence in the lives of those who have gone before us. We do not discover how to live deductively, by reasoning from an abstract set of principles. Otherwise, this earth life would not have been necessary. Eve said, "Were it not for our transgression we never should have had seed, and never should have known good and evil, and the joy of our redemption, and the eternal life which God giveth unto all the obedient." (Moses 5:11.)

In an introduction to Levinas's book *Nine Talmudic Readings,* his translator, Annette Aronowicz, draws out of his work three keys to understanding a text.[1] I want to discuss those keys in the context of our Latter-day Saint scriptural tradition. They have an obvious sense to them but also a deeper sense, which I hope to bring out.

The first key is paying close attention to detail in the scriptures, to the particular words and phrases that are used. This approach is the opposite of abstracting various doctrines or principles from the scriptures. Though there may be reasons for abstracting this type of information, we need to realize that doctrines or principles lose meaning when they are taken out of their context. They become a shadow, a disembodied reflection of what they were before. As Arthur Henry King, Shakespeare scholar and former president of the London Temple, says, "What is the object of the parable of the prodigal son? It is to give us, by means of a piece of the highest art, Christ's own art, the Lord's own art, an experience—an experience of what it is like to repent, of what it is like to forgive, of what it is abominably like to envy—so that we may wish to repent and forgive and wish to shun envy. Who was ever persuaded to repent by discussing an abstract concept of repentance? Who was ever persuaded to forgive by studying an abstract idea of forgiveness? . . . The parable is intended to be, not an illustration of a principle, but an example to be followed and a feeling to be conveyed. If we miss the experience, we have missed the point of the parable."[2]

When we do not pay careful attention to detail, we run the risk of misinterpretation. For instance, John 5:39, "Search the scriptures; for in them ye think ye have eternal life: and they are they which testify of me," has been quoted to support the proposition that we should read the scriptures. But is that what it is really saying? Why does Jesus say, "for in them ye think ye have eternal life" rather than "for in them ye have eternal life"? If we look at the context in which this scripture was given, we find that it was a response to the Jews' persecution of Jesus for healing on the Sabbath. A modern translation of the Bible clarifies the phrase "think ye." The New International Version translates this scripture as follows: "You diligently study the scriptures because you think that by them you possess eternal life. These are the scriptures that testify about me, yet you refuse to come to me to have life." Instead of an injunction to study the scriptures, this scripture is a sober warning against reading them blindly, ignoring what they have to say about our own circumstances in life and failing to see the light that is manifest to us.

In paying careful attention to detail, to the actual words that are there, we allow the scriptures to have a greater emotional effect on us. For example, noticing the repetition of words and phrases can affect us in this way. Let me illustrate with three scriptures. The first describes the reunion of Jacob and Esau after years of separation, precipitated by jealousy and an angry quarrel. Genesis says, "[And Jacob] bowed himself to the ground seven times, until he came near to his brother. And Esau ran to meet him, and embraced him, and fell on his neck, and kissed him: and they wept." (Genesis 33:3–4.)

This scripture was undoubtedly familiar to Jesus during his earthly ministry, and he used words from it in the parable of the prodigal son to describe the Father's reception of his erring son: "But when he was yet a great way off, his father saw him, and had compassion, and ran, and fell on his neck and kissed him." (Luke 15:20.)

The book of Moses reveals an even more ancient source for this way of describing a family reunion and at the same time projects it to the end of time. In Enoch's vision of the latter days, he sees his city, soon to be taken to heaven, return, and he sees himself and his people united with the inhabitants of the New Jerusalem, their brethren in Christ, separated by millennia in time. The Lord says to Enoch, "Then shalt thou and all thy city meet them there, and we will receive them into our bosom, and they shall see us; and we will fall upon their necks, and they shall fall upon our necks, and we will kiss each other; and there shall be mine abode, and it shall be Zion, which shall come forth out of all the creations which I have made; and for the space of a thousand years the earth shall rest." (Moses 7:63–64.)

Seeing each of these scriptures in context with the others deepens their meaning and import. Commenting on a similar pattern of repetition in great literature, Arthur Henry King said, "When you read great literature and find echoes in it over the centuries, sometimes over the thousands of years, it is an extraordinary experience. It goes deep."[3]

The second key to interpreting the scriptures, exemplified by Levinas, is to let them shed light on current problems and concerns. We do not do this by abstracting principles out of the scriptures and mechanically applying those principles to our lives but by absorbing their words and spirit totally into the changing situations of our lives. In fact, it is the ability of the scriptures to enter a multiplicity of situations and historical contexts that makes them great. If we fail to bring the scriptures to bear on our lives, they are dead to us, and our discussion of them will be dead to others. My husband tells me that Neal Maxwell once characterized the type of discussion that goes on in some high priest quorums as intellectual ping-pong. It is that kind of discussion we want to avoid.

I believe that the mark of how well we know the scriptures is not the kind of answers we can give in Sunday School but the frequency with which scriptural phrases and situations and concerns enter into our own lives and our perceptions of the world. Recently, our family attended a wedding in an unfamiliar city. My husband, driving the car, was absentmindedly following a relative who was driving the car in front of us. I asked, "Do we know where we're going?" My thirteen-year-old daughter in the back seat piped up, "Oh, we're just following the yellow brick road." An appropriate response to the situation, her comment placed what we were doing in the context of "The Wizard of Oz," which she had seen a number of times. In a similar manner, I remember lying in a hospital bed with a very bad case of pneumonia, worrying about four young children at home, and thinking, "Oh God, where art thou? And where is the pavilion that covereth thy hiding place?" (D&C 121:1.) Those words kept coming to me. I was living that experience in the context of Joseph Smith's imprisonment in Liberty Jail.

My husband and I have a friend who once complained about some bureaucratic regulation by saying it was "according to the law of the Medes and Persians, which altereth not," referring to the law which forced Daniel into a lion's den, in spite of the king's desire that he not go there. (Daniel 6:12.) In recent years, the discussion of justice and mercy in the Book of Mormon has weighed on my mind as a parent. My husband and I have often noticed that we assume the roles of justice and mercy when it comes to our children. Most often, he is mercy and I am justice. That doesn't always make for a smooth marital relationship. Mercy thinks justice is being too hard on the child, and justice thinks mercy is being too lenient. In the scriptures, the Father represents justice and the Son mercy; and sinners, as we all are, need to hear the call of both. If one overpowers the other, repentance is impossible. The tension between justice and mercy always seems to be there in a family. Perhaps it is a tension as necessary for a child's development as it is in life for our own.

We need to exercise care and thought in applying the scriptures to our lives. This truth came very forcefully to my mind ten or fifteen years ago when I read a newspaper article about a Utah father who decided to sacrifice his infant son as Abraham had Isaac. The child died, and the father ended up in a mental institution. What went wrong here? For one thing, it seems that the father had not come to moral terms with the scriptures. That is necessary, but often it requires a struggle, because the scriptures often challenge our understanding of right and wrong. It is not at all as easy as we sometimes make it seem. Many people find the Old Testament morally repugnant, because they have not paid the price to come to moral terms with it. They say, "This document, or parts of it, cannot possibly teach me anything" and forfeit the deeper understanding of right and wrong that would result if they wrestled with it for a while, as Jacob did with the angel to receive a blessing. For years the story of Abraham and Isaac troubled me. I worried, "Would the Lord ever ask me to do anything that I felt was wrong?" After a period of concern and prayer over this question, I came to understand that what the Lord required of Abraham was not a sacrifice of conscience but a sacrifice of heart, and that is what he would require of me. That is, I might be required to sacrifice what I most love in this world, but he would not ask me to act in a way I could not come to see as being right. In coming to terms with the Old Testament, Jewish commentary, like that of Levinas, can be very helpful, because Jewish rabbis have been struggling with the Old Testament for centuries.

The third key for understanding the scriptures, then, is studying the tradition of commentary that has gone before us. For Latter-day Saints, that means studying what the prophets and other inspired teachers have said about the scriptures. It might also mean studying what Jews and other Christians have said about the scripture they possess. Sometimes this commentary is not too helpful, but sometimes it is very helpful; and it is a kind of arrogance or insecurity that keeps us from taking truth from all sources available to us. We should not approach either Latter-day Saint or non-Latter-day Saint commentary looking for quick, easy, and final answers—scholarly or doctrinal. The greatness of the scriptures lies in their eternal relevance and thus in the possibility for endless commentary on them. Commentary in a religious tradition is like a continuing discussion, and we participate in that discussion when we bring our own experiences and our intellectual and spiritual resources to bear on it.

I once read a non-LDS commentary on the book of Jonah. At one point the commentator drew a parallel between the book of Jonah and the parable of the prodigal son,[4] which led me to reflect on several other parallels. Both stories portray repentant sinners (the people of Nineveh in the book of Jonah and the younger son in the parable of the prodigal son), a judgmental person (the prophet Jonah in one case and the elder brother in the other), and a loving person (God in the story of Jonah and the father in the parable). Both stories end with the loving person asking the judgmental one a question that the reader must answer also: Is mercy not a better course than punishment? These parallels broadened my understanding of the mercy that God expects of his people and of the strong tendency of "righteous" people to judge. It also renewed my appreciation for Christ's extraordinary ability to draw on the Old Testament—his own religious tradition—in teaching his people. As the description of the reunion of the father and son in the parable of the prodigal son echoes the description of the reunion of Jacob and Esau, so the plot and theme of the parable echo those of the book of Jonah. These echoes must have impressed the people Christ taught, giving authority to his message and new life to Old Testament scriptures.

Another commentator I have appreciated is Howard W. Hunter. His remarks about the parable of the prodigal son in a 1960 general conference address greatly moved me and allowed me to see this parable in the context of my own life. He said, "When the prodigal boy, in that parable which most perfectly tells the story of the sinning, and repentant life, 'came to himself,' his words were, 'I will arise and go to my father.' (Luke 15:18.) While he is yet afar off, the waiting father sees him coming and is moved with compassion. Repentance is but the homesickness of the soul, and the uninterrupted and watchful care of the parent is the fairest earthly type of the unfailing forgiveness of God. The family is, to the mind of Jesus, the nearest of human analogies to that divine order which it was His mission to reveal."[5] I used to wonder if the prodigal son's homesickness was genuine repentance; from Elder Hunter I learned that all repentance is homesickness.

Sometimes commentary can be as inspired as scripture and continue the revelation which the scripture began. One example of that is the commentary of latter-day prophets on the scripture in Isaiah, which says, "The wolf also shall dwell with the lamb, and the leopard shall lie down with the kid; and the calf and the young lion and the fatling together; and a little child shall lead them. And the cow and the bear shall feed; their young ones shall lie down together: and the lion shall eat straw like the ox. And the sucking child shall play on the hole of the asp, and the weaned child shall put his hand on the cockatrice' den. They shall not hurt nor destroy in all my holy mountain: for the earth shall be full of the knowledge of the Lord, as the waters cover the sea." (Isaiah 11:6–9.) Modern prophets give this scripture a whole new dimension by teaching that the promised peace between humankind and animals will not come automatically but as a result of our increased kindness to animals. For instance, Joseph Smith said, "Men must become harmless, before the brute creation; and when men lose their vicious dispositions and cease to destroy the animal race, the lion and the lamb can dwell together, and the sucking child can play with the serpent in safety."[6] Brigham Young, Joseph F. Smith and George Q. Cannon also spoke on this subject, and I have been deeply impressed by these prophets, who in many ways seem to have anticipated the environmental movement of our day and give it a religious dimension.[7]

Emmanuel Levinas began his life's work with enthusiasm for Western culture, but the holocaust taught him its moral deficiencies. Within his religious tradition, Judaism, he found the moral perspective that could prevent a recurrence of the holocaust. I hope his insights will be helpful to you, as they have been to me. Behind them all is a willingness to let the scriptures speak and to be humble before them. That is the attitude that invites the Spirit to attend us.

NOTES

1. Emmanuel Levinas, *Nine Talmudic Readings,* trans. Annette Aronowicz (Bloomington and Indianapolis: Indiana University Press, 1990).

2. Arthur Henry King, *The Abundance of the Heart* (Salt Lake City: Bookcraft, 1986), p. 166.

3. Ibid., p. 87.

4. Leslie C. Allen, "The Books of Joel, Obadiah, Jonah and Micah," in *The New International Commentary on the Old Testament,* ed. R. K. Harrison (Grand Rapids, Mich.: William B. Eerdmans Publishing Co., 1976), p. 235.

5. Howard W. Hunter, in Conference Report, Apr. 1960, p. 125.

6. Joseph Smith, *History of the Church of Jesus Christ of Latter-day Saints,* 7 vols., 2d ed. rev., edited by B. H. Roberts (Salt Lake City: Deseret Book Co., 1978), 2:71.

7. Sandra Bradford Packard, "The Salvation of Animals," unpublished manuscript in possession of the author.

The Book of Job and God's Hand in All Things

MELODIE MOENCH CHARLES

The book of Job seems to be two stories rather than one. It begins and ends with a frame story, written in prose. (Job 1–2; 42:7–17.) This frame story surrounds an interior story written as poetry. (Job 3:1–42:6.) In the frame story, God and Satan meet up, and God brags about how loyal Job is to him. Satan says that Job is loyal because it pays to be loyal. God has bought Job's love. Experience has taught Job that blessings are the automatic reward of his loyalty. If there weren't such rewards, Satan claims, Job would curse God.

God challenges Satan to do whatever he wants to Job and Job will still be loyal. So Job's fortune disappears in a puff of smoke, and his children are all killed in a freak accident. Job remains loyal.

Trying again, Satan says that if God lets Job feel physical pain, Job will curse God. God gives Satan permission to hurt Job. So Job's body is terribly afflicted, and yet Job blesses God.

Having made his point to Satan, God restores Job's fortunes, gives him back double the possessions he had lost, and gives him new children.

What does this story teach? That Job was virtuous, and that righteous people who are loyal to God prosper. Job prospered as the story began, and after a temporary devastation, Job regained the prosperity he deserved. This is an example of covenant theology: God covenanted with the Israelites that he would bless them in return for their righteousness and loyalty and that he would punish them in return for their wickedness and faithlessness. The Old Testament is full of statements and examples

Melodie Moench Charles, whose master's degree is in Old Testament from Harvard Divinity School, has published articles on the Old Testament, women and scriptures, and Latter-day Saint theology. She and her husband, Robert Charles, have four children. She serves as Primary pianist in her Texas ward.

of this theology.[1] In the interior story, the system of appropriate rewards for righteous behavior has failed Job. In the dialogues Job has with his friends, no one shows any awareness of Satan's existence, and all assume that God is directly causing Job's misfortunes. Furthermore, they all assume that God has a reason for causing Job so much pain.

Job suffers; he curses the day he was born; he complains bitterly because he can't see any good reason why God should torment him; he protests his innocence; he asks God why God is tormenting him; he complains that God won't answer his questions or come to his aid. In between Job's speeches are speeches of Job's friends. They defend covenant theology. They remind him that because the righteous prosper and the wicked suffer, he must have done something to deserve this; if he would repent, then God would restore him to his former comfort and happiness.

Finally, God appears to Job in a whirlwind and says, in essence, "I created everything. Job, what can you do compared to that? What do you know compared to what I know?" God does not answer any of Job's questions and does not take sides in the debate about covenant theology. Instead He insults and taunts Job for being merely a creature. Job responds that he had not understood. Having seen God, he despises himself and repents.

Although on most levels I am very fond of the book of Job, I am not fond of it as history. I find it repugnant to believe that God and Satan made a bet about whether Job would crack under stress. I am very unsettled at God's badgering and belittling Job when He finally does respond to him. I don't believe that God rewarded Job's faithfulness by giving him double the possessions He had taken from him and a new set of children. And I don't believe that made everything all right again.[2]

I see Job as representative of all humankind. As Pulitzer Prize-winning poet Archibald MacLeish writes in *JB*, "Oh, there's always someone playing Job. . . . There must be thousands! . . . Millions and millions of mankind."[3] Job is any righteous person who suffers through no fault of his or her own. I believe that the dialogues between Job and his friends represent and reflect dialogues sufferers have had with themselves, with God, with their churches, and with those around them as they have tried to make sense of their suffering.

The value of the book of Job for me is its teaching that there is no necessary correlation between what people deserve and what they get.

It shows that righteous people do suffer and that there may be no reason behind their suffering. It provides no ammunition for the belief that suffering is evidence that God is punishing someone. It does not support the belief that God tries individuals to test their faith or to improve them. The book legitimizes asking the toughest of life's questions, and at the same time it shows that there are often no good answers. I find, too, that much of the value of Job for me is not actually *in* the book of Job. The part of the book of Job I like best is what it draws out of me as I participate in the dialogue between Job and his friends. If I read the book of Job with my mind engaged (and that is not always easy—difficulties in the text often make it unintelligible), it is impossible not to join the fray—to agree with some arguments, to reject others, and to add my own. What I want to share here is something that is not in the book of Job at all but rather is what the book of Job has caused me to think.

In the interior story, Job and his friends all believe that God is the immediate and direct cause of the calamity befalling Job. Job's friends believe that God gives humans their just rewards or punishments during their mortal lives. They tell Job that God will redeem the righteous from famine and protect them from war (5:20); God will ensure that the wicked will not prosper for long nor enjoy their ill-gotten wealth (20:5–29); God will repay people according to their deeds (34:11); God will correct the faltering righteous: if they listen to him and serve him, he will make their lives prosperous and pleasant; if they will not listen, they will perish by the sword, for the godless in heart die young, and their life ends in shame (36:6–14).

Before Job was afflicted, he believed as his friends do: God rewarded the righteous and punished the wicked during their mortal lives. But since Job did not deserve his suffering, he had to revise his beliefs. He threw out the belief that God dispensed rewards and punishments justly; however, he kept the belief that God was the one doing the dispensing. God was still the cause of what happened to Job, but now Job had no explanation for why God would devastate him. Job said, "Who knoweth not . . . that the hand of the Lord has wrought this?" (12:9.) Job cried to his friends, "Have pity upon me, have pity upon me, O ye my friends, for the hand of God hath touched me!" (19:21.)

In the Book of Mormon, God promises the Nephites and the Latter-day Saints that he will bless his people when they are righteous and punish them when they are not. The Nephite cycles of prosperity and hardship demonstrate this system at work.[4] We are also taught to expect, as Job did, that at least some of the blessings we receive for righteousness will be material good fortune and not just spiritual comfort. Tithing is our best example of increased prosperity being promised to the obedient.[5]

From the nineteenth century, Doctrine and Covenants 59:21 says that God's wrath is kindled against "those who confess not his hand in all things." Doctrine and Covenants 87:6–8 teaches that God chastens people by famine, plague, earthquakes, and storms. (Compare D&C 43:25–26.) The *Millennial Star*'s regular column, "Signs of the Times," pointed to various natural disasters in the news — volcanoes, floods, tornados, and famine — as being God's judgments upon humans.[6] Orson Hyde, in "A Timely Warning to the People of England," attributed England's hardships to "the withering touch of the Almighty."[7]

More recently, quoting President Joseph F. Smith, Elder Boyd K. Packer told Latter-day Saint scholars that those who are wise and careful "see in every hour and in every moment of the existence of the Church . . . the overruling, almighty hand of Him who sent His Only Begotten Son to the world."[8] Like Job's friends, some Mormons today respond to their afflicted fellow Saints by suggesting that their affliction is God's punishment. William Timmins, a Latter-day Saint dying of cancer, wrote: "Some ward members have openly asked me, my wife, and some of my children what we have done wrong that the Lord is punishing us by taking me away."[9]

The idea that God's hand is in all things is easy for people who are comfortable. When we are healthy and prospering, when our children are making us proud, we might think that God has blessed us because we deserve it. When distant others, people not very much like us, are struggling, we might think that God has put them in that situation because they have somehow deserved it. But what if we're righteous and we're suffering? How might we respond, and what are the consequences of our responses?

First, like Job, we may ask, "What have I done to deserve this? Why has God done this to me?" Rather than believing that our suffering is random and impersonal, we may prefer to believe that God designed it specifically for us for a good reason. Because we are uncomfortable with purposeless suffering, we come up with reasons to give our suffering meaning. We attribute our suffering to God's plan.

If God gives us the situations we deserve and we are suffering, then we must have done something to deserve it. We were wrong to think we were righteous. Personal disasters are our fault: "If I'm suffering, I must be guilty." We might think, "God has caused my infertility because I postponed having children so my husband and I could finish school." "God wouldn't heal me because I didn't have enough faith." In this mindset, we suffer not only the pain of whatever disaster has befallen but also the burden of guilt and a diminished sense of self: the sufferer is unworthy of a better situation; the sufferer deserves the suffering.

If we see suffering as punishment, we may interpret a loved one's suffering as punishment for ourselves: "Because my daughter has leukemia, maybe God is punishing me for something." If we believe that God causes trouble for someone we love in order to punish us, then we must also believe that we are more important to God than that suffering loved one is. We must believe that God is willing to devastate one innocent person to punish those guilty people who love that person.

As Church members, we may believe that group hardships in the early Church were a divine punishment for group guilt. The early Saints believed that it was because of their sins that Zion's Camp couldn't redeem Missouri for them, that their cooperative financial ventures failed, and that polygamy was ended. If the group had been more committed, more faithful, more righteous, more determined, then God would have blessed each of these endeavors with success. Rather than explain these failures by economics, politics, weather, social climate, geography, or the soundness of the plan to be followed, many of the Saints narrowed the explanations to two: God failed them or they failed God. Since God wouldn't fail them, then they must have failed God.[10]

If I believe that *my* suffering is punishment from God that *I* deserve, then it is only logical to judge the rest of humanity by the same standard as well. According to this line of reasoning, anyone who is suffering is being punished for sin. And if sinners deserve their suffering, then I would be disrupting God's plan if I gave them either compassion or assistance. One example of this thinking is the "You made your bed— now lie in it" approach to others' misfortunes.

Nevertheless, Elder Packer said in a general conference address about handicaps that we are wrong to believe that suffering is necessarily a direct result of sin. "There is little room for feelings of guilt in connection with handicaps. Some handicaps may result from carelessness or abuse, and some through addiction of parents. But most of them do not. Afflictions come to the innocent.... The idea that *all* suffering is somehow the direct result of sin has been taught since ancient times. It is false doctrine."[11]

Second, we may try to make sense of suffering by thinking that God has caused difficulty in our lives for a positive purpose. We or someone else will ultimately benefit from it. If we are righteous, "all things shall work together for [our] good." (D&C 90:24.) We might think, "God gave our family this sick child to bring us together." "God called my father home to heaven to do missionary work." "God gave my teenager AIDS so that he could teach other teenagers that immoral behaviors can have tragic consequences." "God needs my child in heaven more than I need her on earth." Although some people find comfort in these kinds of reasons, I think that it's risky to presume either that God has caused a tragedy, if he hasn't told us he has, or that we know his motive, if he hasn't told us that either.

Margaret (Meg) Rampton Munk, a Latter-day Saint poet, died a few years ago of cancer. In the sermon she wrote for her own funeral, she asked her friends not to tell her children and husband that she died because God needed her in heaven more than they needed her on earth. She didn't believe that was true. She died because cancer was stronger than her body's ability to fight it; God knew that her family needed her on earth.[12]

We may suggest that God gives people difficulties to refine and improve their character: "God caused my disability to teach me humility." "God gave me a child with attention deficit disorder to teach me patience." It is true that some people who suffer are ennobled by what they endure; however, just because some people are ennobled through suffering does not compel us to believe that God caused their specific suffering to ennoble them. Not all suffering has an ennobling purpose nor an ennobling result. What of the suffering of children? Carlisle Hunsaker, formerly an institute teacher at the University of Utah, argues that starving children are not better off spiritually because they starve. They don't need to starve to learn something or to improve their character, and their suffering cannot be part of God's plan for them.[13]

The notion that God routinely causes catastrophes for his children's benefit or punishment makes God a monster. The material world provides plenty of suffering that occurs naturally. Why would God add more misery to the world and aim it at specific people? The mortal parents I know do not manipulate their children's worlds to cause them pain so that they may grow by experiencing it, and it is hard to conceive of a heavenly parent doing that for his children.

Third, we may respond to suffering by becoming embittered toward God. People who speak of "the patience of Job," including the New Testament author James, must be thinking of the frame story, for Job is not patient in the interior story. Job is bitter. He rails, "I will speak in the anguish of my spirit; I will complain in the bitterness of my soul." (7:11; cf. 10:1.) He tells God, "Let me alone, that I may take comfort a little, before I [die]." (10:20–21.) "God hath delivered me to the ungodly, and turned me over into the hands of the wicked. I was at ease, but he hath broken me asunder: he hath also taken me by my neck, and shaken me to pieces, and set me up for his mark." (16:11–12.) People who are bitter might think, "God could have healed my child, but he didn't choose to." "God let my husband abandon me and my family." "God let us lose our retirement money when the company went bankrupt." "What good has it done me to be righteous? I've been loyal to God, but look at what he has done to me."

As Latter-day Saints we are not bound to believe, as Job did, that God causes specific suffering. Our God is not responsible for everything that happens. Instead of deciding why God caused our suffering, we can say, "I don't know why it happened." That is hard for us to admit, for we think we should have answers for all of life's important questions. And yet "We don't know why" is the response Elder Neal A. Maxwell offered a family when their father was killed and their mother was paralyzed in an accident while they were mission presidents in Africa. Brother Maxwell assured this family that God loved them, quoting Nephi, "I know that [God] loveth his children; nevertheless, I do not know the meaning of all things." (1 Nephi 11:17.) He encouraged everyone to turn their focus from "Why did this happen?" to "How can I help?"[14]

Natural law at work causes accidents and disasters. When drought limits harvests, people starve. When cars crash, people get hurt. Some proportion of the population will be infertile, and some proportion will get cancer. In spite of their parents' teachings, some children will use their agency to make destructive choices. Rather than assigning responsibility to God and trying to think of his motive, we can look at cause and effect. Elder Packer explained, "The very purpose for which the world was created, and man[kind] introduced to live upon it, requires that the laws of nature operate in cold disregard for human feelings. We must work out our salvation without expecting the laws of nature to be exempted for us."[15] Carlisle Hunsaker asks us to accept "randomness as a fact of existence."[16]

Does this view push God too far out of our lives? I think not. We still have faith and hope that if we're in trouble, God might interrupt the natural chain of cause and effect and choose *our* child to be healed. Even if he chooses not to disrupt the natural chain of cause and effect in our lives, he need not be irrelevant to us. God can still help the surgeon do her very best in operating on our child. God can help us be the wisest, most loving parents it is possible to be. God can inspire a researcher to put the right combination of chemicals together to cure a cancer. God can give our teenagers the courage to make good choices. God can inspire us to offer material and spiritual comfort to others. In all of these, God will have an effect on suffering, though in each a responsive human is necessary, too. God can influence us to respond to suffering in our lives with courage, dignity, compassion, and charity.

NOTES

1. For instance, see Deuteronomy 5:9–10; 7:12–15; 11:13–17; Isaiah 48:22.

2. In 1922 the First Presidency, responding to a question about biblical literalness, said that while they thought that Job and Jonah were real people, it was possible that they were teaching vehicles, as were the characters in the parables. See Thomas Alexander, *Mormonism in Transition: A History of the Latter-day Saints, 1890–1930* (Urbana and Chicago: University of Illinois Press, 1986), p. 283.

3. Archibald MacLeish, *JB* (Boston: Houghton Mifflin Co., 1958), p. 12.

4. For example, D&C 3:18; 103:7–13; 104:5, 8, 23, 25, 31, 33; 105:2, 9; 109:25–33; 121:2–3; 13–23; 124:90; 2 Nephi 1:10–22, 28–32; Alma 45:10–14; 50:22; Helaman 4:23–26; 6:33–36; 15.

5. The most famous statement of this expectation comes from Mary Fielding Smith as told by her son, Joseph F. Smith. She explained: "If I did not pay my tithing, I should expect the Lord to withhold His blessings from me. I pay my tithing not only because it is a law of God, but because I expect a blessing by doing so. By keeping this and other laws, I expect to prosper and to be able to provide for my family." "Tithing Blessings," *Friend*, Mar. 1981, p. 36. Because this story is frequently retold in Church publications and lesson manuals, this expectation clearly has official sanction.

6. See, for example, *Millennial Star* 1 (1840): 65–67; 96–100; 2 (1841): 24.

7. In *Manchester Mormons: The Journal of William Clayton, 1840–1842*, ed. James B. Allen and Thomas G. Alexander (Santa Barbara: Peregrine Smith, 1974), pp. 5–6.

8. Boyd K. Packer, "The Mantle Is Far, Far Greater Than the Intellect," *Brigham Young University Studies* 21 (Summer 1981): 261.

9. William M. Timmins, "On Death and Dying," *Ensign*, Apr. 1989, p. 32.

10. Doctrine and Covenants 103:4–8, 12–14, 36 and 105:2–9 present this explanation for calling off the campaign to redeem Zion in Missouri. Historian B. Carmon Hardy noted that George Q. Cannon, Joseph F. Smith, and Matthias Cowley all gradually began to promote this explanation for God's allowing the Church to discontinue the practice of polygamy. Many Latter-day Saints came to believe that God allowed the practice to end because the Saints weren't living it valiantly (B. Carmon Hardy, "Self-Blame and the Manifesto," *Dialogue*, 24 [Fall 1991]: 43–57). Some Latter-day Saints, after the 1978 revelation allowing black males to hold the priesthood, said that the revelation would have come sooner if the Saints had been willing to be nonracist. This statement put a burden of guilt on the membership — their wickedness had kept a discriminatory practice in place. The book *Building the City of God* claimed, "Church leaders have consistently emphasized . . . selfishness, unfaithfulness, and unrighteousness" as the reason that the Saints' cooperative financial ventures were failures (Leonard J. Arrington, Feramorz Y. Fox, and Dean L. May [Salt Lake City: Deseret Book Co., 1976], pp. 38–39).

11. Boyd K. Packer, "The Moving of the Water," *Ensign*, May 1991, pp. 7–8.

12. My sister, Nelda Bishop, shared this information with me after she attended the funeral. Similarly, William Timmins said that "death is just part of life." Although some might be comforted by the idea that God needs someone in heaven for an important work, he said, "It is not comforting to my wife and children, who need me here and now." (Timmins, p. 32.)

13. U. Carlisle Hunsaker, "Mormonism and a Tragic Sense of Life," *Sunstone* 8 (Sept.-Oct. 1983): 31–35.

14. Dean and Lorraine Brooks shared this information about Dean's father's funeral with me.

15. Packer, "The Moving of the Water," p. 8. If we did not expect the laws of nature to operate in virtually every case, we could not function. We would never know what to expect; precedent and previous experience would mean nothing. If God micromanaged the universe, routinely manipulating nature and history, we would rarely experience the natural consequences of our choices.

16. Hunsaker, p. 32.

The Restoration of the Doctrines of Marriage and Atonement

M. CATHERINE THOMAS

Among the early Christians a philosophy arose called *asceticism,* which ultimately dismantled several key doctrines of the true Church. Asceticism holds that the material world is devoid of spiritual value and only by renouncing this world and rejecting the sexual function could a person enter the highest spiritual state. Asceticism contributed to changes in several early Christian doctrines, including the doctrines of eternal marriage and atonement. My purpose is to explain how these changes took place, to show the relationship between marriage and atonement, and to suggest how these doctrinal changes have affected women.

Asceticism seeped into Christianity from at least two (and probably more) sources. First, it came indirectly from a Judaism that had its own ascetic tendencies (e.g., the celibate Essenes at Qumran), and from such Greek-influenced Jews as Philo, a contemporary of Jesus and Paul. Second, asceticism entered Christianity directly from early Christian converts who had been trained in Greek philosophy. Many of the earliest Christian converts who wrote to explain and defend Christianity to their Greek-educated friends tried to couch the Christian message in terms their intellectual friends could accept. Because the most profound and basic truths of the gospel (such as a suffering Savior) cannot be reshaped in Greek philosophical terms, these early Christians succeeded not in

M. Catherine Thomas received her Ph.D. in early Christian history from Brigham Young University. She has taught ancient scripture at BYU and at the BYU Jerusalem Center and has directed travel study tours to Israel. She and her husband, Gordon K. Thomas, are the parents of six children. Catherine serves as a Gospel Doctrine teacher and as first counselor in her stake Young Women presidency.

clarifying and preserving the gospel but in distorting it. It soon became unsophisticated to accept the plain truths surrounding the ministry of the Lord Jesus Christ. President Ezra Taft Benson described the process: "The world shouts louder than the whispering of the Holy Ghost. The reasoning of men overrides the revelations of God, and the proud let go of the iron rod."[1]

In particular, asceticism influenced the thinking of the early Christian authors on marriage and procreation. They believed that a better world would arrive if people would quit perpetuating the present fallen order by their acts of reproduction; that is, it would be better to let the material world and fallen man die out. The higher spiritual order would come on earth when the old one, the one Eve had precipitated, had ceased.

If man's body was bad, then of course God could not have a physical body. With the rejection of the material world and man's flesh, the ascetics denied God a body. Greek philosophy also insisted that God must be totally unlimited and absolute and that, therefore, he could not be limited to and by a body. In addition, there could be only one such being, because if there were more than one, they could not both be ultimate and absolute.[2] Thus the Christians had a problem when it came to drafting creeds on God's form because the scriptures plainly taught three divine persons. Therefore, at Nicaea (A.D. 325) the first official council of the Christian Church officially sanctioned the nonmaterial, three-in-one God. A great mystery—manmade.

An example of a descendant of the Nicene Creed is the Thirty-nine Articles of the Church of England. This creed is typical of orthodox Christian creeds and has a familiar phrase: "There is but one living and true God, everlasting, without body, parts, or passions; . . . and in unity of this Godhead there be three Persons, of one substance, power, and eternity: the Father, the Son, and the Holy Ghost."[3]

If God was something entirely other than man, then man could not become like him: man did not exist on a continuum with God. The diabolical aim was to distance man from God and to scramble men's and women's understandings of their own exalted destiny.

The body of the Son of God came under attack as well. Justin Martyr, one of the earliest Christian writers (mid second century), wrote that Christ had submitted to the conditions of the flesh that included the need for food, drink, and clothing, but one physical function, namely, the "discharging the sexual function He did not submit to; for, regarding the desires of the flesh, He accepted some as necessary, while others, which were unnecessary, He did not submit to. For if the flesh were deprived of food, drink, and clothing, it would be destroyed; but being deprived of lawless desire, it suffers no harm.... Let not, then, those that are unbelieving marvel, if in the world to come He do away with those acts of our fleshly members which even in this present life are abolished [by some]."[4] These Christians could not accept their own sexuality nor see the divine purposes in human sexuality; so, of course, they could not accept God's sexuality.

In the third and fourth centuries after Christ, the desert wildernesses of the Middle East filled up with celibate men and women. The practice of asceticism distinguished men and women from the common herd and identified them with the elite. Ascetics found that they had greater prestige as holy persons, and the women, greater autonomy over their lives and their bodies.

Ascetically inclined people reinterpreted and even tampered with various biblical texts to justify themselves and persuade others to their ascetic way of life. Such men as Tatian and Marcion, both writing in the second century after Christ, believed that Christian asceticism was the only way of spiritual deliverance and actually doctored the scriptures to recruit people to a virginal life. Tatian, for example, changed Luke 2:36, which concerns the prophetess Anna who lived with her husband seven years from her virginity, meaning *from* her marriage, to say that Anna remained a virgin *with* her husband seven years.

Men like Tatian and Marcion, although undoubtedly neurotic in their hatred of women, nevertheless were amazingly influential in persuading others to the practice of asceticism. Here is a passage from Tertullian, another second-century mainstream Christian writer, on the sin inherent in women: A woman should "go about in humble garb, and rather to affect meanness of appearance, walking about as Eve mourning and repentant, in order that by every garb of penitence she might the more fully expiate that which she derives from Eve, — the ignominy, I mean, of the first sin, and the odium . . . of human perdition. In pains and in anxieties dost thou bear [children], woman. . . ? And do you not know that you are [each] an Eve? The sentence of God on this sex of yours lives in this age: the guilt must of necessity live too. *You* are the devil's gateway: *you* are that unsealer of the [forbidden] tree: *you* are the first deserter of the divine law: *you* are she who persuaded him whom the devil was not valiant enough to attack. *You* destroyed so easily God's image, man. On account of *your* desert — that is, death —

even the Son of God had to die."[5] Thus Tertullian lays the blame even for the death of Christ on women. Clearly, misogyny was a factor in the practice of asceticism, based (at least theoretically) on an apostate understanding of the woman's role in the Fall and of the function of the Fall itself.

An apostate group among the earliest Christians called docetists (from Greek *dokew,* "seems") claimed that Christ only seemed to be physical. This idea invaded mainstream Christianity. Hilary of Poitiers, a fourth-century Christian theologian, wrote of Christ's suffering that "He felt the force of suffering, but without its pain," as if a weapon were to pierce water or fire or air. "The body of Christ by its virtue suffered the violence of punishment, without its consciousness. . . . He had not a nature which could feel pain."[6]

Once God lost his body and could not suffer, the mainspring of the Atonement was effectively removed. A substitute for the Atonement was devised in a practice called penance, apparent in the instructions to women in the passage from Tertullian quoted above. Doing penance meant self-punishment rather than actually acquiring virtue. Assigned to penitential tasks by a celibate clergy, women and men sat in sackcloth and ashes at the church door, groveled at the feet of the clergy, or abstained from marital relations, sometimes for months. Through these punishments, early Christians expiated their sins. The practice of penance replaced the true doctrine that Jesus suffered and paid off the law of justice, releasing to women and men a great divine enabling power to pursue the divine nature.

If we had the full text of what constituted the original Bible, I think we would see that changes have been made in at least two main doctrinal areas: first, in the doctrine of the Atonement, especially the accessibility of the grace of Jesus Christ, and, second, in the doctrine of the body of God and the relationship of the Father and the Son; and as corollary, the doctrines of the deification of mankind, eternal marriage, and eternal procreation.

These changes in doctrine influenced the whole subsequent development of mainstream Christianity, as we can see today in the enduring practices of penance and celibacy and perhaps in our own possible discomfort in thinking of Jesus in a married relationship.

Because the doctrine of God's body is so pivotal, it is often the first doctrine that has to be restored before an apostasy can begin to be healed. In the Sacred Grove, Joseph could obviously see that there were two separate, glorified, anthropomorphic beings in the Godhead before either of the Gods had said a thing. In a split second Joseph grasped a truth that could end eighteen hundred years of speculation and pointless philosophizing, centuries of making mysteries out of plainness.

With the restoration of the Gospel came a whole complex of related ideas and practices that greatly expanded the knowledge and power of the believers. Two of these ideas, marriage and atonement, have a significant relationship to each other. *Atonement* is a made-up word invented by the translator William Tindale. It first appears in Tindale's English version of the Bible in 1526. He used the word *at-one-ment* to translate the Greek word for reconciliation. The word *atonement* is literally *at-one-ment.* Generally, wherever it is used in scripture, it pertains to the work that Christ did to bring fallen, estranged man back into spiritual oneness with God, first through the Holy Ghost and then literally into God's presence. The Greek word for reconciliation *(kataláge)* means to reunite two who were once in harmony but became estranged. The English prefix *re,* as in re-conciliation suggests this same idea of returning to a relationship. The Greek word underlying our English *atonement* suggests not only that Christ brings us to heaven but that he is going to restore us to a relationship and organization that existed before the world was. Therefore, the word rendered *at-one-ment* by the early translators of the Bible could perhaps have been more accurately rendered *re-at-one-ment* or *re-union.* That is, atonement seeks to restore us to a spiritual relationship with the Father and the Son in this life and to that organization and harmony we had together in the premortal world (after the war in heaven).[7]

Things must be done on earth as they are done in heaven so that that which is earthly may be made heavenly. Since at-one-ment is the condition in which heavenly beings live, we may consciously and deliberately assist in bringing at-one-ment to pass, in whatever way we can, on the earth. The Lord has said: "I have committed the keys of my kingdom, and a dispensation of the gospel for the last times; and for the fulness of times, in the which I will *gather together in one* all things, both which are in heaven, and which are on earth. And also with all those whom my Father hath given me out of the world." (D&C 27:13–14; emphasis added.) It is our privilege as the covenant people to participate in that restored work. "If ye are not one ye are not mine." (D&C 38:27.)

Thus, we further the Savior's work of atonement when we live together in a state of at-one-ment. We do atonement work when we marry and work at that marriage. Without the commitment to marriage, the Lord's atoning work could not go forward on the earth. The purposes of creation would have been wasted. Eternal marriage, after all, is both a type and a function of at-one-ment. It is a type in that it constitutes two separate, fallen beings—a man and a woman—brought into oneness with each other and with God through the grace and power of Jesus Christ. It is a function of atonement in that, through the divine enabling power of the Atonement, a man and woman make their marriage eternal. The Savior said, "Have ye not read, that he which made them *at the beginning* made them male and female, and said, For this cause shall a man leave father and mother, and shall *cleave* to his wife: and they twain shall be *one* flesh? Wherefore they are no more twain, but *one* flesh. What therefore God hath joined together, let not man put asunder." (Matthew 19:4–6; emphasis added.) The word *cleave* is an atonement word that means "to cling to closely, tightly." Paul wrote to the Corinthians, countering currents of asceticism already gaining momentum in the Church: "Neither is the man without the woman, neither the woman without the man, in the Lord. For as the woman is of the man, even so is the man also by the woman; but all . . . [are] of God." (1 Corinthians 11:11–12.) Conversely, when we put relationships asunder, we violate this spirit of at-one-ment.

We also participate in at-one-ment in the temple where we seal ancestors and posterity in the great family chains that Brigham Young says Joseph Smith showed him in a vision to be part of the premortal organization: "Be sure to tell the people to keep the spirit of the Lord; and if they will, they will find themselves just as they were organized by our Father in Heaven before they came into the world. Our father in Heaven organized the human family, but they are all disorganized and in great confusion.

"Joseph then showed me the pattern, how they were in the beginning. This I cannot describe, but I saw it, and saw where the Priesthood had been taken from the earth and how it must be joined together, so that there would be a perfect chain from Father Adam to his latest posterity."[8]

About the premortal organization of the covenant people, of Israel, Elder Bruce R. McConkie wrote: "Israel is an eternal people. She came into being as a chosen and separate congregation before the foundations of the earth were laid; she was a distinct and a peculiar people in the preexistence, even as she is in this sphere."[9] Were many relationships of the covenant people created spiritually before they were created physically? It would seem so. Part of the great work of the Atonement, then, is to restore those heavenly relationships and thus, ultimately, to restore women to their exalted positions in eternity.

Therefore, when a woman lives in patience and love with others, in peace, meshing with those around her, forgiving, she does the work of at-one-ment. The more she makes each relationship sweeter, more tender, and dear, the more she lives at-one-ment. As women nurture children and live in resonance with them, they do this work. As women draw others to the love of the Savior, they live at-one-ment. As men and women come together to the temple, for themselves and for loved ones, they come closer and closer to the divine embrace.

As the true doctrines of marriage and atonement declined through such apostate influences as asceticism, many men and women rejected the traditional roles of womanhood. Women lost their eternal bearings and a knowledge of their eternal status. With the Restoration came a greatly enhanced view of marriage, of the exalted position and destiny of women, and of their calling to the work of atonement.

NOTES

1. Ezra Taft Benson, "Beware of Pride," *Ensign*, May 1989, p. 5.

2. Stephen E. Robinson, "The Great Church Councils," unpublished manuscript in possession of the author.

3. John H. Leith, ed., *Creeds of the Churches*, rev. ed. (Chicago: Aldine Publishing Co., 1973), pp. 266–67.

4. Justin Martyr, *On the Resurrection*, trans. M. Dods, in *The Apostolic Fathers with Justin Martyr and Irenaeus*, rpt. lithograph (Grand Rapids, Mich.: Eerdmans Printing Co., 1985), 1:295.

5. Tertullian, "De Cultu Feminarum [On the Apparel of Women]," trans. S. Thelwall, in *Fathers of the Third Century*, ed. Alexander Roberts and James Donaldson, rpt. lithograph (Grand Rapids, Mich.: Eerdmans Printing Co., 1976), 1:1.

6. St. Hilary of Poitiers, *On the Trinity*, 10:23, in *St. Hilary of Poitiers: Select Works*, trans. E. W. Watson, L. Pullan, et al., ed. W. Sanday, rpt. lithograph (Grand Rapids, Mich.: Eerdmans Printing Co., 1983), pp. 187–88.

7. See Alma 42:23, which clearly says that the Atonement brings men back into the presence of God and thus they are restored into his presence.

8. Brigham Young, Journal History of The Church of Jesus Christ of Latter-day Saints, Feb. 23, 1847, Salt Lake City, Church Historical Department, p. 2.

9. Bruce R. McConkie, *A New Witness for the Articles of Faith* (Salt Lake City: Deseret Book Co., 1985), pp. 510–11.

An Inheritance in Zion

JILL MULVAY DERR
MAUREEN URSENBACH BEECHER

In July 1830, Emma Smith received from God the promise and comfort of great blessings. In the revelation to her through her prophet-husband, Joseph Smith, the Lord addressed her by name, "Emma Smith, my daughter," assuring her that "all those who receive my gospel are sons and daughters in my kingdom." "Thou art an elect lady, whom I have called," Emma was told, and she was promised, "Thou shalt receive an inheritance in Zion." The revelation concluded, "This is my voice unto all," extending the promises given Emma to other faithful daughters. (D&C 25.) The "inheritance in Zion" promised to Emma and her sisters is central to the story of Relief Society.

God's assurances that his faithful Saints will receive a divine inheritance are scripturally abundant. For Latter-day Saints such promises took on enlarged significance when the Prophet Joseph Smith received a February 1831 revelation outlining the law of consecration and stewardship. Faithful Saints who voluntarily consecrated their properties to the Church would in turn receive properties or stewardships proportionate to their needs, and a hoped-for accumulated surplus would be used to build the Church and help the poor. Attempts to live the law as an economic system failed at Kirtland, Ohio, and Independence, Missouri. But the promise remained sure: the man or woman "that is a faithful and wise steward shall inherit all things." (D&C 78:22.)

Jill Mulvay Derr, a research historian with the Joseph Fielding Smith Institute for Church History at Brigham Young University, is coeditor of Women's Voices: An Untold History of the Latter-day Saints, 1830–1900. *She and her husband, C. Brooklyn Derr, are the parents of four children. She teaches in her ward Relief Society.*

Maureen Ursenbach Beecher, a professor of English and a research historian with the Joseph Fielding Smith Institute for Church History at BYU, is the author of Eliza and Her Sisters *and coeditor of* Sisters in Spirit *and* New Views of Mormon History. *She and her husband, Dale F. Beecher, have two children. She is a teacher in Relief Society.*

Just as New Testament scriptures entreat us to inherit "the kingdom of heaven" rather than the physical "promised land" of the Old Testament, so Latter-day Saints learned that consecration and stewardship provided a pattern, not simply for settling Ohio and Missouri, but for living the Christ-centered life of the spirit. In this sense, the law of consecration and stewardship is not dormant, awaiting reinstatement at a future time when Saints are more prepared. This law is still operative. It is the pattern by which women and men learn to live holy lives. Consecration and stewardship are the way we lay hold of our "inheritance in Zion."

As Latter-day Saints consecrate the spiritual and temporal gifts they receive for the building up of the kingdom, they receive new gifts of responsibility: stewardships. Moroni writes in the Book of Mormon of the "gift of [the Lord's] calling." (Moroni 7:2.) Women in this dispensation first received the gift of callings and responsibility in connection with the founding of the Relief Society in Nauvoo, Illinois, in 1842. Sisters of diverse ages and backgrounds and from widely spread Nauvoo neighborhoods united in the new organization and consecrated their individual and collective time and means to the Church. Their efforts blessed the poor and furthered the building of the Nauvoo Temple, establishing the sacred pattern of consecration and stewardship that would distinguish the labors of many subsequent generations of Relief Society sisters.

When we consecrate, we start with whatever we have, however little, and discover that if we dedicate it to the Lord's service in consecration, it will expand to meet the need. "Starting from scraps," as historian Audrey Godfrey observed, and patching them together to meet community needs was the almost universal Relief Society experience.[1]

Lucy Meserve Smith, writing of her Provo Relief Society, told of their collections in behalf of the 1856 handcart pioneers caught by early snows in the mountains near South Pass. As soon as the freezing Saints' dilemma was announced in general conference, she wrote, "the sisters stripped off their Peticoats stockings and every thing they could spare, right there in the Tabernacle and piled [them] into the wagons to send to the Saints in the mountains. . . . As our society was short of funds then we could not do much, but. . . . My councilors and I wallowed through the snow until our clothes were wet a foot high to get things together. . . . [T]he four Bishops could hardly carry the bedding and other clothing we got. . . . I never took more satisfaction and I might say pleasure in any labour I ever performed in my life."[2]

From scraps the resourceful Relief Society women furnished their homes and their communities. Their endless braiding of rugs, making of quilts, wasted not, and for the most part, their families wanted not. "Spinning and weaving our scanty supply of wool, gathering up old tin and making it into cups" were ways of contributing. Priscilla Merriman Evans, Relief Society secretary in Spanish Fork, recorded: "President Lucretia Gay worked ten days cording and spinning wool for shirts. She furnished 1/2 pound of wool, worked four days cording and spinning hair for lariats for the brethren. . . . She also helped to make a pair of pants and she made one pair of mittens."[3]

The Sunday eggs, traditionally a woman's to claim, replenished Relief Society coffers, and, as Susa Young Gates noted, "certainly the faithful female of the hen species arose to the occasion."[4] During the early decades of the twentieth century, Utah and Idaho women gleaned in the fields to garner the last sheaf of the harvest against a time of famine, while Tahitian and Hawaiian sisters were reported making "quilts and mats, fans, and all kinds of handiwork"[5] and "weaving hats and also diving for pearls to increase their [charity] funds" and contribute to the building of the Hawaiian Temple.[6]

What was true materially was also true spiritually — from scraps of talent and bits of knowledge consecrated to the Lord's service, the women extended themselves to serve the common good. Emmeline B. Wells recorded in her diary the 1874 challenge of Eliza R. Snow to write an editorial for the *Woman's Exponent*:

"Mon. Aug. 24. This morning I commenced writing. I seemed concerned about the Editorial for fear I should not please the Committee. . . . Tues. Aug. 25. I am still writing getting on pretty well, been not feeling very well in my mind; and not in health, my head seems confused and I am very nervous indeed. . . . Wednes. Aug. 26. Today I finished my writing and Annie took it to the Office. I am glad to have it off my mind."[7]

This from the woman who in three years would take over the newspaper and operate it successfully for nearly forty years, as well as assume leadership of Utah's woman suffrage movement, play a significant role in the national women's movement, and eventually preside over the Relief Society worldwide.

The success of Relief Society programs has ever depended on the willingness of one woman, or one group of women, to take those first timorous steps toward fulfilling what must seem at the outset an overwhelming stewardship. Who among us has not felt, with the poor servant of the parable, the temptation to hide the lord's talent in the earth? Not such a one was Sarah Kimball, who as a ward Relief Society president in Utah in the 1870s saw opportunity in the time her sisters spent sewing carpet rags from the "ever faithful basket." Though pre-scribed Relief Society lessons as such were nearly forty years away, Sister Kimball saw her stewardship as activating the minds as well as the hands of her women. They sewed their rags and stitched their quilts to readings from scripture, from Parley P. Pratt's *Key to the Science of Theology,* and even from the contemporary *Phrenological Journal.*[8]

A generation later, Rhoda Ann Burgess, having settled among a few Saints in Pine Valley, recorded a "reading meeting" with her sisters, "according to the instructions of Sister Zina D. H. Young who stands at the head of all." The meeting was "Called to order by Sister Ann Snow. Singing 'For the Strength of the Hills.' Sister Snow then called on me to read. I first read Sister Zina's address to the Sisters, then a piece from the Y[oung] L[adies] Journal . . . after which Alice Gardner read the first lecture on Faith . . . after which the sisters all joined in talking over what we had read and of the goodness of our Heavenly Father to us."[9] Out of such simple endeavors grew the educational programs of the Relief Society. Thus does "the gift of calling" create an inheritance. The varied talents and garnered scraps women consecrate to the Lord in steward-ship expand not only to meet local, temporary needs, but beyond their moment in history to become a legacy of inspired leadership and the good fruits of the Spirit.

The Relief Society work itself becomes part of the promised in-heritance in Zion. Maternity and child care was a Relief Society priority in the 1920s. Amanda Neff Bagley, in her sixth year as president of the Cottonwood Stake Relief Society, heard General President Clarissa Williams suggest that stakes might eventually operate local maternity homes. The idea, however intimidating, caught hold—Amanda had seen two women die of birth-related causes—and she moved into action.

With President Williams' blessing, Sister Bagley proposed to her stake president, Uriah G. Miller, that the Church purchase the Neil McMillan home and property, a "cool, quiet, restful location" within their stake, for the stake Relief Society to convert into a maternity hospital. The Presiding Bishopric and the First Presidency authorized the purchase, and sisters throughout the Cottonwood Stake rallied to provide funds, furnishings, and supplies for the new hospital. On 10

December 1924 the hospital was dedicated. There were no funds for salaries at first, so Mary F. Greaves and Agnes M. Merrill volunteered free nursing service. Amanda and her counselors did the washing until a laundress could be found, and board members worked without pay for months. The first month only one patient came for care, but after the initial struggle for acceptance, the hospital was well patronized, and in 1926 Sister Bagley lobbied successfully for a seventy-five-hundred-dollar addition to accommodate a delivery room, an isolation room, more wards, and a nursery—the cooks were complaining about the nurses' bathing babies in the hospital kitchen.[10] Murray's Cottonwood Hospital and its Center for Women are the present-day descendants of Amanda Bagley's sense of stewardship, her willingness to risk.[11]

With five talents, or two, or only one, Relief Society stewards have held themselves accountable. Whether undertaking to improve the health of mothers and children in the 1920s, or faithfully stocking emergency cupboards and completing welfare sewing in the 1930s, or expanding professional social services in the 1950s, or building in the 1970s a monument to inspire in women a sense of their strength, or knowing in 1992 that we can't teach the *whole* world to read but setting out anyway—these are the things that Relief Society stewards do. We begin where we are. From bits and fragments, Relief Society women established the groundwork of the three-million member organization intended to bless the world. "Wherefore, be not weary in well-doing, for ye are laying the foundation of a great work. And out of small things proceedeth that which is great," said the Lord. (D&C 64:33.) In spite of fear and uncertainty, one step after another, we go on.

To be a multitude of stewards stepping forward without stepping on one another's toes is a challenge, indeed, a requirement. "If ye are not one ye are not mine," the Lord declared. (D&C 38:27.) None in the kingdom is independent of the rest. "All must act in concert," the Prophet Joseph taught the Relief Society, "or nothing can be done."[12] "In concert" means neither running off in all directions nor marching in lockstep formation. "In concert" suggests harmony, counterpoint, syncopation—diverse parts joined in beautiful union. Our efforts as Saints to cooperate, to connect in the work of the kingdom are often clumsy, not always graceful. We collide, but as we meet, we resolve, and grow. Relief Society workers learned—are learning—to mesh their stewardships with those of their brethren of the priesthood quorums. Sometimes it is hard.

Before 1900 Relief Society General President Zina Young and

Church President Lorenzo Snow realized together the women's need for a building to house their organizations. Sarah Kimball had articulated the dream: "We want to have a house and we want land to build it on and it should be in the shadow of the temple," she had said in 1896.[13] President Snow promised the choicest site available, on Main Street, directly east of Temple Square. The Church would give them the deed as soon as they raised twenty thousand dollars toward the building's costs. They "could be as sure of it," the secretary recorded his saying, "as you will be of happiness when you get to heaven."[14]

At the October 1900 conference the Relief Society general presidency launched their campaign. The women's reception was immediate and enthusiastic. Relief Society, Young Women, and Primary sisters contributed. Records show stake contributions. Individual women gave — some fifty cents, some a dollar — the amounts in a steady stream to be recorded in the cash book. It seemed not to matter that the distant sisters might never themselves see the building: "The Relief Society Central Building will reflect credit on the daughters of Zion," the women agreed.[15]

For the next six years the contributions continued, until fourteen thousand dollars had been raised, eight thousand of it by the Relief Society. Then disturbing rumors reached the ears of President Bathsheba Smith that their plans had been shelved. A letter to the First Presidency asked if it were true, that they were not to have their building. Word came back: the rumors were true. A Presiding Bishop's building was to be built on the land they had been promised and would incorporate within it the women's offices.[16] An associate reported that Sister Smith was "overcome with grief."

"Some members felt very much grieved over the way matters stood," reported the secretary in the minutes. "We felt pledged to those who had contributed the money for a building that was to be their own," explained Sister Smith's first counselor, Annie T. Hyde. Talk of "changes for which the board were not accountable" expressed the helplessness the women felt. The following week's minutes included the revealing comment that "some unnecessary paragraphs [have been] expunged from previous minutes."[17]

Had not Joseph Smith himself introduced the idea of a house for them, back in Nauvoo? Had not President Snow promised them one here? Were they not well on the way to their required twenty thousand dollars? It is not difficult to imagine the heightened emotion of their discussions.

However, had not the Prophet Joseph also taught them to be united with their brethren? Indeed, they were to receive instruction "thro' the medium of those appointed to lead." "Not war, not jangle, not contradiction," he had said, "but meekness, love, purity, these are the things that should magnify us."[18] Even more to the point, "You need not be tearing men for their deeds, but let the weight of innocence be felt; which is more mighty than a millstone hung about the neck." And again from the Nauvoo society's minutes, "All must act in concert or nothing can be done—that the Society should move according to the ancient Priesthood."[19] So the sisters reconsidered objecting and chose rather to acquiesce and begin making plans for the space they would occupy in the new Bishop's Building. It would fall to a later generation to see the fulfillment of the promises made to their mothers.

How do we enlarge our understanding of such setbacks and disappointments, experiences which have been as much a part of Relief Society's past as the astounding successes? In more than one instance, enterprises and responsibilities, stewardships cherished by the sisters as their own, have been yielded to another steward. Just as the proposed Woman's Building became a suite of rooms in the Bishop's Building, the old Relief Society halls were relinquished and sisters began furnishing Relief Society rooms in ward meetinghouses. Relief Society charity work and social services have been assimilated into comprehensive churchwide programs. "I think almost the last letter I got as president of Relief Society was a plea to have the [Relief Society] magazine again," Belle S. Spafford said in 1976, two years after her release as general president and six years after consolidated Church magazines replaced the separate magazines of various organizations within the Church.[20]

Even wise and faithful stewards witness stewardships come to a close. Relief Society presidents, counselors, and teachers are released and reappointed. Assignments and responsibilities change, and often, as Sister Spafford indicated, the changes are painful. Without a doubt, there have been moments in the history of Relief Society when its members have felt disinherited, forsaken. Perhaps inheritance can only be fully appreciated if we understand something of disinheritance. The Savior's parable of the prodigal son hints that the older, faithful brother did not comprehend the value of his inheritance, whereas the younger brother, having lost all, expecting nothing, marveled that his father gave him a ring, a robe, and a fatted calf. Our mother Eve understood the importance of opposition in all things "and was glad, saying: Were it not for our transgression we never should have had seed, and never should have known good and evil, and the joy of our redemption, and the eternal life which God giveth unto all the obedient." (Moses 5:11.) The experience of our Savior Jesus Christ is a study in incongruity, irony, and opposition. He is "in and through all things": the King born in a humble stable, the Wonderful Counselor once despised and rejected, the Good Shepherd and the Lamb, the Father and the Son, the First and the Last. "And with his stripes we are healed." (Isaiah 53:5.)

When our mother Sarah understood that she would at ninety years of age bear a son, she laughed, as did Abraham. "After I am waxed old shall I have pleasure, my lord being old also?" The answer came as a question: "Is any thing too hard for the Lord?" Sarah and Abraham, through their faith and learned meekness, were blessed with a son. Out of a barren womb the lineage of Israel came forth, and Sarah became, as God promised, "a mother of nations." (Genesis 18:12–14; 17:16.) The faith of our mothers has taught us that even those who inherit the desolate waste can bring forth choice and excellent fruits of the spirit.

As the Second World War progressed toward the death struggles of Hitler's Reich, while American Relief Society sisters rolled bandages and knit sweaters and prayed in the safety of their homes for their servicemen abroad, German sisters clung to each other in fear and mortal danger. Recalling those bleak days in Bernberg, Germany, Sister Ruth Lippke wrote: "You can't imagine how alone we felt. We had no communication with the Church—no transportation—no priesthood. Women laid hands on each other to pray for the sick. We used old lesson books when we met in each other's homes."[21] The sisters in Bernberg pooled their scanty food and fuel so they could meet together in the evenings in a warm room to study, sew for the needy, and eat a frugal meal. On one occasion they scraped together enough rations to make a birthday cake for a faithful, elderly brother. "He cried, when he ate the first slice," wrote Sister Lippke.[22]

Somehow, in the midst of the chaos and fear of war, our sisters abroad carried on their work of charity, study, and care of their families. In May 1940, shortly after the Netherlands surrendered to Germany after five days of fighting, Gertrude Zippro, district Relief Society president in Holland, traveled sixty miles from Amsterdam to devastated

Rotterdam, where two sisters and a brother lived. She wrote her brother: "I did not have a moment's rest until I knew how the family was [in Rotterdam]. There were no trains because the track had been twisted and mangled. . . . One could not find a bus or automobile, so I had no recourse but to use my bicycle. . . . It took me nine hours to go to Rotterdam, and that whole time the German army roared by me on motorcycles, tanks, tractors, etc. . . . I could not believe my eyes. . . . Even though we know that these things will happen, our prayers still plead to God that it will end soon."[23] The end was five long years away.

As the district Relief Society president in the mission, Gertrude was concerned not only about her family, whom she found safe, but about all the Saints in Holland.[24] She continued to visit the branches regularly, by bicycle, by train, and even by canal boat, in spite of growing difficulties. Her son John provides more detail in his account of her life: "It became increasingly dangerous to be out at night as the occupation continued for five years, and many women were molested or raped. . . . Can you imagine my mother braving those circumstances and going out at night on her bike many times, to visit another branch? . . . She told us one evening of her experience as she returned from one such visit to a Branch by train. It was in the winter and mighty cold. . . . This night as she was returning home by train, the shooting started. The train stopped immediately and the people jumped out, including mother. She crouched at the side of the tracks, making herself as small as possible, lying there in the cold, wet and muddy ditch, with bullets striking all around. . . . I wonder if she even thought about what she [had] told us — 'Do not worry. I'll be perfectly safe.' The train sustained some damage from bullet holes to broken windows, but Mom was not scratched. Yes she was cold and wet and somewhat dirty, but she was alive. . . . [T]here was no hesitation the following week when she had to go again to visit other sisters somewhere else."[25]

In the Book of Mormon parable of the wild and tame olive trees, the servant questions his Lord about why he has grafted one of the branches onto a wild tree in such a poor spot. The Lord responds: "Counsel me not; I knew that it was a poor spot of ground; wherefore, I said unto thee, I have nourished it this long time, and thou beholdest that it hath brought forth much fruit." (Jacob 5:22.) Perhaps in the poor soil we are most nourished and nurtured.

From the Lord, through the faithful stewardship of our mothers, the daughters of Zion have inherited richly. Not lands and buildings, not magazines, or money. Our Relief Society sisters—Rhoda, Amanda, Bathsheba, Belle, Ruth, Gertrude—have left to us an inheritance of good fruits of the Spirit: love, joy, peace, longsuffering, gentleness, goodness, faith, meekness, temperance. These are not the fruits of womanhood but of sainthood, fruits of the Christ-centered life available to women and men alike. The scriptures contrast these fruits with works of the flesh: wrath, strife, and envyings. (Galatians 5:19–23.) Joseph Smith learned by revelation that "jarrings, and contentions, and envyings, and strifes, and lustful and covetous desires among [the Saints]" pollute their inheritances. (D&C 101:6.) Our sisters' meekness has not been weakness but a great strength of wise, faithful stewards, willing to give *all* that they possess for the building of the kingdom of God on the earth. The Savior drew from the words of the psalmist to tell us who would be blessed: "The meek shall inherit the earth; and shall delight themselves in the abundance of peace." (Psalm 37:11.)

Ours is a heritage of abundance: of peace, of wisdom and knowledge, of faith and testimony, of partnership with our brethren in building the Lord's kingdom under the direction of his holy priesthood. It is the inheritance of charity, "the pure love of Christ," which "endureth forever, and whoso is found possessed of it at the last day, it shall be well with him [or her]." (Moroni 7:47.) By praying for, receiving, and exercising charity, we become like unto the Son, in purpose one with the Son. He will receive all that the Father has and so will we if we become like him. The Lord tells us that we—Mary, Katharina, Tchitrilanka, Lyli, Louise, Anna—we are his inheritance. We are the fruits of his harvest, his jewels, his own. Faithful stewards are no more servants but the sons and daughters of God, heirs and joint heirs with Christ to "inherit thrones, kingdoms, principalities, dominions, all heights and depths," fulness and "exaltation and glory in all things."[26]

NOTES

This essay is drawn from a fireside address in honor of the Relief Society sesquicentennial, presented by the authors 7 May 1992 at the BYU Women's Conference and published in full in *BYU Today* 46 (July 1992): 30–40. Most of the historical information has been extracted from Jill Mulvay Derr, Janath R. Cannon, and Maureen Ursenbach Beecher, *Women of Covenant: The Story of Relief Society* (Salt Lake City: Deseret Book, 1992), and special recognition and thanks goes to Janath R. Cannon for her significant contribution to this essay.

1. Audrey M. Godfrey, "Starting from Scraps: The Mormon Village Relief Society," paper presented at 1980 Sperry Symposium, Brigham Young University, Provo, Utah.

2. Lucy Meserve Smith, "Historical Sketches of My Great Grandfathers," holograph, Special Collections, Marriott Library, University of Utah, Salt Lake City, Utah. Her autobiographical account is published in Kenneth W. Godfrey, Audrey M. Godfrey, and Jill Mulvay Derr, eds., *Women's Voices: An Untold History of the Latter-day Saints, 1830–1900* (Salt Lake City: Deseret Book Co., 1982), pp. 261–71.

3. "Autobiography of Priscilla Merriman Evans," typescript, pp. 7, 8, Utah State Historical Society, Salt Lake City, Utah.

4. Susa Young Gates Papers, typescript, Utah State Historical Society, Salt Lake City, Utah.

5. "Notes from the Field," *Relief Society Magazine* 4 (May 1917): 277–78.

6. "Notes from the Field," *Relief Society Magazine* 5 (March 1918): 156.

7. *Women's Voices*, p. 295.

8. Fifteenth Ward Salt Lake Stake Relief Society Minutes, 1868–1873, 28 May 1868, 11 June 1868, 25 February 1869, 12 August 1869, LDS Church Archives, Salt Lake City, Utah.

9. Journals of Rhoda Ann Burgess, 6 February 1894, typescript, courtesy Lois S. Beck, Alpine, Utah.

10. Emily M. Carlisle, "Report on Cottonwood Stake Maternity Hospital," *Relief Society Magazine* 18 (July 1931): 415–16. This information is drawn from the work of Janath R. Cannon.

11. *The Cottonwood Health Care Foundation*, p. 1.

12. "A Record of the Organization and Proceedings of the Female Relief Society of Nauvoo," holograph, LDS Church Archives, 30 March 1842. Used with permission; hereafter cited as Nauvoo Relief Society Minutes.

13. Relief Society General Board Minutes, 1892–1911, 3 October 1896, holograph, LDS Church Archives. Used with permission.

14. Ibid., 26 March 1901.

15. "R. S. Reports," *Woman's Exponent* 30 (1 January 1902): 70–71.

16. Bathsheba W. Smith, Martha H. Tingey, and Louie B. Felt, to the Presidency of the Church . . . , 23 January 1907, First Presidency General Administration Correspondence, LDS Church Archives.

17. Relief Society General Board Minutes, 1892–1911, 1 and 15 February 1907.

18. Nauvoo Relief Society Minutes, 28 April 1842.

19. Nauvoo Relief Society Minutes, 30 March 1842.

20. Belle S. Spafford Oral History, interviews by Jill Mulvay Derr, 1975–76, typescript, p. 187, James Moyle Oral History Program, LDS Church Archives.

21. Conversation between Ruth Lippke and Janath R. Cannon, 21 November 1982, Albuquerque, New Mexico; information courtesy Janath R. Cannon.

22. Ruth Lippke to Janath R. Cannon, 2 March 1983; courtesy Janath R. Cannon.

23. Gertrude Zippro to Pieter Lodder, 31 May 1940; courtesy Janath R. Cannon. Sister Zippro's letter was reported in the September 1940 *Relief Society Magazine* by the Church mission secretary. It was the first news to Church headquarters from the Netherlands after the invasion.

24. In the May invasion, more than seven hundred people had been killed in Rotterdam and seventy-eight thousand people had been left wounded and homeless; the entire center of the city was flattened. See Larry Collins and Dominique Lapierre, *Is Paris Burning?* (New York: Simon & Schuster, 1965), p. 23. The LDS Church meetinghouse on the St. Jansstraat was completely destroyed.

25. "Life Story of John Zippro," unpaged ms. courtesy Janath R. Cannon.

26. Romans 8:16–17; D&C 132:19.

Women's Lives, Women's Stories: The Extraordinary in the Ordinary

JULIE J. NICHOLS

....

[Because] so much of women's history . . . is sewn into quilts, baked in breads, honed in the privacy of dailiness, used up, consumed, worn out, . . . [reading and writing it] becomes essential to our sense of our-selves—nourishment, a vital sustenance; it is a way of knowing our-selves.[1]

The personal essay, unlike personal journals, letters, and oral histories, is not an artless form. It transforms the raw material of personal experience in the double crucible of carefully chosen language and the light of mature retrospection. A finished personal essay requires revision, a literal re-seeing; not only does the product enlighten and engage its reader but the process of writing and revising itself generates changes in the writer as she re-views her self, her place in her community, and the meaning of her experiences.

We live by stories; every person has a story that matters. Phyllis Rose in *Parallel Lives: Five Victorian Marriages* suggests that we are constantly in the process of "imposing a narrative form onto our lives" in order to make sense of experience. "Questions we have all asked ourselves such as Why am I doing this? or even the more basic What am I doing? suggest the way in which living forces us to look for and

....

Julie J. Nichols, a doctoral candidate in creative writing at the University of Utah, has taught creative writing and literature at the Waterford School, the University of Utah, and Brigham Young University. She and her husband, Jeff W. Nichols III, are the parents of four children. She serves as a Relief Society teacher and Primary pianist.

forces us to find a design within the primal stew of data which is our daily experience."[2]

Stories affect us differently than do mere assertions of principle, more profoundly than mere dogma; stories influence our actions, help us make sense of the world, and enable us to share our experience and understanding. Carol Bly, author of a fine collection of essays, *Letters from the Country,* points out that in our time, women are socialized to write their stories — "Women must write our history . . . , so that we have it — the way an athlete must have muscle."[3] At the same time, Bly notes, men are *dis*couraged from writing theirs, precisely because writing one's story requires a certain amount of evaluation and self-judgment. Bly's conclusion is that, in writing their stories, women learn to evaluate and judge and are thus in many ways better prepared to recognize and help counter the ills of a male-dominated world.

But certain aspects of our culture can bar even women from enlightening themselves through personal narrative. Since 1984 I have taught English 218R — Introduction to Creative Writing, with an emphasis in literary nonfiction — at Brigham Young University. In these classes, I have watched both women and men resist coming to terms with the contradictions of their lives. For Latter-day Saint women, in particular, such resistance comes from three general sources: lack of time, because setting aside large blocks of quiet, self-reflective time is difficult when you're busy rearing children, caring for a home, and, more often than not, working outside the home; lack of knowledge about women's stories, which are infrequently mentioned in the scriptures and only recently began making their way into Church lesson manuals;[4] and fear of recrimination, from family or from official sources for expressing negative emotions, disagreement, or nontraditional thought processes.

In my classes, I try to help would-be memoirists overcome these barriers by providing structured time, abundant reading material, and plenty of theory and practice. Working together, we establish that personal narrative is the prototypical discourse.[5] We learn that telling a story we deem important forms the basis for *all* discourse. We read the works of women writers whose lives constitute their material, from Julian of Norwich and Margery Kempe in the Middle Ages to Annie Dillard and Alice Walker in twentieth-century America, as well as such Latter-day Saint women writers as Emma Lou Thayne, Mary Bradford, and Helen Candland Stark. We perform writing exercises that allow memory and feeling to rise to the surface and find form in words. (The suggestions in Natalie Goldberg's *Writing Down the Bones: Freeing the Writer Within* and *Wild Mind: Living the Writer's Life*, and in Gabrielle Rico's *Writing the Natural Way* are my personal favorites.) Though these exercises are not always successful, when my women students finally push through their resistance and produce fine essays such as the ones quoted from below, we all reap remarkable rewards.

The first reward that lies in producing a polished personal essay is pleasure—on many levels. Lorinne Taylor Morris took English 218R twice because the first time she took it, she struggled with an essay about her mother's death for months, saying to me several times, "I don't even know what I'm trying to say here." I encouraged her to continue to work with it, praising the understated tone and the importance of the story itself. When she finally came to a satisfactory ending, she said, "Now I know what I meant. I thought I was writing about how I always felt left out and how I tried to let my dad's efforts be enough. But I needed my mother to help me know who I was. I know that now. This is an essay about me as a woman."

Regeneration
LORINNE MORRIS

I was five years old when my mother died. Her death didn't seem to change my world much then. I just received more attention from relatives and neighbors, was all. In the two years since she had been diagnosed, she had evolved from my caregiver to a sick person whose bedroom I had to stay out of while the cancer ate at her body. I learned over those two years she could not care for me, so by the time of her death, I thought I had become used to living without her.

My father had begun taking over for Mother by making the family meals. He also woke us up and got us ready in the morning. I insisted on having my hair in ponytails like my two older sisters, and though he tried to part my hair into even halves and get the ponytails straight, they always came out crooked. After he left the bathroom I'd climb onto the counter and tug up on one ponytail and down on the other. It just wasn't the way it was supposed to be.

As the years passed my needs changed, and so did my father's role in my life. In junior high one day, I received a wink from a boy who sat a row in front of me. My friends told me this was because he liked me and wanted "to go" with me, but I didn't know what "to go" with someone meant. I found Dad that evening outside doing chores just as the sun was setting and leaving just enough light to see his faint shadow. I guess he sensed the seriousness in my voice, because he put down the bucket of feed and sat on the upper rail of the fence while I unfolded the dilemma of my day. I can't remember now what he said, but it was dark before we came in.

When I became a quiet, emotional teenager, I realized my mother's death meant her absence from my life. During my high school years when I wanted some comfort, I often imagined what it would be like to have a mother. I would sit at night on the front steps and imagine my mother coming outside to sit by me. She would quietly open the front door, sit down next to me, and put her soft, middle-aged arm around me. I wasn't really sure what she would do next, maybe tell me not to cry or listen to me for awhile. I would eventually stop my dreaming and go to find my dad.

But last summer the absence was relieved for a moment when I learned to bottle tomatoes. I used the old empty jars from my grandma's fruit room that had been on the shelves for years. They were covered with dust and spider webs. Some even had tiny dead bugs in the bottom. It took me hours to wash them all. Then I took them to a neighbor's house where she taught me how to blanch the tomatoes to remove the skins, then to quarter them and press them into the bottles. She showed me how to take a knife to remove the air bubbles before steaming them to seal their lids. Together we bottled more than a hundred jars.

I took my bottled tomatoes back to my grandma's fruit room, and one by one I placed them on the dusty shelves. As I bent over, picked one of the bottles up, and placed it on the shelf, I saw my mother. Like me, she bent to pick up a bottle, placed it carefully, and stood back to admire the work she had done. At that moment she was there with me, doing the things she had done that I was now beginning to do. I understood that we are connected in ways that go far beyond death, and I whispered, "Welcome home, Mom," and she whispered, "Welcome home, Lorinne."

Pleasure, the first reward of a story well told, is often not only cerebral but also physical — leaving both writer and reader feeling peaceful and relaxed. Lorinne experienced further pleasure; as she wrote, she discovered a new sense of herself, a sense that she belongs, even though her mother died long ago, to the community of mothers and daughters participating in the rituals that many Utah LDS mothers and daughters share. For the first time, she recognized her rightful place in that community.

Anthropologist Barbara Meyerhoff has formulated the notion of "the great story," the set of stories by which we live our lives.[6] LDS women may be centered by stories such as: "women should be in the home," "church attendance is a measure of spirituality," "families are forever," or "repentance and change are always possible." Lorinne's essay partakes of the "great story" that says, "Everyone needs a mother; no one can take a mother's place." Meyerhoff goes on to say that personal narrative is a "little story," a story that is true for one person instead of for an entire culture. People's "little stories" can affirm or challenge the "great story." The following untitled essay by Kathy Haun Orr corroborates the "great story" that mothers are perfect. Like Lorinne's essay, it also provides pleasure — in this case the pleasure of humor:

My mother can do everything. Every year my sisters and I got Easter dresses made especially for us and dresses at Christmas for family pictures. She made the bridesmaid dresses for my oldest sister's wedding because they couldn't find any they liked in the stores. The dresses were lavender with white lace trim, tea length, with a long, full ruffle and a v-waistline to match my sister's wedding gown. Then there's me: I've never even touched a sewing machine except to turn my mom's off when she forgot. The first time I sewed a button on was last semester when it came off my coat and my roommate wouldn't do it for me.

My birthday cakes were always decorated with whatever I requested, from Mickey Mouse when I was three to a two-tiered cake with frosting floral arrangements when I turned sweet sixteen. I did take a cake decorating class with my best friend our senior year of high school. I loved the class, and the teacher, but my roses looked like big lumps of lard, and my clowns always fell over like they were too tired to sit up.

My mother is the very definition of domestic goddess in the kitchen. Leftovers taste great, everything's nutritious and yummy, and she can make desserts that make your mouth water just looking at them. Until I left home for college, the only things I could cook were toast, grilled cheese sandwiches, and chocolate chip cookies. When I got up to school, my roommates mocked me in the kitchen and gave me quizzes on all the different utensils and their true use.

My mother is into all sorts of crafts, like grapevine wreaths and quilts and the artwork for her silkscreening business. I know how to use a glue gun—I used one once to hem some pants.

Kathy concludes the essay by saying that despite the gaps between her mother's achievements and her own, her mother's love and encouragement are qualities she fully intends to pass on. The essay is fun to read and allowed Kathy to safely express her marginal position within a pervasive "great story" that LDS mothers are domestic goddesses.

Both these essays focus on a key role in a woman's life: the mother role. Being a mother is a pinnacle of accomplishment for a Latter-day Saint woman. Unconsciously or consciously, many LDS women examine their own propensities for this role with varying degrees of satisfaction or trepidation, seeking first (like Lorinne and Kathy) to connect with their own mothers and then to come to terms with the differences among their own mothers, their own individual leanings, and the "great story" about motherhood. Writing personal narrative encourages and facilitates this process.

It is especially liberating for my women students to realize that personal narrative needn't always affirm the "great story." According to Meyerhoff, the "little story" can also radically question the "great story." Often its power lies in its ability to interrogate the inadequacies in the larger cultural narrative. Several of my students who have been emotionally and physically battered have written essays probing the differences between their experiences and the LDS "great story" of the family as the source of protection and nurturance. In all of their efforts, they have sought to name the origins of their wounds and find balm for them. It was the process of their writing that finally helped these women find the power to initiate real healing.

Personal narrative can also teach. Kristin Langellier, professor of speech communication, notes that family stories may inspire or warn family members about the consequences of certain actions and also keep stories alive that are important to the family's solidarity.[7] Often, of course, my students write about their role as mother. The following story, which teaches and inspires, explores the spiritual strength that can come as we seek answers to problems in that particular role:

The Committee
MARSHA BENNION GIESE

Hannah's screams echoed in my ears long after I hung up the phone, strident newborn cries that demanded help. A moan rolled out from someplace deep inside me, surprising the hard silence of my hospital room. I'd been checking on her condition with her nurse in an intensive care unit many miles away. "We're having trouble with her I.V. sites," she told me, "we're just running out of good places to stick her and her sites don't last long. We've been trying to restart her for about an hour." I knew that meant strapped down flat under bright lights, her perfect new skin repeatedly pierced with no success. Tears ran down my cheeks and nose onto the receiver as I listened to her report and the background anguish.

"How many times have you tried?" my voice choked to a whisper.

"Well, three times, actually," she answered regretfully. "I've called for some help and we're trying for a place on her head now."

Baby torture. My good-bye was barely audible. "Tell her Mom loves her and is sorry . . . " Grief curled my freshly stitched body and squeezed at my chest. I bit into my fists through stretched sheets spreading dampness out in rings like oil on water. We'd endured so much to get this baby here, and now there was more. A new series of hurdles seemed to extend out beyond my view.

The I.V.s were crucial as they bore her only source of nourishment during recovery from post-birth surgery on an incomplete esophagus. She clearly wanted to eat. She'd been born by emergency C-section ten days early due to placental failure, delivered weak and thin and hardly able to move from nearly starving to death in my womb. I'd been alerted to her danger when she'd quit moving within me, and from a building sense of urgency that got me to the doctor just in time. Now she searched desperately for comfort at Children's Hospital, sucking fiercely on her fists, bedding, the side of her incubator, trying to fill her still empty stomach, covered with surgical drains, I.V.s, monitor leads, alone and hungry and in pain. I needed to be there. I wanted to hold her, feed her, ease the harshness of mortality. I'd been waiting so long.

It took us a long time to conceive her older sister, Megan, but once she came we thought we were home free—no more baby trouble. Not so. The years passed. I felt I wasn't finished and that there was a sibling for Megan possible, but month after month my hopes rose and fell—little cycles of death that took their emotional toll. We had tests. I had blessings. Stacks of temperature charts, drugs, and surgeries. Frightening bills. Hi-tech fertility care and finally, an in-vitro procedure. Nothing.

Five years into all of this, my Aunt Mary fell profoundly and terminally ill with pancreatic cancer. Beloved by all her family, talented and politically active, she was a matriarchal figure to me, unhesitant to raise her powerful voice in song or strong opinion. I was able to care for her during her last days. She hated the waiting and terrible loss of strength. Five days before her death she whispered her thanks for my care and sighing a laugh, asked if there was anything she could do for me in return. I assured her she had already done, just by living her life and being who she was—but I added, "Well yes, there is one thing. When you get where you're going, would you see if you can do anything about getting us our baby? I mean, whatever it takes—if it's a bureaucratic problem, get a committee together. Find out who's in charge of this and shake things up. Start a petition. Let's just get on with getting our baby here. We're ready. I don't know how it works, but see what you can do, okay?" Aunt Mary's lips sketched a smile, and she rolled her eyes. "I'll see," she breathed. It was our last real conversation.

That was June. In August I was once again on a gurney wheeling to surgery for another in-vitro procedure. My husband stood at my side gripping the hand that was untaped as the embryologist rolled his big stainless steel box up past us, gave us a thumbs-up sign, and flashed four fingers. We had four of our fertilized eggs in his incubator ready to implant in my tubes. One of them was Hannah.

It had been a roller coaster pregnancy. The euphoria of finding out we'd been successful. We saw heartbeats on two of the embryos before nearly losing both in early miscarriage. Bedrest and weekly ultrasounds, phlebitis and childbirth refresher classes. Painting the nursery, unpacking a carefully stored layette. Months of great anticipation and anxiety—looking toward the time of completion when I could study a new little face, watch Megan bond, and rejoice with our extended families. Expectations stopped two days ago. Now we lay in separate hospitals, kept from each other by our respective tenuous health. My only physical ties to her were phone lines, my only communication her compelling screams. I'd lost awareness of my own surgery to the pain of her distance.

Prayers formed as the cries persisted in my head. "Help her, help me, ease her pain, send comfort please."

Then as I repeated these petitions, my focus turned inward from my barren room. It seemed to me that suddenly I could see Hannah in the I.C.U. from just a few feet away. Tiny and bare in her isolette, tubes and wires snaked out from her fragile body mooring her to the sophisticated equipment clustered above and to one side. But she was sleeping. Calm and relaxed on her tummy with her knees tucked slightly under her. And she was not alone. Around her with their backs to me stood a trio of women in long white gowns, their heads bending toward each other occasionally in consultation. I recognized them: my late grandmothers Nana and Mimi, and to the right, Aunt Mary. They hovered protectively at her side, shoulder-to-shoulder with each other and with the two nurses tending her equipment. As I watched, they reached to touch her, crooning her name, singing lullabies and reassuring her that life would not always be as painful. This would pass. I knew that this was the committee come to guard her and comfort both of us. My tears subsided; my muscles relaxed. I turned my gaze outward to the night-black windows and pondered the mystery of time and distance and mortal limitations.

Over a year later I hear Hannah's approach down the hall. Her newly acquired lumbering resembles Frankenstein's gait. Her curly head pops around the corner, face alight with mischief. "Boo!" she declares and falls backward on her bottom. "Boo! yourself. I'm happy to see you," is my reply as I bend to swing her up over my head. Quick and joyful and round with breastmilk, we bear no trace of the awful struggle it took to get here. I bring her laughing face close to mine and look into perfect blue eyes and see eternal love and the mercy of God.

Such stories validate the teller's life, and move the hearers to wonder and reverence that we *aren't* alone on this planet; our needs are met, often, in ways we don't expect.

Stories which teach and inspire might begin also with a question: why are things the way they are in this family or community? Telling personal stories that pursue answers may clarify complex questions. Beth Ahlborn Merrell's essay does just that.

No Name Maria
BETH AHLBORN MERRELL

Ten years after my own baptism I buried myself in the waters again . . . and again . . . and again. It was a great opportunity for me to recall the importance of baptism. I did my best to prepare myself, that the spirits waiting on the other side would not be mocked.

I was baptized thirty-seven times for Maria. She had no last name. No birth date or place. No family information. Only the location of her grave.

I inquired of these Marias. A temple worker told me that these Latin American women had been buried in graves without proper markings. Because there was no information, they were baptized with the symbolic name Maria. I couldn't help but wonder if I had done any good in being baptized as proxy for thirty-seven women who had no names.

Before leaving the temple, I received a printout with the information on the thirty-seven women I had served. No need looking over the names. All Marias. But I did look at the locations. Panama, Guatemala, Nicaragua — almost all Central

American countries. At the bottom of the list were five women from Tegucigalpa, Honduras. My heart jumped and burned.

August 29, 1924. Tegucigalpa, Honduras. Julia Eva Valasquez, seven years old, stood on the banks of the mountain river that ran through her family's estate. Her older brother, Roberto, fished while Julia twirled on the banks, watching the ruffled layers of her silk dress floating like magic in a rippling circle. Confident that she would dance with the best one day, she moved to the Latin rhythm that played inside her head. Bending close to the water, Julia smiled at the face she saw mirrored on the glassy surface of the pond: dark hair curled daintily around a heart-shaped face the color of creamy coffee. She flirted with her reflection, placing a lotus blossom behind her ear.

Julia never heard the revolutionist behind her. Perhaps the music inside her head played so loudly that it drowned out any snapping twigs that might have warned her of the silent murderer. One moment she was looking into the reflection of a smiling girl, the next she was seeing the reflection of a revolutionist raising a machete over her body. His double-edged knife whistled as it fell toward her head.

Instinctively she rolled, blocking the blows with her right arm. Roberto flew to protect himself and his sister, but his struggle was brief against the attacks made by men who came to proclaim their right against the suppression of Honduras's upper class. I've never heard anything about how my great-grandmother and Uncle Roberto found help. Roberto carried deep scars in his skull for life. Julia's dreams of dancing were shattered; she lost her right arm from the elbow. Their white mansion burned to the ground; their parents and siblings died in the flames.

I often wonder how my great-grandmother managed without two good arms and without the extended family support upon which Latins depend. But the details of my heritage are scarce. She died before I learned to speak Spanish. She died before my first-generation LDS mother taught her the gospel. She died without telling us the names of her parents and siblings. She died, and this is all I know of her life.

Records in Central American countries are incomplete at best. Government documents are burned periodically in the chaos of political revolutions. And when the fires die, the dead who leave no families are often buried in common, unmarked graves.

I looked back at my printout. I asked to be baptized for a relative, but my mother told me it was impossible given our dead-end genealogy. I did not receive a heavenly visitation from a member of Julia's family; I have no physical proof that I served a relative in the temple. But in my heart I am grateful that gospel blessings are not limited to those who have proper burials or grave sites. I look forward to the day when I can perform temple ordinances for another no-name Maria.

In this essay, Beth comes to the conclusion that the ordinances performed in the temple are not in vain. In doing so, she establishes connections with the community of her family, as do Lorinne and Kathy, as well as with the community of Latter-day Saints who work in the temple. Beth also negotiates with a puzzling aspect of the "great story," and she asserts herself as someone who can respond to her circumstances and make a story that provides answers as it holds and moves its readers.

Further, by making that story a woman's story, she refutes the "great story" that canonized writings (scripture or official Church histories or manuals) are the only authoritative ones. To write ordinary women's lives thoughtfully and imaginatively makes them extraordinary, gifts not only for posterity (the *raison d'etre* for most injunctions to write personal narrative) but also for interested contemporaries.

Stories like these need to be heard. Great pleasure, great strength comes from writing and sharing these stories. We need to give ourselves and each other time and encouragement for writing the stories of the women of our communities. We can form writing groups; we can let our families and friends read our work; we can send it off to the *Ensign* and other forums. We can request that more of these stories of ordinary modern women be included in Relief Society manuals and supplements. By doing so we reap great rewards, for ourselves and all women. We validate ourselves and add to the truth of the "great stories" that make up our lives as Latter-day Saints, as women, and as extraordinary individuals.

NOTES

1. Bettina Aptheker, "Imagining Our Lives," *Woman of Power* 16 (Spring 1990): 32.

2. Phyllis Rose, *Parallel Lives: Five Victorian Marriages* (New York: Vintage Books, 1984), p. 6.

3. Carol Bly, *The Passionate, Accurate Story* (Minneapolis, Minn.: Milkweed Editions, 1990), p. 47.

4. One of the five 1992 Relief Society sesquicentennial goals has been to gather stories from LDS women, including humorous anecdotes, spiritual events, and special challenges unique to local Relief Society units. Copies were to be sent to Relief Society headquarters.

5. Kristin M. Langellier, "Personal Narratives: Perspectives on Theory and Research," *Text and Performance Quarterly* 9 (October 1989): 243.

6. Barbara Meyerhoff, as quoted in Riv-Ellen Prell, "The Double Frame of Life History in the Work of Barbara Myerhoff," in *Interpreting Women's Lives: Feminist Theory and Personal Narratives,* ed. Personal Narratives Group (Bloomington: Indiana University Press, 1989), pp. 241–58.

7. Langellier, p. 264.

The Choice of Forgiveness: A Personal Account

MIDGE PATRICK

My name is Midge Patrick, and I would like to stand but I can't. On 25 July 1987, our family was involved in a catastrophic automobile accident, and, as a result, I have no feeling from my chest down. My husband was killed; I lost a son. I was driving. My seven surviving children and I spent months in hospitals, to be reunited as a family again just before Christmas.

During this time I was faced with overwhelming decisions and problems. I must admit that forgiving myself was actually one of the easier challenges that I faced. I wasn't sure that I could face what lay ahead, especially trapped in a body that didn't work. I longed to be with the children, some of whom were also in critical condition. I longed to hold them, knowing how frightened and alone they must feel. I needed to draw strength from them. I wanted so desperately for John to still be with me, for I knew that together we could overcome anything. I fantasized that he would come through the door of my hospital room – hoping desperately that it would happen, yet knowing that it would never be.

I learned very quickly that the question "Why?" has no tangible answer. The only real answer to "Why?" is faith. We place our lives in the hands of the Lord, having faith that he knows what is best for us in the long run. I also had to accept that some things in this life simply cannot be changed. How many times I must have said to myself, "if only." If only I could relive a few seconds of my life, things would be so different – but life does not rewind so we can revise our parts, and dwelling on "whys" and "if onlys" is unhealthy.

Midge Patrick received her bachelor's degree in nursing from Brigham Young University. A homemaker and mother, she serves as Relief Society education counselor in her Provo, Utah, ward.

"Whys" and "if onlys" keep us dwelling on regret so we cannot forgive ourselves and move forward in faith, prayerfully trusting in the Lord. The Lord, with His infinite love for us, will never leave us. I was able to forgive myself because I literally felt the Lord's kind, gentle arms around me during this time. I never had before, nor have I since, felt such an outpouring of love from the Lord. The car crash was not planned—it was an accident—so there was no real reason to blame myself. With the Lord's help, I knew that. My soul was touched, my spirit healed, and I came to feel at peace with our circumstance as it was.

Other seeming accidents—coincidences, providences—prepared us to survive this catastrophe. For instance, the last thing my husband and I had discussed, as I was dropping him off at the airport, was our new insurance policy. Had he paid the premium? I wondered. "Why don't we have it taken out as a monthly deduction," I suggested. "That way we won't even miss the money." He had paid the premium: $13.01, and that's all we ever paid. That $13.01 policy helped me to build a home that I can function in as a quadriplegic.

Other things for our benefit were also in place when the accident occurred. There was, for instance, a doctor in St. Louis, where we were hospitalized, the one pediatric orthopedic surgeon in a thousand who would even have tried to save my daughter's foot, the top of which had been severed. Others would have immediately amputated. He took muscle from her back and grafted it onto her foot. Because of his faith and skill, she is walking. He was only at that hospital for a few months. Was it chance that he was there? Was it chance that he came in several nights after the surgery to say, "I don't know why I did what I did. I hadn't gone in to do that procedure. I just did something very different from what I planned on." Was that an accident? I don't think so.

So many things were in place for us that I knew that the Lord loved us. Kind Church members in St. Louis did for my children that which I could not do—sending cards, visiting, giving continuous care to the children day and night, housing and feeding relatives as they came to help put our lives back together. The hospital staff stood in awe as these people, who didn't even know our family, gave service in such an organized and loving manner.

Through priesthood blessings, circulation was restored to crushed legs that were scheduled to be immediately amputated and a comatose child was blessed to regain consciousness and productivity at the time lifetime custodial care in a nursing home was being discussed. A beautiful woman trained as a nurse practitioner and with a master's degree in neurological nursing joined our family, changing her life so ours could be better. She works as a director of nursing at a state facility during the days and provides love, support, and care for the family in the evenings. It is not chance that she is with us. How could I not forgive myself? To fail to so so would jeopardize the future of my family.

Many who are victims of natural consequences struggle not only to forgive themselves but to forgive God. Was our accident the Lord's fault? I don't believe he caused it, but surely he could have stopped it from happening. Every prayer I remember offering throughout my married life had included the plea that my husband John and I would remain together to rear our children. It frightened me deeply to think of being the sole person responsible for many children. Very little in life equals the thrill of holding a newborn baby, and it is a joy to watch children grow and learn. But it is hard to deal with them alone. John and I were supposed to do that together. In fact, I had envisioned that after the last child went away from home, my husband might then have a heart attack—perhaps even as she walked out the door. I felt certain that the Lord would spare him until then. Well, He didn't. Does that mean that my prayers weren't answered, or that the Lord doesn't love me and my family? I don't think so. It means that we are to start from zero again and work out a new life plan. We switch to Plan B. I guess I am glad we have an alphabet with 26 letters so that we can have several other plans to follow. I am at Plan F going on G right now!

The next person I had to forgive was my husband. It really wasn't fair for him to check out early. In the hospital the day of the accident, I had a dream vision—I struggle to describe it—an insight, revelation, life-beyond-life experience, impression. I was dressed in a beautiful, white, flowing dress, simple in design yet very elegant. John was in white pants, shirt, and tie. I was ascending, he was descending, both of us with arms outstretched toward the other. We almost clasped hands, but before we touched, he told me, "No, you can't come now. You have to go back." Although he spoke the words, I knew that we both had made the decision.

Now, on a good day, I feel Christian-spirited and can forgive him for leaving. I can even see the wisdom in my staying. My soul is filled with benevolence. But, on a bad day, I get really agitated with the whole situation. (Perhaps that's why he chooses to come only on good days.) He chooses to be present—I feel his spirit—at baptisms, confirmations, and weddings. He is with me when I talk in church. He's there for nice times. His spirit touches my spirit, say, during an opening song in church, and I find myself unexpectedly in tears. People around me are baffled, but the kids look down the row to where my wheelchair is parked in the aisle and murmur, "He is here again, and she has lost it!"

These moments are sweet but also frustrating. It is really unfair. I don't know why he can't come also on days when the kids are misbehaving. Why is he never there when I would like to paste them against the wall, and I can't? I have thought of one way to involve John, however. I sometimes say to the children, "You should always try to do the right things and never place yourself in a compromising situation. You never know when your father may be at your side." They usually reply, "Right, Mom!" But it's worth a try. Someday it may help them out of a tight spot. Maybe if I were a little less frustrated, he would come and help during the trying times. Or maybe I haven't experienced the worst times, and he is saving himself for when I have run my course and am on Plan Z . . . I hope not.

So, when all has been said and done, am I really capable of forgiving? Are any of us? I think so. I feel I have forgiven John, but I am still overwhelmed with frustration at times. And frustration is not the same as anger. I don't hold the Lord accountable. I don't hold myself accountable. If I did, I would draw others into my suffering and despair. I will not let my children suffer because I am not willing to forgive myself and get on with life.

Does the Lord believe we are capable of forgiving? At least eighty-two scriptures deal with forgiveness. To give it so much mention, the Lord must know it's not easy. Doctrine and Covenants 98:40 specifies that we should forgive seventy times seven, or four hundred and ninety times. That's a lot. In my youth, I didn't think I would ever need to forgive anyone that many times. But, as a mother with children between the ages of four and nineteen, I gained a new perspective. Before they are four, children are still cute, but there are fifteen uncute years between four and nineteen. Let's be very conservative: if you forgive a child only *once* a day, you have forgiven him or her fifty-four hundred times. And that is only if you get Mother's Day and your birthday off. I'm not skipping Christmas because we all know that Christmas can be extremely stressful. I have seven children; my forgiveness-once-a-day tallies at forty-three thousand times. These may be small matters most of the time, but holding on to anger or frustration taints your present and shapes your future.

No matter what your circumstances, you cannot escape opportunities to forgive and be forgiven in both large and small matters. How you deal with that fact colors the quality of your everyday life. You must forgive yourself for yelling at your children for spilling milk. You must forgive yourself for having a confrontation with your neighbor. You must forgive yourself for feeling angry at your employer or for not seeing eye-to-eye with your spouse. Failing to forgive may handicap us in important ways. When we are filled with anger and frustration, the Holy Ghost cannot be with us. As much as the Lord would like to help us, he cannot, for the circuit between earth and heaven is full of emotional static.

Let's consider handicaps. I have a handicap that is visible. I am considered a quadriplegic. I have no feeling from my chest down. When people first see me in a wheelchair, the obvious is suspected—I can't walk. As we get to know each other better, they learn that the disability includes much more than just being unable to walk. For instance, if I do not shift my weight occasionally as I sit in the wheelchair, I can very easily develop pressure sores that require months to heal because of poor circulation. I have no conception of hot and cold and consequently can burn myself without realizing it. I put my elbow on a hot burner one day, and the next morning I woke up to find an ugly burn—almost to the bone. As I looked at it, I thought, "That must really hurt!" The examples could go on and on.

Just as I have learned alternate ways to function, such as driving with hand controls, your spirit also will change to accommodate a "hidden handicap," and your whole way of dealing with life can change. The word *adversity* is very close to the word *adversary*. The adversary would certainly like to win when we are dealing with adversity. By not forgiving, we are unconsciously inviting the adversary into our lives. It is very easy to blame the Lord when things don't go right in our lives, just as it is easy to blame others for our unhappiness. Our happiness and well-being are our individual responsibility. The Lord has given us the instruction booklet and the tools with which to attain happiness— the attainment is up to us.

By harboring resentment or hurt, you place a handicap on your spirit. You leave your soul open for other problems, to other hurts, to other miseries, to other pain that you cannot even imagine. These emotional handicaps can be hidden to you, but they can affect many areas of your life. They can cause depression, physical illness, and spiritual illness. They can interfere with interpersonal relationships or self-esteem. When your spirit is afflicted with the disease of not forgiving, your spirit accommodates to protect itself, and your whole personality and life-style can change in ways you would not consciously choose. Bitterness and anger can easily replace charity.

I have a frustrating physical handicap, but I choose not to have a hidden spiritual handicap. By choosing to forgive myself and others, I am assuring that my spirit will not suffer.

Very Easy, Very Vogue

LOUISE PLUMMER

Exactly three years ago I was called to be a counselor in the Provo Oak Hills Stake Relief Society presidency. I did not know which counselor I was until I was asked to sit on the stand at stake conference. The president, Deanne Francis, handed me a stack of manuals; the top one was light blue with a title in bold black letters: *CREATIVE HOME-MAKING FOR HAPPY LIVING.* I gasped and turned to Deanne. "I'm the homemaking counselor?"

She smiled what I now think of as an oily smile and whispered, "I know you're a grasshopper, but you'll do just fine."

After the meeting, I met Tom, my husband, at the back of the chapel. "I'm the homemaking counselor," I told him.

He put his arm around my shoulder. "Don't worry," he said. "I'll lend you some of my recipes."

When my four sons heard, they responded in panicked unison: "This doesn't mean you're going to start cooking again, does it?"

Later that afternoon, Tom and I went for a walk around our neighborhood. As we turned a corner, we met a group of neighbors, the bishop among them. When they saw me, they burst into guffaws. "I never thought I'd see the day when Louise Plummer would be the homemaking counselor," the bishop said. "What are you going to do?" Snicker, snicker, snicker.

"Well," I said, "first I'm going to make a baby quilt, and then I'm going to have a baby! Come on, Tom, let's go home and make a baby."

The next day I browsed through the Relief Society handbook and manuals. I browsed through *CREATIVE HOMEMAKING FOR HAPPY*

Louise Plummer teaches writing at Brigham Young University. She is the author of two young adult novels, The Romantic Obsessions and Humiliations of Annie Sehlmeier *and* My Name Is Sus5an Smith. The 5 Is Silent, *and a book of essays,* Thoughts of a Grasshopper. *She and her husband, Tom Plummer, are the parents of four sons.*

LIVING. It is divided into four sections; one is "Food Preparation and Storage," in which I learned that it's never too late to learn to cook. I read through the section titled "Home Management and Beautification" and learned how to keep my house plants healthy. I read through a section called "Varied Interests," which gives instructions on how to build a manger from bread dough clay. I did not, you'll be glad to know, find any instructions for making those glass grapes our mothers were so fond of.

Where my self-esteem really took a dive was the section on sewing and stitchery, called "Homespun Is Home Fun." While I feel little guilt over disliking cooking—"Let them eat Ho Ho's" is my motto—and while I have not made mangers from bread dough clay, I *have* made glazed hearts to hang on my Christmas tree from a no-cook cornstarch and salt dough recipe, which I will be happy to share with you if you'll each send me a dollar and a self-addressed, stamped envelope, in care of the English Department at BYU. And while I have learned from experience that some neglect and a yearly shower of Malathion is healthy for plants—it is overwatering that rots them—I have never come to terms with my unwillingness to sew, because buried deep, deep in my soul is the belief that I should know how to sew.

So I tried to recommit myself to the idea of sewing after I was called to be the homemaking counselor. I made a sample quilt of twelve red schoolhouse squares, completely sewn by hand, because I have an adversarial relationship with my sewing machine. I quilted it free-style without a quilting hoop or frame. It is a crooked, lumpy little quilt—not a quilt to be shared with *real* quilters—and so it hangs above my sofa in my writing cottage in Manti, where no one can see it but me, and here it gives me a lot of private satisfaction.

I recommitted myself to the art of sewing even more recently. Two weeks ago, I decided that I would wear a dress that I had sewn to this conference, and this is it: a semi-fitted, slightly tapered dress, mid-knee, with shoulder pads, princess seams, back zipper and hemline slit, self-lined above-elbow sleeves, black linen with white contrast front and back. Very easy, very Vogue.

The project was as risky for me as bungee jumping and just as exhilarating. I have not had a good night's sleep since I made the decision. For the last two days I have had a migraine headache complete with vomiting. This dress is why.

In eighth grade, I was required to take sewing for one semester.

All the sewing was done at school. We had two projects to complete: one apron and one gathered skirt. I got a D in the class. A *D!* I don't know what I did wrong with the apron, but I know I sewed the buttonhole on the wrong flap of the skirt, so it buttoned from back to front.

I didn't sew again until I was married and felt that sewing my own clothes would save us money. It seldom did, because I bought nice fabrics, and if what I made wasn't exactly right, I wouldn't wear it. It was seldom right. Finally, in the early seventies, Tom begged me to stop sewing. "We buy everything twice," he told me. "First you sew a skirt; then you discard it because you hate it, and then you go buy a skirt. Why not just pay for one skirt?" He was right, of course.

So why this continuing obsession with sewing when I am so obviously not suited for it? Because I also have a rich history with sewing that binds me to my mother. Up until the time I got married, my mother sewed all of my clothes. In fact, my earliest memory is of my mother sewing me a lamb costume for the church Christmas play. I stood by her side looking up at her left hand as it pressed the white flannel under the needle while her right hand pushed the wooden knob of the sewing machine wheel around.

Later we rode the bus to the Yardstick in downtown Salt Lake and chose from their selection of Bates cotton. Then we walked through Woolworth's to J.C. Penney's where she would buy a small bag of cashews, which we shared on the bus ride home. She sewed me plaid dresses with white collars. She sewed me a pink taffeta gown for my aunt's wedding. She sewed me wool peg skirts in junior high. She sewed me a black velvet skirt with a white brocade top for the junior prom at the University of Utah. My husband still remembers that dress with affection.

My mother loved me; she sewed for me. It was one of her ways of nurturing me. Did I appreciate this wealth, this embarrassment of riches of having well-made clothes while I was growing up? Did I say thank you?

I thanked her last Saturday night when in desperation I called her on the phone and said, "If you have ever been my mother, if you have ever loved me, you will help me!"

"What is it?" she asked.

"You have to sew in the sleeves to this dress that I'm making for women's conference. Please, please, please."

What did she do? She burst into laughter. I didn't care, because in the end she said yes. So I drove up Sunday, and she put in these sleeves while I sat by her side and watched. My mother loves me. She sews for me.

Will I wear this dress again? I don't know. I can feel it puckering even as I speak. I have gained a little weight, and I feel like an aging Porky Pig disguised as Pepe La Pew. Even my twelve-year-old son said, "Mom, you look like a skunk."

Will I ever sew again? Probably. Two of my sons have requested that I make them shorts, even though they must have been aware over the last two weeks of my picking out seams with a paring knife and swearing not so softly under my breath. They want me to spend time on them, to know that I love them.

I don't need to sew again for Relief Society, though. That is the one thing I've learned as the homemaking counselor. The program is varied. In our stake there are women tying quilts for community shelters and for Deseret Industries at homemaking meeting. They are reading books together, listening to lectures about politics, art, and music together. We write in our journals together, and next week in our ward, a group of us are going to read poems about spring together. I have a place in this program. I don't have to know how to sew to belong.

When I first conceived of this talk, I wanted to end it by telling you that there had been a rumor in the Church that Patty Perfect did not exist, but I had looked in the mirror and in my reflection I had seen a nearly perfect Patty, because I had sewn a dress. Well, I did look in the mirror, but what I saw was a woman dressed like a skunk, a woman who struggles to be perfect in all things but who can only get it together with a few things. I will have to learn to sew perfectly in the hereafter. Through grace. I'll pick a simple pattern. Very easy, very Vogue.

The Price We Pay through Competition

DONLU DeWITT THAYER

It was a hot Saturday in July, but it was someone's birthday, and so, against my better judgment, I went shopping with several of my children at Price Savers in Provo, Utah. The parking lot was crowded, almost full, but we were lucky enough to arrive just as a brown station wagon was pulling out of a place right across from the front door. I waited a few seconds while the station wagon backed out and then began to pull my van into the space. Suddenly, a small blue sedan shot around from behind me, cut across my path and into the space. I stared at the driver in disbelief; she grinned and waved a clenched fist at me while her three children in the back seat cheered.

There is more to this story, though, for I have to admit that I did not just drive away to find another spot. I honked my horn as I passed her. I muttered something about drivers in this state deserving everything my California roommates ever said about them. I silently hoped that when we finally got parked, my foe would still be in sight and I could catch up to her and say something really nasty to her. But they were inside by the time we could walk from the other end of the lot back to their spot (*our* spot). I wanted to kick her tires. I hoped I would recognize her if I saw her in the store.

Fortunately, I didn't see her again. And, in a very short time, I was sorry that my reactions to such a little thing should have led me to make an enemy in my heart of a complete stranger. And I was very sorry that my children had seen it happen. It is tedious sometimes living under the watchful eyes of impressionable children. My behavior teaches

Donlu DeWitt Thayer has taught English composition courses at Brigham Young University. A free-lance writer and editor, she has recently published her first novel, In the Mind's Eye. *She and her husband, Douglas Thayer, are the parents of six children. She serves as a Gospel Doctrine teacher in Sunday School.*

· 129 ·

my children who I am and shows them, to the extent that they trust me, how they should be. I want my children to know peace and love in their lives. I worry when my peace departs and my love fails, because I want my influence to bless the lives of my children, not to hurt them.

So why did my peace depart and my love fail in the parking lot at Price Savers? Not merely, of course, because of the frustration of having to walk an extra fifty yards. Even more, it was my annoyance at having been vanquished. Because, who wants to lose, ever? And isn't it *natural* to feel that way?

It has been said that at the heart of Christianity is an impossibility — a commandment governing not mere behavior but emotion, the human heart. This commandment, the commandment to love, covers not only what and whom one wants to love, naturally loves, but also one's enemies, those whom it is unnatural to love. The gospel of Jesus Christ teaches, in fact, that without charity — the pure love of Christ — as the motive for everything we do, we are nothing, no matter what else we might acquire — such as the ability to move mountains by faith or speak in tongues, for instance. (See 1 Corinthians 13:2; Moroni 7:44, 47.) Loving this way requires putting off the "natural man," which is an enemy to God, to follow the enticings of the Holy Spirit and become a "saint through the atonement of Christ the Lord," to become "as a child, submissive, meek, humble, patient, full of love, willing to submit to all things which the Lord seeth fit to inflict." (Mosiah 3:19.)

Even the closest mortal associates of Jesus seemed to have trouble with this idea. To his disciples, contending over who among them was greatest, Jesus said: "Unless you reverse your present trend of thought and become as the little children, in no case shall you enter the kingdom of heaven. Therefore, he who is of such a nature as to humble himself like this little child, esteeming himself small inasmuch as he is so, thus thinking truly, and because truly, therefore humbly of himself, this person is the greatest in the kingdom of heaven."[1] Mark records what is probably the same incident: "They came to Capernaum; and when he was indoors, he asked them: What were you talking about on the way? They were silent, for they had been talking on the way about who was the greatest. He sat down and called the twelve and said to them: Whoever wishes to be first must be last of all and servant of all. And taking a little child he set him in the midst of them, and embraced him, and said: Whoever accepts a child like one of these in my name, accepts me."[2]

Conversely, Jesus warned his followers that "if one leads astray one of these little ones who have faith in me, it is better for him to have a millstone hung about his neck and be drowned in the sea."[3] This will happen, this leading astray, as acknowledged by Luke: "It is impossible that there should come no causes to make man go astray; but woe to him through whom the causes come. . . . Watch yourselves."[4]

What does it mean to lead astray the little ones? We should re-member, first of all, that the "little ones" are not only children but all who are humble followers of Jesus Christ. (See Doctrine and Covenants 121: 16–19.) The word rendered by Lattimore as "lead astray," by Wuest as "be a stumbling block to, cause to stumble" and by the King James translators as "offend" is the Greek *skandalon,* the source of our word "scandal." How do we "scandalize" the little ones? A dictionary definition reminds us that scandal is "discredit brought upon religion by unseemly conduct in a religious person. Conduct that causes or encourages a lapse of faith or religious obedience in another." To his disciples, con-tending over who among them was greatest, Jesus said, "Watch your-selves." To myself, contending over a silly parking place, I say, "Watch yourself."

It is a beautiful April afternoon, and the nine-year-old soccer players run onto the field, happy, energetic, ready for their first game of the season. The young coach gathers the boys and girls around for a pregame pep talk. His words float toward me in the air: "I've seen the team you're playing today, and they're mean lookin'. And they hate you. And they say they're gonna kill you. What do you say to that?" "We'll make 'em eat their words!" scream the children. "We'll tear 'em apart!"

I don't think the coach means to invite the children to actual hatred and mayhem. I don't think he even realizes that he is lying to them (he hasn't seen the opposing team; they have not even arrived). This is just hype, just sports talk, meant to stir up feelings of athletic rivalry, feelings that have been described as "clean hatred"—clean because they are directed not against actual people but only against symbols, such as a number or a jersey.[5] I wonder, though. In fostering such "clean" hatreds, might we not be teaching the way to develop "real" hatred? That is, of course, how perfectly peaceful people are taught to wage war. But, as we learn from the Book of Mormon, for a disciple of Christ, war is to be waged only at the command of God, in self-protection, and then not in glee but courageously, in great sorrow.

I understand that this young soccer coach is only doing his job, and that this is only a game. But what is a game? What is the relationship of "playing" to "real life"? We draw parallels all the time, make analogies to teach serious lessons about life from our experience in games. So am I wrong to be concerned about the violent language of the young players, which seems fully justified by most of the adults around them, as does the fabrication that induced them? The justification comes from what the language is intended to achieve—victory and a consequent pride in achievement. In other words, the end, or result, is supposed to justify the means used to achieve that end.

It seems to me, however, that for a disciple of Jesus Christ, an end can never justify a means. In fact, in the Christian way of life, there is no end in this sense. The means is everything. Those who follow Christ, who is the Way of Truth and Life, are in the path of righteousness; that is to say, their lives are lived out in repentance. Repentance is not a goal or a product; it is a process. In every moment of the life of a committed follower of Jesus Christ, the means to achieving the end *is* the end. Exaltation, then, often called the end, or goal, of our existence, is not a destination but rather the perfection of a process, the perfection in ourselves of the way of truth and light. That is not something we can quantify. We cannot say, "I am 86 percent exalted. How much exalted are you?" Or "I am just five yards (or fifteen minutes, or six trips to the temple) from exaltation. Race you to the finish!"

We will become exalted if we sanctify ourselves, make the requisite covenants and keep them, consecrating all we have and are to the establishment of Zion, and endure to the end. In this process, we learn that all we do must be motivated by pure love, else, in the end, we are nothing. If we try to "get" eternal life with the wrong motives, we will fail. Eternal life is a state of being, a quality of existence, not a quantity of spiritual acquisitions, not the great end zone or the ultimate parking place in the sky.

Competitiveness arises in a time-bounded world of limited resources. All of us on earth have voluntarily "fallen" into this world of limited time and space; we have taken upon ourselves estrangement from God to live and learn in an economy of scarcity,[6] where the survival of one creature can mean the extinction of another. There is only so much room on Mother's lap, so much time in Father's day, so many places on the team, on the stage, in graduate school, so much potential demand for a particular product, so much room at the top. So, we all compete for temporal things in this temporal economy of scarcity. But in the economy of God, there is enough for all, and to spare. It is an economy of abundance. "I am come," Jesus said, "that they might have life, and that they might have it more abundantly." (John 10:10.) "I the Lord am willing to make these things known unto all flesh; for I am no respecter of persons, and will that all men shall know." (D&C 1:34–35.) God is not protecting his status at the top. He wants us all to come where he is, to eat and drink and be filled, nevermore to hunger or thirst. "Henceforth I call you not servants; for the servant knoweth not what his lord doeth: but I have called you friends; for all things that I have heard of my Father I have made known unto you." (John 15:15.) Jesus stands at the door and knocks; it is for us to yield to his desire for us, and receive that which he gives liberally to all.

Is there a competitive instinct, then? If there is, is it an aspect of the natural man that is an enemy to God, or is it something else, perhaps something meant to drive us to excellence we wouldn't otherwise know? Or could it be both? It is clear, I think, that competition is a natural response to scarcity, perhaps a result of an instinct for self-preservation. I wonder, though, if seeking to destroy others physically, emotionally, even symbolically, to achieve victory in situations that do not involve life and death should be seen as self-preservation.

Sometimes competition seems exactly that — *self*-preservation. Even losing something as trivial as a parking place can feel like a loss of self, or at least of self-esteem. Perhaps, when we compete, we are merely having fun, rejoicing in comradery, playing to test our strength, our courage, our skill. Or, perhaps we are trying to establish our*selves,* make identities for ourselves as winners, so that we can then have what is called pride in performance, pride in ourselves.

In spite of what most of us have come to believe, competitive attitudes and the resulting pride (or agony, depending upon the outcome) are not intrinsic parts of either working or playing. It is possible to work, to achieve, to improve minds and bodies, to excel, even to play games, without competing. "How fast did you run, Susie?" should be a question that invites a child to say "As fast as I could!" not a question that invites Susie to find her worth in a number that compares her, favorably or unfavorably, with another. I remember the joyful experience of sabotaging an elementary school field day by running onto the field with a handful of ribbons, handing them out to all the losers as I ran along with them. "Wow!" said one little person. "I never won anything before in my life!" We can play, exert ourselves, stretch ourselves, without keeping track of the rankings, without keeping score. We have only to become as little children, playing for the joy of it—after all, we are created for joy, taught Father Lehi to his much-tried son Jacob— instead of for the conquest of another.

"By proving contraries," said Joseph Smith, "truth is made manifest."[7] And so we engage in tests of strength, agility, ability, engage in debates to find the truth. But as soon as we abandon the search for truth and substitute for it the quest at all costs for *victory*, we have lost our pure motive. In the eternal scheme of things, when we have lost that, we have lost all.

On Saturday morning, 1 April 1989, the prophet of the Lord delivered a message. "I know the Lord wants this message delivered now," he said. The message was a warning to "beware of pride . . . the universal sin, the great vice . . . the great stumbling block to Zion." President Ezra Taft Benson warned his hearers that pride is a "very misunderstood sin" and admonished them to avoid sinning in ignorance by coming to understand the central feature of pride, "enmity—enmity toward God and enmity toward our fellowmen. *Enmity* means 'hatred toward, hostility to, or a state of opposition.' It is the power by which Satan wishes to reign over us."

Pride, said the prophet, "is essentially competitive in nature. We pit our will against God's. When we direct our pride toward God, it is in the spirit of 'my will and not thine be done.' . . . Our will in competition to God's will allows desires, appetites, and passions to go unbridled." The enmity in "this very prevalent sin of pride" is directed not only toward God but "toward our fellowmen. We are tempted daily to elevate ourselves above others and diminish them. . . . The proud make every man their adversary by pitting their intellects, opinions, works, wealth, talents, or any other worldly measuring device against others."[8] Then, to emphasize the competitive nature of pride, the prophet quoted C. S. Lewis: "Pride gets no pleasure out of having something, only out of having more of it than the next man. . . . It is the comparison that makes you proud: the pleasure of being above the rest. Once the element of competition has gone, pride has gone."[9]

In our culture, we are schooled from the cradle to maintain the rivalry and pride that gets and keeps us moving, accomplishing. We grow up perceiving rivals in our families, on the playground, in the classroom. Quite naturally we find that enemies — adversaries — is what our legal system is all about,[10] and our political system, too. What does this mean? When I have asked such a question, I have been accused of wanting to eliminate all fun from life and even of trying to undermine the American economy. I do not want to do either of those things. I do, however, want to suggest that there are dangers in establishing or submitting ourselves unnecessarily to structures that can perpetuate, and even create, emptiness.

Michael Novak, a great baseball fan and a "staunch defender of competition" has observed that in contemporary America, "our sports are lively with the sense of evil, [providing] an almost deliberate exercise in pushing the psyche to cheat and take advantage, to be ruthless, cruel, deceitful, vengeful, and aggressive."[11] If that is true, we need not think this evil applies only to athletes participating in steroid scandals or to such sports spinoffs as the mother who hired someone to kill the mother of her daughter's cheerleading rival. For some of us, we need to think back only as far as our last experience in a crowded parking lot, or a red-tag sale, or our last Little League game. Which brings me back to memories of athletic coaches and parents I have observed while watching my children play sports. I have heard adults, Latter-day Saints, men and women, urging young athletes to "become animals," screaming at them to fight, to kill, shouting obscenities, berating young people (who are supposed to be having fun) for missing a shot, making a wrong move, failing. Objecting to such behavior, I am accused of seeking to deny my children the opportunity to learn about real life.

But, once again, whatever "real" conflict my children will encounter in mortal life, what I hope for them is that their hearts will be prepared for joy. It is difficult for me to see how they will find joy in ruthless striving for victory or in vain attempts to establish their own worth at the expense of others. I think they will find joy only when love is the motive for all their actions — in work, in play, in "pretend" life, and in "real" life. And how will they learn love? By being loved, I think, and so learning their real, intrinsic worth, beyond compare, and by being taught correct principles and then being trusted to learn and live according to them.

I worry about the view of human nature revealed in teaching children by luring them, bribing them, manipulating them, threatening them, rewarding them into good behavior (and therefore, it is supposed, into righteousness). "I know," said a very good elementary school teacher once when I said this to her. "I'd like them to be good for nothing, too." But, I am told, what you have to do to get kids moving is to promise them a reward. Better yet, invite them to a contest and induce them to be winners. The fact that in doing that we are much more likely to set them up to be losers is ignored.

In serious competition, winning isn't everything, as the famous coach Vince Lombardi said—it is the *only* thing. For a truly competitive person, victory is the single goal that provides the most important motive for action in relationship to others. All sorts of means are justified in reaching this goal. These need not be the means to change, progress, learn, grow; too often, they are merely the means to win.

I once taught in Sunday School a lovely young woman, gentle in her spirit, an exquisite pianist. I worried about the amount of time and energy she put into her music, mostly in preparation for competitions, because of the isolation it required. I asked about her plans for the future. She told me that of course all pianists dream of a concert stage career, but even if that were not to come to her, what she was doing now would have been a wonderful way to have spent her young life. A very healthy attitude, I thought. She wasn't playing the piano to please her parents and teachers. She wasn't trying to find personal glory at the expense of anyone else. She truly loved making music. I stopped worrying about her.

She went off to conservatory to follow her dreams. Eighteen months later, back in Provo, she phoned me, weary and disenchanted. She had left the conservatory, and she didn't think she could ever touch the piano again. All the scrutiny, all the comparisons, evaluations. It took the joy out of making music, she said. It wore her down. It wasn't the real musicians who could succeed at that school, she said. It was the real competitors.

Most people will concede that competitiveness *can* be bad, if it gets out of hand, if it gets ruthless. But that wouldn't stop most people from valuing competition itself, or from helping their children develop competitive attitudes. And perhaps it is true that competition is only bad for people like me, who have a predisposition to becoming *fiercely* competitive. (If only I could learn to be a "good sport," to lose graciously, without feeling—or at least without exhibiting—pain!)

Someone who considers "fiercely competitive" a compliment once asked me when I was going on like this, "What's the matter with you?

Don't you want your kids to succeed in life?" Here it was again. That response angered me. I wanted to argue with this person and win my point. I know how to win arguments. In high school debate we practiced winning arguments, even if we didn't believe what we were saying. That was supposed to be fun, and our victories would bring academic glory to the school. I could win, but I didn't like doing it when my heart wasn't in it. I know that I might be able to win the argument about my children and success, too. But, deep down, I know that this would not change my opponent's heart. I know, too, that the momentary triumph I would feel at arguing someone into the ground would soon turn bitter. I would feel ashamed and want to apologize. How could that be, since I would be *right*? But I know it would happen.

It is easy to rationalize what is called the competitive instinct: it's a hard world. We need to make our way, not only for our own sakes, but for the sakes of others who depend on us. We get tired; we just want to get things done. We work hard. At the end of a day, we want the kids to go to bed, so we stage a race to the bedroom and reward the one who wins. Thus we plant in others the seeds once sown in us: Who can be first? Who can be best?

Or how about, Who can be the most reverent? One of the more interesting challenges presented by the consolidated schedule is Primary Sharing Time. There are all those children, together, in the house of the Lord, on the Sabbath day. Afraid that the children will not respond, will not be good, we make plans. We motivate singing by dividing up the children to see which group can sing best. We have scripture chases, play gospel-concept Concentration, Book of Mormon Double Jeopardy, Church History Tic-Tac-Toe. Having worked so hard to provide these activities, we are dismayed when the children, wanting to win the games we have set for them, end up shouting at one another, and we berate them for failing to be reverent in Heavenly Father's house.

As children grow, as they learn to assert their own wills, find themselves, protect themselves, advance themselves, it is likely that they will find that yielding to God and to others in love can become more and more difficult, until there is real pain, real struggle, something to conquer, before the yielding comes. They will have learned, perhaps, that they must at least compete with themselves in order to obtain "excellence." But is that true? Is that necessary?

Let's ask another question. Can we love someone we are trying to defeat? If we compete with ourselves, are we not divided against ourselves? A house divided against itself cannot stand.

When, in desperation, I began some years ago to thread my way back through the labyrinths that had brought me, with all my religious beliefs and practices intact, to the pit of despair, I found competition lurking at every turn. First competition for love and grades and attention and men and success, and then the ultimate competition, the competition with self—just me and my "list," that impossible list, the list that I made every morning, literally or figuratively, the list that goes on forever, stretching out before me into eternity. A person with a quantifying, list-making mentality can easily fail just by comparing her list to someone else's. Or, if she needs a boost, she can use the same method to "succeed" momentarily.

In the old days before we moved north to Edgemont, my neighbor Ruth Clegg, old enough to be my grandmother, used to make me sit down and smell the flowers in her sun porch while she took my three babies into her kitchen and fed them foods I didn't allow. Ruth had a small cluttered house full of music, plants, potting soil, hot rolls, books, Scout projects, and happy people of all ages. In Ruth's house, I knew peace.

My next three babies were born in a different neighborhood, while we lived in a house too big ever to keep clean enough. For a while, the backdoor neighbor was a beautiful thin woman who cleaned the toothpaste off the bathroom mirror and vacuumed the family room every noon before her husband came home for lunch. Her hair was perfect every morning at seven—I could see it through my bleary eyes from my kitchen window to hers. What was worse, she was always happy. As happy, it seemed to me, as Ruth Clegg.

But I wasn't happy. A fourth child, a fifth, a sixth (just as the oldest turned nine). I couldn't keep it up, the house, the Church callings, the editing, the music, the needs of the children. I resented "morning people" like my happy neighbor; I resented all thin people with clean houses; I couldn't do it. But I had to. My worth depended on my being as "good" as they were, and even better. My neighbor was herself, living her life as she wanted, happy. She didn't invite me to a contest, but somehow I perceived a contest, and I couldn't stop competing (and therefore, failing). Added to the unavoidable stresses of that time of my life, then, was the avoidable stress of my need to compete.

As I have suggested, competition is the process of identifying and labeling failure. When I became depressed, I had pretty much decided that it was impossible for me to be anything but a failure as a Latter-day Saint housewife. At other things, I had been successful, but wifing and mothering were too ambiguous, too difficult to quantify and measure. How could I ever be successful at them? I was so accustomed to finding my worth (my "self") in the comparisons and rankings of competition that I couldn't figure out who I was anymore. I was lost, worthless, depressed.

A contest, a competition, is arbitrary. In an athletic or academic or aesthetic contest, where is the truth? What have we actually discovered by deciding a victor—the best, the prettiest, the fastest, the most, the largest, the highest? Assuming that we have decided something measurable about physical strength, mental ability, or beauty, is this value intrinsic, or assigned? Does it actually represent "worth," in a fundamental (eternal) sense?

Competing to establish worth by superior performance never works, in the long run, because it denies reality. The God we emulate is not the Great I Do but the Great I Am, a self-existent being, beyond compare. "These two facts do exist, that there are two spirits, one being more intelligent than the other; there shall be another more intelligent than they; I am the Lord thy God, I am more intelligent than they all." (Abraham 3:19.) This is not an invitation to a race. It is a description of what is. It is for us to be still and know this reality.

The Book of Mormon offers two great teachings that are important here: the necessity of opposition in all things, and the evils of contention. King Benjamin, among others, warned against the spirit of contention, which is of the devil. And, in appearing to the Nephites, the resurrected Jesus repeated the teachings we find in the New Testament as the Sermon on the Mount, among them the teaching to "resist not evil" and to "turn the other cheek." To the devil himself, we are to say, "Get thee behind me, Satan." This means that we are not to contend with evil on *its* terms. To do so is to partake of its spirit, which is death and destruction.

Yes, Father Lehi did teach that there must needs be (is, of necessity) opposition in all things. Joy is defined against pain, perhaps even derived from it. The fight with sin is real. It will be long and must go on. We do live in a world full of conflict, paradox. But it is important that in perceiving the opposition in all things, we do not see an opponent in every person. If we have a competitive world view, there is danger that we will do this, danger that we will perceive life's paradoxes incorrectly, or misconstrue them. We can, for example, perceive polarity where it doesn't exist, seeing ourselves in competition with something we are actually part of, thus destroying any possibility of real community with others.

Without the *necessary* opposition in the universe, "all things must have vanished away," taught Lehi. (2 Nephi 2:13.) This necessary opposition is the "opposition" of female and male, of the electron and the nucleus, or of the nuclear members themselves, a relationship that holds the universe in order, that keeps the atom from collapsing, a relationship that says, "There is something, and not nothing." This kind of opposition calls for conjunction, for harmony, for balance to bring forth truth. But we must take care not to see in this necessary opposition the kind of arbitrary or "rival" opposition that creates competition. Creating rivalries destroys the meaning of the polarity. When we see the relationship between the sexes, for instance, in any sense as a war, we are not able to yield ourselves to learning what there is to learn from the otherness of sexuality.

We do not find eternal life by waging war against each other. We do not find truth by attempting to conquer paradox. We can only break ourselves in the attempt. As we break ourselves, and as we break from others, we break the body of Christ. This is not a holy breaking, a sacramental one, but an unholy one, a desecration.

Ancient Christianity sometimes created pictures of the righteous laughing in derision at the sinners burning in hell. But the vision of Lehi tells the truth. The derisive laughter comes from the sinners in the great and spacious building, mocking those who, holding steadfast to the word of God, move towards eternal life in the way of truth and light—in the love of God. It is this vision, this view of the world, that I want my children to learn. It is a sacred, mature, Christian view of life. It is not a vision that prevails in American culture, but it is a vision that is taught in scripture, ancient and modern. "God will have a humble people," says our living prophet, President Ezra Taft Benson. "Either we can choose to be humble, or we can be compelled to be humble.... Let us choose to be humble. We can choose to humble ourselves by conquering enmity toward our brothers and sisters, esteeming them as ourselves, and lifting them as high or higher than we are.... My dear brethren and sisters, we must prepare to redeem Zion. It was essentially the sin of pride that kept us from establishing Zion in the days of the Prophet Joseph Smith. It was the same sin of pride that brought consecration to an end among the Nephites.... Pride is the great stumbling block to Zion.... We must cleanse the inner vessel by conquering pride. We must yield 'to the enticings of the Holy Spirit,' put off the prideful 'natural man,' become a 'saint through the atonement of Christ the Lord,' and become 'as a child, submissive, meek, humble.' "[12]

What does it mean, to become as a child? It means, in part, learning (or relearning) how to play for the sheer joy of it—running our hearts out, taking pleasure in strengthening our bodies and minds, encouraging others along the way. It means not just being good sports but being generous of heart. It means learning to value the process over the product, giving up "precision—particularly precision in the service of determining who is best—in exchange for pure enjoyment. He who plays does not ask the score. In fact, there is no score to be kept."[13]

My experience as a mother has taught me that this way of being is natural to children, more natural than their "competitive instincts." I recall, among many examples, the time our two oldest sons staged a tricycle race when they were three and four years old. The elder, constantly finding himself ahead, would stop, turn around, encourage his brother, wait for him to catch up, sighing. His only complaint was that it was taking a long time to help his brother enjoy this race.

It is my view that all of us are born with a desire to grow and develop and find truth. If children are presented with rich opportunities for learning, by people who are interested in giving all they know so that the children can become happy, productive, loving adults, the children will grow, blossom, develop. Unless children are damaged in some way, they quite naturally learn. If they are led and instructed, they follow their gifts, becoming musicians, athletes, mechanics, artists, according to their interests and opportunities. They quite naturally, as they outgrow the normal and necessary egocentrism of infancy, find joy in helping, sharing. The rewards of competence and cooperation lead the children on, if the children are not deprived, abused, or overstimulated by adults seeking to use and manipulate them for their own purposes.

It is not competition and its attendant griefs that prepare children for the real world. It is, rather, love and acceptance in our early years that allow us to deal with rejection later on. It is an initial sense of security that gives us the strength to face adversity, and this security is precisely what competition inhibits.

We have come to earth to learn to make Zion, the place where the pure in heart can dwell. The pure heart is the *true* heart, independent in its own sphere, acting on its own, without external coercion. The work and glory of God are to help us purify our hearts, to bring us out of bondage into freedom, to bring to pass immortality and eternal life for us. The work of God in the universe, then, is the work of creation, of bringing new life, not conquest, out of relationship. All other work is vain, empty. No other success can compensate for failure to love. If we seek first the kingdom of God and his righteousness, all else will be added unto us.

It might be well for those who would be saints of God to consider what they mean by offering to establish or find worth in the victories of one human being over another in what would otherwise be benign activities. "Every contest that is staged...involves the creation of a desired and scarce status where none existed before."[14] If we take the contest model as our model for reality, we will always see the wrong reality.

President Benson has told us that we must become humble. And it is obvious that we cannot acquire humility by paying attention to (quantifying, and being proud of) our efforts at humility. We cannot find humility by subjecting ourselves to humiliation and certainly not by attempting to conquer and humiliate others. True humility is found only in the self-forgetfulness of a self-existent being. We can only find ourselves by losing ourselves—not by exhausting ourselves in resentful service, but by giving ourselves freely to increase the joy in the universe. We walk in the way of truth and life—"truth" because it is in harmony with what is, "life" because all other ways end in death. This is the way of repentance, of creating in ourselves new hearts and new minds. We do this for ourselves, and we help others to do it, by avoiding contention. We resist creating unnecessary scarcity in the world—for ourselves, our families, our friends, our constituents, our congregations, our readers. In this way we can find a more abundant life.

At first, we don't see how we can do this. It is difficult to have faith in a way of being we have not known. If we had the faith, we could change our hearts; we could sacrifice all earthly things, even our competitiveness. But how can we find such faith without the strength and understanding that come from having made the sacrifice? We are caught. How can we change? This is a paradox.

The way out of the paradox is to accept it, receive it, experiment upon it, working with others to test ourselves, our ideas, our methods of accomplishing things. As we move along, we will not always agree. We are different. But we need not contend. If we are to be exalted, we must, even with our differences, become one. We must, by the grace of God, find communion, find moments when love brings Zion, when love discloses the kingdom of God among us. We explore our differences, test our strengths, "proving contraries" to find truth. We live together, play together, in love.

For the real story of the universe is not who gets which for what—top kingdom, middle kingdom, bottom kingdom. The story of life and creation is glory—the glory of the sun, the glory of the moon, the glory of the stars. Let us play in the universe, says the heart that is true. Let us, undivided from one another, go on to glory.

NOTES

1. Kenneth S. Wuest, *The New Testament: An Expanded Translation* (Grand Rapids, Mich.: Wm. B. Eerdmans Publishing Co., 1961), pp. 45–46. This translation is an attempt by Wuest, "teacher emeritus of New Testament Greek" of the Moody Bible Institute, to render the connotations of the Greek as accurately as possible in English, regardless of how cumbersome or unpoetic the result. Thus, what the King James Version renders as "be converted," Wuest translates "reverse your present trend of thought." Likewise, the KJV "to humble oneself as a little child" is explained by Wuest to mean "he who is of such a nature as to humble himself like this little child, esteeming himself small inasmuch as he is, thus thinking truly, and because truly, therefore humbly of himself, this person is the greatest in the kingdom of heaven." Sometimes when a passage of scripture is very familiar, a new rendering can bring insight. I found this to be the case here.

2. Richmond Lattimore, *The Four Gospels and the Revelation* (New York: Farrar, Straus, Giroux, 1979), p. 26. Lattimore is an eminent scholar, a translator of many important Greek texts.

3. Ibid., Matthew 18:6.

4. Ibid., Luke 17:1–3.

5. This idea was expressed by Ronald Reagan, as quoted in Brenda Jo Bredemeier and David L. Shields, "Values and Violence in Sports Today," *Psychology Today*, Oct. 1985, p. 23.

6. I have borrowed the terms "economy of scarcity" and "economy of abundance" from Rollo May, *Love and Will* (New York: Dell Publishing Co., 1969), pp. 306–7.

7. Joseph Smith to L. Daniel Rupp, 5 June 1844, published in Joseph Smith, *History of the Church of Jesus Christ of Latter-day Saints*, 7 vols., 2d ed. rev., edited by B.H. Roberts (Salt Lake City: Deseret Book Co., 1978), 6:428.

8. Ezra Taft Benson, "Beware of Pride," *Ensign*, May 1989, p. 4.

9. C. S. Lewis, *Mere Christianity* (New York: Macmillan, 1952), pp. 109–10.

10. Alfie Kohn, *No Contest: The Case against Competition* (Boston: Houghton Mifflin, 1986), p. 85.
11. Ibid., p. 163.
12. Benson, pp. 6–7.
13. Kohn, p. 86.
14. Ibid., p. 75.

Adult Spiritual Development

A CONVERSATION WITH
FRANCINE R. BENNION
AND MARTHA N. BECK

Francine: Eve lived in a garden with her husband, and both of them walked and talked with God; but they lacked knowledge of both good and evil until Eve began their journey out of Eden and into adult spiritual development.

Much later, Elijah called down fire from heaven. It burned water-soaked wood and water-soaked bullocks, and consumed them, and all the people fell on their faces and said, "The Lord He is God." Then Elijah prophesied rain to end a long drought. First there was a little cloud, then the skies blackened with clouds and wind, and a great rain did come. The hand of the Lord was on Elijah. But Jezebel sought to kill Elijah, and he fled into the wilderness, sat down under a juniper tree, and requested that he might die: "Now, oh Lord, take away my life, for I am not better than my fathers." Then Elijah, also, began a journey of adult spiritual development, traveling forty days and forty nights, meeting a strong wind that rent mountains and broke rocks, and after the wind an earthquake, then fire, before he heard a still small voice, the voice of the Lord. (1 Kings 18–19.)

Much later, developing his own journey line upon line until death, Jesus made his second prayer in Gethsemane slightly but significantly different from his first. (Matthew 26:39, 42.) As he hung nailed to the cross, according to Matthew, some of his last words were a question: "My God, my God, why ... ?" (Matthew 27:46.)

Most of us have our own questions: Why? How? Who? In the midst

Francine R. Bennion teaches history of civilization in the honors program at Brigham Young University. She and her husband, Robert C. Bennion, have three children.

Martha N. Beck teaches sociology at Brigham Young University. She and her husband, John C. Beck, are the parents of three children.

of realities we hadn't expected, many of us find the questions exceedingly important to adult spiritual development.

Let us define our terms.

By *adult* we do not mean a matter of age. The world can be wider for adults than for children, but for some it becomes more narrow. By *adult* we mean persons who have met realities better and worse, more diverse and complex, than they expected as children. If you have not already met such realities, you will if you live long enough. We're defining *adult* in this discussion as a matter of experience.

Development is change. In our context here, *development* means change from limited awareness and relative ignorance toward those larger capacities with which God moves among saints and sinners, people who worship and people who abuse, mock, misunderstand, or ignore; among fires, earthquakes, worlds coming into being, and galaxies without number to us. Spiritual *development* means change as we move towards knowing God and becoming more like God, rather than remaining simply children.[1]

Spiritual is more difficult to define. We will not use the word to mean measurable things such as tithing, meetings, home evenings, baptism, Church callings, scripture reading, or even beneficent acts, for any of these may or may not be spiritual. What we are concerned with here is awareness, relationships, and states of being. We use *spiritual* to mean our sense of ourselves, God, and the universe, and therefore our inner experience. We use *spiritual development* to mean reaching for the prime realities that underlie our existence.

Spiritual does not mean the same thing to all people, but generally it means transcending ordinary, day-to-day things. In some parts of the world, people use a higher, "holy" language, different from that of mundane life, to speak of spiritual matters. In English we use ordinary words — love, truth, joy, peace, for example — but these are tied to our limited human experience, and as a result, we may limit our conceptions of the spiritual to what we have already experienced or imagined.

The point of our spiritual development is enlargement of our souls, increasing capacity for truth, love, God, freedom. It is awareness that we are not simply humans dealing with other humans in a physical world that we don't comprehend or control, but that we are all related to God, that we are living in His universe, that His universe is ours, that He gives us means to know ultimate realities and transcend our present limitations. The point of spiritual quests, the point of spiritual development, is not to be gods already but to be reaching toward those larger realities and to be connected to them by our very search for them.

I affirm the reality of that connection whether we're in the middle of joy, or pain, or opportunity, or struggle. The connection is there if what we are seeking is adult spiritual development, if what we are seeking is not simply the comfort and safety of easier times. The connection is there when we want or need it most.

I affirm the importance of what we give to each other on our journeys. I affirm our capacity to make the journey, to increase the richness and strength of our souls. I believe adult spiritual development is the reason we are alive.

God knows our journeys and the ultimate spiritual realities we seek, but we may differ greatly in our own conceptions of them. Devout Buddhists journey toward nirvana, a state of oblivion without individual identity, without pain or external reality. Taos Indians look to living in harmony now and in ultimate harmony after death, not in the kinds of hierarchy so prized by much of the world, not in various levels of personal glory or status where some are more important than others, but rather helping and enhancing each other here and now, and ultimately being folded together in blessing with water clear, air clear, and all beautiful.

Even as Latter-day Saints, we differ. Some look for joy and absence of suffering and pain, while others ponder joy with a God who *feels* the suffering of struggling humans. Some think of black marks and gold stars, while others focus on matters of the heart. Most assume that their own conception is the only ultimate possibility.

Those ultimate realities are not what we're here to talk about today, but they have much to do with spiritual development because where we think we are going has a lot to do with our more immediate destinations and what we do to get there.

Martha and I are not here to prescribe one way to become spiritually developed. The process is individual, and one person's way may not be another's, even if both are using the same maps and tools. We want to share with you some of our own experience and those of others we know, which may help you in your own journeys.

We'd like to begin by suggesting what spiritual development is not. You can understand a thing only if you understand what it is not.

Martha: I've become something of an expert on this aspect of spiritual development. You see, several times during my life I have been absolutely sure that I knew exactly what spiritual development was — in fact, I was pretty confident that I'd achieved it. As I prepared for this conversation, I looked back on all those times, and I felt a bit like Mark Twain when he said that he knew he could quit smoking because he'd done it a thousand times. I guess the very fact that I've tried so many routes to spiritual development shows that I'm not particularly spiritually developed. The truth is that during my lifetime I have come up with a whole array of prescriptions for spiritual development, but none of them worked very well. There is some benefit, however, in having made a lot of mistakes, because maybe by talking about them here I may help some of you avoid some of my own errors — and together we may come closer to finding a better path than I have taken to this point.

My first strategy for achieving spiritual development was one we all learn as children in Sunday School. Children need to be taught rules and are not really capable of testing those rules against experience to form their own judgments. My first set of criteria for spiritual growth never got beyond this. For a long time, I believed that what I had to do to obtain salvation was to keep a lot of rules. It was that simple. If I kept every rule that I could learn, I was bound to achieve happiness, exaltation, and divine status in a matter of minutes. If keeping all the rules I knew didn't seem to be enough, the answer was to learn more rules and keep them as well.

I tried that strategy. I tried it for a long time. I tried it throughout all my teenage years, and it served passably well as a means to spirituality. But at the end of those years, as I began to encounter the world in the body of an adult — at least, a young adult — I found this structure weakening and becoming inadequate to support the realities I was learning. In response, I intensified my rule-keeping. I thought perhaps that I wasn't praying enough, and so I prayed more often. When I still didn't attain nirvana, I thought I might not be praying the right way. I read texts on prayer techniques and tried different methods. I prayed standing, sitting, and on my knees. I prayed in my heart and out loud. I prayed in a shaft of sunlight and in the dead of night. I prayed in various different ways, and yet I still felt that my spiritual development was stalling. So I kept the Word of Wisdom with more care, and when that didn't work, I kept other "words." I remained kosher, halal, and vegetarian. I kept every rule I could find. And still, I did not feel inner peace or unity with my Father in Heaven. I felt lost and alone and frightened. And I had no explanations for the sorrows and the struggles I saw in the world—not my own nor those of the people around me. Keeping rules simply wasn't enough for me.

Francine: Martha, how were you defining *rules?*

Martha: A rule was anything handed to me by an authority figure—in print, especially. If I could get it in print, I was sure it would work.

Francine: Did you ever see any contradiction between two rules?

Martha: When you're keeping one rule, you think about that rule, and when you want to keep the next rule, you just stop thinking about the first rule and keep the second.

Francine: How long was it before you wondered if you understood the rule in the same way God might?

Martha: That took me about a year. By that time I was in the hospital. Keeping so many rules finally pushed me to a complete physical and emotional collapse.

Francine: Why were you keeping the rules? What were you conscious of as the reason for keeping the rules?

Martha: Keeping the rules was one of the rules. But—as Francine is very rightly pointing out and as Eve discovered in the Garden of Eden—even the rules of God seem to be in contradiction some of the time, and you have to exercise logic, agency, and prioritizing in deciding which rules you should keep. When I discovered that as a young adult, I had to come up with another prescription for spiritual development—a prescription to tell me which rules I should keep. The first idea I seized upon as my ultimate priority was to please everybody. It became my motto. I could have had it tattooed across my face: "PLEASE EVERYBODY."

Francine: I have known two young married women who kept the rules and pleased everyone until they found one rule in conflict with another and had to make a choice. Both women joined polygamist cults—a matter of great pain for their families. The same virtues they had seen as paramount in their youth, to obey authority figures and to please and make others happy, were the very things that encouraged them to believe what a very authoritative polygamist told them—to marry him in order to please God and obey God. It is important to define the virtue of whatever it is you are trying to do, especially to define differences between child-like pleasing, child-like obedience, and adult spiritual development.

Martha: That is especially important for women. In our society, women often seem particularly compelled to please others as a means to feeling worthwhile. Many of us decide which rules to keep by determining whom we most want to please. We may then adopt whatever strategy it takes to avoid displeasing or coming into conflict with those people. That was my own way of thinking for some time, and I met many others who were following a similar course. All of us hoped that this pleasing behavior was the road to spiritual development, to the peace I mentioned earlier. It failed me as badly as my strict rule-keeping had, and for the same reason: people's expectations of me came into conflict.

I will never forget the trauma I experienced over this issue as a graduate student. I felt, and priesthood blessings had confirmed to me, that God approved of my educational goals and that I was in his company as I tried to raise my little girl and fulfill the expectations of my teachers in graduate school. That very year was the year that the Church's stance on women remaining in the home and eschewing careers was very much strengthened. I had a deep testimony, and I wanted to please the people in the Church who were at least hinting to me that my pursuit of a graduate degree might be a little bit outside the bounds of orthodoxy. I also wanted to please my advisors, who had been my friends and mentors and whose ideas were completely contrary to those of the Church. I wanted to please my husband. I wanted to please my child. I wanted to please my parents, my parents-in-law, and all my other numerous friends and relatives. But it seemed that none of these people wanted me to do exactly the same thing. I remember going behind a bookshelf one day after a class, lying down on the floor, and thinking, "Okay, now I have to die, because I cannot please anybody anymore." I was exhausted and bewildered. By trying to please everyone, I had pleased no one.

Then I tried another way to spiritual development. This is a method you can find in the texts of mystics and various religious gurus throughout history. What I decided to do was to completely withdraw from life. After all, doesn't it seem logical that the best path to spiritual growth might be to avoid all the distractions of the material world and focus on the ways of God? This was the model of the celibate monks of the Middle Ages. In order to be a saint, one must detach from everyday existence, from the clutter and bother that occupies most ordinary people. According to a lot of religious traditions, this is the only way to focus completely on God and thus achieve spiritual maturity.

I discovered two major problems with this strategy. First, I was a mother, and the joys and difficulties of raising children did not mesh well with a hermit's way of life. Second, even when I could get a moment for myself and think of absolutely nothing in the real world – just focus completely on my own spiritual development – I became unbelievably bored. Now, I am not sure exactly what our Heavenly Father is like, but one thing of which I am convinced is that God is not boring. So I decided that I must still be doing the wrong thing, because otherworldly mysticism (at least the way I was doing it) was boring my socks off. I became so bored that I knew I had to change something if I wanted to come closer to God.

Of course, I couldn't go back to keeping all of the rules or pleasing everyone, so I came up with something new. I decided to reject everything and become a rebel. My first response to anything anyone said during this grand new experiment was to reject it. I rejected all rules as a matter of principle. Because keeping rules and pleasing people hadn't been an effective path to spiritual development, I thought this kind of rebellion would be a good way to discover myself. What I actually found was that I was as much a slave to the rules and regulations and opinions of others when I was trying to reject them as when I was trying to fulfill them, because my life still centered on those rules, prescriptions, and opinions.

A final method I used to achieve spiritual development was making conclusions about the world around me based on my experience and then carrying those conclusions through the rest of my life. This method was also flawed. Let me illustrate with a hypothetical example. Suppose Mabel grew up during the Depression. Based on her experience of poverty and need, Mabel might decide that scarcity was the ultimate destroyer and, correspondingly, that the ultimate goal of life is financial security. If she never questioned that belief, Mabel might grow up to believe that goodness is identical to hoarding resources. As a consequence, she might have a hard time giving material as well as spiritual things. I have known women like this. They live in fear of losing security, and their inability to be generous without feeling resentful sometimes hurts others. But they are not bad women. They are simply acting on deeply held beliefs that are no longer effective. To free themselves, they must question some of the ideas that once helped them survive, and that is frightening. In a spiritual way, it violates the very idea of security that is so important to people who have experienced loss and need.

Of course, we have all experienced these things at some time, in some form. There are ways in which we all yearn for security. I, for instance, had sought spiritual development as the quickest route to spiritual certainty. I have found that, paradoxically, this very urge to find a definite, unquestionable spiritual road is one of the biggest obstacles to my own true spiritual development. It doesn't work. It is based on attempts to control, to manipulate life and its exigencies. I have tried that most of my life and have found that life is prone to hand me a lot of circumstances that are not in my control. In fact, often my willingness to surrender control has been the basic factor in negotiating such experiences.

Francine: What do you mean, "surrender of control"? Surrender to somebody, or surrender trying to have control?

Martha: Surrender to the fact that I have no control. So, now that I have told you all about my expertise in spiritual development, I have arrived at a conclusion: I know absolutely nothing.

Francine: No. That isn't true. Don't be proud of knowing nothing, Martha.

Martha: But Plato says that man gains his first measure of intelligence on that same day that he admits to his own ignorance. Therefore, by admitting my own ignorance, I have achieved intelligence. I think I've got it this time.

Francine: But Martha, if you know absolutely nothing, how can you know you know nothing? Acknowledging that you don't know everything is very different from saying that you know nothing.

Martha: So what do we know? What is spiritual development?

Francine: First I want to add one more thing that spiritual development is not. It isn't being in a given state and staying there. Any state of development you arrive at is one step in an eternal journey, and when you think of finally becoming spiritually developed, whatever goal it is that you have in mind is only one step. You don't "arrive." No human on earth is a spiritual adult in the sense of "being there." Only God.

Martha: Then do we abandon hope? What is the process? How do we achieve this thing? Or is it to be achieved at all?

Francine: I like the metaphor of being on a road. When our children were young, we thought we would give them a real treat and take them to Yellowstone. I had never liked Yellowstone particularly, but I loved the ride there past the Tetons. Here we were going past the magnificent

Tetons, driving through meadows and past moose, and our children kept saying, "When are we going to get there? When are we going to get there?"

Whatever you are doing is a process, and if the desire of your heart is spiritual development, you are getting there even when the road is long or boring, even when you slip, even when you fall, or when you are in a pit or on a plateau, going fast or going slow. You are getting there. Even when you felt you might just as well die, Martha, you were getting there.

We develop spiritually by meeting reality, and none of us "knows" reality yet as God does. What we "know" is limited by what we currently think and see, and we may change and revise considerably as we go on living. If you are trying to forgive someone who has hurt you terribly, or trying to love your difficult and jealous mother-in-law, if you are trying to live with a husband who fell in love with another woman but did not leave you and now wants to make the marriage work and you wonder if you can live with that—if you are facing such struggles or worse and thinking you should already know all reality, should already be spiritually perfect, be now as God is, then perhaps you are wanting to be in Yellowstone without taking the long adult journey to get there. If you get up in the morning and all day long you are pulled here and there by other people, if you have no pull of your own even for a minute, you may ask yourself, "Am I getting anywhere?" It has been very important for me that when I am even sitting on the floor weeping, I am getting there.

Martha: I agree with you that spiritual development is a journey. But there is something else that is implicit in your comments—that a spiritual journey not only moves us forward but changes us fundamentally. It is like the journey of a caterpillar to a butterfly as well as the journey of an object across time and space.

Francine: True. But sometimes we are given the impression that we are on the opposite way, moving from butterflies to caterpillars by being alive.

We have inherited two contradictory frameworks in our scriptures. One says that by being born we fall, that by choosing for ourselves we fall, that by seeking knowledge we fall. The other says that by choosing to be born, we courageously chose to take God's gifts, to know evil and good, to become ourselves and accept the gifts of God and Jesus. I particularly like the scriptures that support the latter framework, the one I choose to live by.

I like the caterpillar-butterfly metaphor. Butterflies struggle in escaping the cocoon. I feel God wants us to escape ignorance, fear, bondage, inexperience. Spiritual development is not a matter of denying our own thoughts and desires. It is a matter of meeting and knowing things as they are, with our own vision, and enlarging our capacities with the help of God and Jesus. Without them we could lose ourselves, could freeze ourselves along the way, could be overwhelmed.

Martha: One of the stories that has helped me understand the spiritual journey is a myth told by the Plains Indians about a little mouse. The mouse hears a roaring that none of his mouse friends seem to notice. He discovers that the noise comes from a great river, which represents the spirit. By jumping high in the air, the mouse is able to see a range of sacred mountains, and among them is the lake where this river of the spirit originates. The mouse sets out on a quest to reach the lake, a quest which symbolizes his spiritual development. He has a lot of adventures along the way, but the two adventures I remember best are instances in which he finds part of himself by choosing to lose part of himself.

He meets two great beasts—a buffalo and a wolf. Both of them can help him reach the sacred mountains—but both of them are ill. To be healed, each needs the eye of a mouse. When he hears this, the mouse surrenders his eyes one by one, first to the buffalo and then to the wolf. After giving his first eye to the buffalo, the mouse creeps along in terrible fear of the great eagles that are going to swoop down and get him now that he is half blind. When he meets the wolf and realizes that he has to give up his other eye, he is truly terrified—but by that time he has become so devoted to his quest that he surrenders his other eye. The wolf leads the blind mouse to the sacred lake. As he is drinking from the lake, his old fears come back to haunt him. He hears the eagles cry above him, and one of them swoops down. The mouse is completely helpless. All he can do is wait to die—and then he feels the eagle's talons hit him. He feels himself rising, but strangely, he doesn't feel dead. Out of habit he opens his blind eyes and finds them coming into focus. He looks down to see the full beauty of the sacred lake, and he hears the animals down below shouting to him as he rises into the sky. They are calling, "Now you are an eagle!"

I heard this story when I was quite young, and I internalized it as a sort of archetypal pattern. It meant nothing specifically to me at the time I learned it, but it had a certain resonance. I think the great myths and epics of all cultures have that same resonance. From Dante's Divine Comedy to the Baghavad Gita, they all have the images of travel and of change, as well as the idea of fashioning ourselves by surrendering our ways of seeing. In Indian legend, the mouse is a creature which sees only what is directly in front of its face. By giving up this nearsightedness, even at the risk of living in darkness, the mouse gains new eyes that can see much further and much more clearly. Giving up your way of seeing — to go into that blindness — creates the potential for another way of seeing that is clearer, perhaps one that can see as far as eternity.

Francine: When the mouse heard the roaring, the other mice were busy doing mouse things, poking around looking for things to eat, and didn't hear the roaring. One thing we often have to give up, which we may think we cannot give up, is busyness. I am not talking about the necessary business of taking care of our survival and the necessary business of listening to and being involved with other persons. I'm talking about the busyness that consumes us, for example, when we are taking a bath or shower, or walking or doing chores. Those who focus even then on what they have to do, on setting or meeting goals, on what has already happened, will lack a pool of silence in the day for anything else. I know what it is to be overwhelmed with too much to do and too little energy to do it. But the mouse could not have made his search if he had been too busy doing mouse things.

One difficulty in spiritual development is how to work at what we necessarily do in the world and still allow ourselves to look at light, or look to ourselves — and listen and taste, not just walk through tasks. When we were young, and over and over again since, many of us have been taught "the" four steps of prayer: address our Father in Heaven, then thank, then ask, and then close in the name of Jesus Christ. That is enough to teach one to begin, but for me as an adult that kind of busyness, that kind of routine prescription of steps to go through, has not sufficed. The most spiritual times in most of my days are the times when I begin a prayer and all I say is "Father," and there isn't anything else for a while but God, and I change. If there is no time for that kind of stillness, because of routine thank you's and askings, then the prayer is not likely to be a time of spiritual development. It will be a time of going through the task, going through the mouse things, not moving on our journeys.

The mouse was fortunate: the buffalo and the wolf knew exactly what was needed. It was just his eyes. As soon as the mouse decided to give up an eye, it flew up of its own accord. If you are having a hard time forgiving someone, or loving someone, or feeling you are worth anything, or knowing God, if you are having a hard time finding courage, you may not know what to give up and what to keep. Giving up an eye, one's way of seeing, is difficult. It is especially difficult if you don't know it is an eye that is needed, and it doesn't fly out of its own accord just because you say, "I am willing. Change me."

Martha: I think life is designed so that a perfect being—Christ or God the Father—could travel through it in joy despite its sorrows. Those who haven't achieved that divine ability to accept the changes in life encounter them as difficulties and barriers; a perfect being may see them as rich opportunities. Life brings us the buffalos and the wolves. The giving up of our eyes—our ways of seeing—comes generally as we recognize that we are in pain.

I had an experience that really brought the story of Jumping Mouse into focus for me. I was a graduate student at Harvard, very ambitious, very fast track. I had had a lot of praise in my life for doing well in school. In fact, I had had so much praise that I had begun to identify myself as an intellectual. I placed almost all my self-worth in that area of my life. During my second year of graduate school, I discovered I was expecting a baby, and in the fourth month of pregnancy, my husband and I learned that the baby had Down's syndrome. Everyone I knew at Harvard, including all of the doctors, my fellow students, and my professors, thought that this was a reason to end the pregnancy. I was in a social environment where people didn't seem to feel that this child could have any value whatsoever, and to a large extent I believed them. I was on that same wavelength. I needed to give up my way of seeing. No, I didn't walk up to this "buffalo" and simply offer it my eyes. The change I went through was not as effortless as taking pity on something and saying, "Gee, I guess I should change. I guess I should give up my way of seeing." It was a terrible rending of my universe, shattering everything I had thought to be true, everything I had thought my life would be like. And yet some spark inside of me told me to go forward. I never considered aborting the child even when I was pressured to do so. I never considered that my baby's life was worthless, although initially I couldn't see the worth in it because I had based my own worth completely on my supposed intelligence. This child was not smart, and moreover he was not going to be handsome, or rich, or famous — not ever. I had to begin a spiritual search, a search to find out what the value of my baby's life really was. I wasn't sure myself why I had made the decision not to end the pregnancy. It wasn't just a religious belief. I felt his worth. I loved that child, and since I thought of myself as lovable only insofar as I was an intellectual, I had to figure out why I loved him. In doing so, I figured out why the Lord loves me. It was not the reason I had thought. My eyes were changed. In that sense I have become a little bit more like an eagle.

Francine: Much of the language we have inherited about religious experience speaks of sacrifice as though it were a way of erasing yourself, a way of erasing your own value or the value of your desires. I like better what you just said. Sacrifice is giving up something you want very much for something you want more.

Sometimes we are most ready for sacrifice and change when we are struggling. But there are other times when we suddenly recognize our current limitations and become excited about our capacities for change.

Not long ago, we were coming back from New Mexico on a road we hadn't used before. We stayed overnight in Montrose, Colorado, by the Black Canyon of the Gunnison. We got up early, eager to get home, and drove up to the canyon first, expecting some little gully.

My first view of the deep rugged Black Canyon of the Gunnison was astonishing. Then we drove to another viewpoint that was even better. Looking, I wondered how as a child I might have felt seeing the size of it and beauty of it. The names of rocks and elements went rolling through my mind — gneisses, garnets, mica. Then there were bushes. There were blades, leaves, roots, bare branches. There were pines, junipers, snowberry, sage. There were birds, bumble bees, beetles, hornets, and flies. I looked at all this diversity in a very narrow canyon well over a thousand feet deep, black blades and fins of stone receding one after another into the distance with spaces between, and mist hanging in the spaces — I looked and could not comprehend it. It was too much. There is too much diversity and too much variety and too much beauty. I couldn't hold it in my mind. I got more and more excited because here was more to comprehend.

Even with my little triple-folding field microscope, even with an electron scanning microscope I could not have seen it all, not quarks, not every ant. There are things too small for human vision and things too large. I couldn't see our galaxy, let alone the clusters of galaxies there in the morning sky.

There is too much for us to see. Spiritual development is not a box canyon, a state of being here and now. We haven't arrived. We are on the road.

For me, some times of great development have begun with a paradox or a contradiction or a time of great difficulty, times when I am trying to put pieces together in a new way and don't know how. But sometimes it is just pure delight in the beauty of the world. I don't think I would have survived the last twenty years with any resiliency if I hadn't been able to walk in the mountains. I need contact with God's creations. If I had no mountains, I would walk and look at the sky. I would walk and look at the trees. If there were no trees, I would find something, even if it were a fly, that took me out of my own creation.

Martha: I think it is in those moments of heightened perception, whether caused by pain or by great beauty, that we find ourselves groping for what it means to develop spiritually. I began life, and continue it, trying to find which way to go in my spiritual journey. The very process of our discussing this is a process of groping toward a definition. What I have decided while talking with Francine about this subject is that this is exactly what spiritual development really is: the process of groping toward a definition. When we speak of physical or intellectual development, we talk of milestones and stages and comparative speeds and finishing points. But spiritual development takes place in eternity. There is no beginning and there is no end; in such a context, milestones and finishing points have no meaning whatsoever. There is no such thing as going too slowly or stumbling too often or falling behind in the course of spiritual development, for the only objective is to find joy in the process of our progression. That joy is something the Church teaches; it is an emphasis unique among all the faiths preached by human beings.

I know people who feel they have become hopelessly, spiritually lost; that they have made some kind of irrevocable mistake or choice that took them off *the* path they were to follow in their mission on the earth. If you believe that, then, with all respect, I must tell you I believe you are wrong. I have faith that as long as we are devoted to the process of spiritual development, no mistake is irrevocable and no straying from the path is hopeless. C. S. Lewis said that in the spiritual realm, "the good man's past begins to change so that his forgiven sins and remembered sorrows take on the quality of Heaven."[2] We believe that the quality of heaven is the quality of the process of growth, and that is accessible to us wherever we may be.

The Chinese philosopher Lao-tzu wrote that the infinite journey begins from beneath your feet. Right now your feet rest on the path that you will take through life. We could trace all our feet along a path that seems to begin in infancy and end with death and which in fact goes on in both directions eternally. But all we have right now is the present. All we can control about our feet right now is the next step we will take. The present is the moment when eternity intersects with time, and that is the only moment in which we can develop spiritually. We can do that by using our agency to choose from an infinite number of courses. Our choices in the present will color the whole path of our spiritual development, past and future. And no two paths are identical. We all are different.

Francine: We are all different and unique, but we are also alike. It is important to acknowledge both the likenesses and the differences, for both enhance our journeys.

Martha: In fact, one of the biggest similarities we share is that we all are here because we have a firm belief that there is one Way. We believe in Jesus Christ, who said that he is the way, the truth, and the life, and that no man cometh to the Father except by him. I'd like to share the way that I interpret that scripture and the way it helps me as I grope to figure out what spiritual development is. I take great comfort from the fact that the way, the truth, and the life are all identical with the One I call my Savior, who loves me. All three of those things — the way, the truth, and the life — are freely given to us, but it is up to us to choose whether we will accept or reject the gifts.

The way I most often inhibit my own spiritual progress is by refusing to accept the gift of the truth. I'm not talking about the grand abstraction of Truth with a capital T — that's beyond me. But the truth also has to do with the ordinary, nitty-gritty details of our lives — the facts of our circumstances, and the way we feel about them. If I don't accept those, I find myself getting lost. When I heard about my son's Down's syndrome, I immediately had the "right" response. I told myself: "Oh, what a blessing. I'm sure that this will be a wonderful experience for our family." I denied the truth, which was that I felt intense grief and terror and anger because of his disability and that in some ways I would rather have lost him to death than face the prospect of raising him, which I expected to be a horrible ordeal. I went through a couple of months of illness and stress and pain before I finally capitulated to an acceptance of the simple truth that my son was handicapped and that I was upset about it. But I can tell you that in the very moment I accepted my pain, I felt the beginnings of my healing. At that moment I understood the paradox that the truth, even if it's painful, can set us free and allow us to feel joy.

The truth about our circumstances isn't the only thing that keeps us moving forward. There is also a Way, a direction in which we want to go, and part of this has to do with something Francine has already mentioned—the desires of our hearts. One day I was reading the Gospels, and somewhat to my surprise I noticed that when Christ dealt with individuals face to face, he almost never told them what to do, although he obviously knew. Instead he would ask them some variation on a certain question: "What do you want me to do for you? What do you want? What are the desires of your heart?" He asked that of a number of individuals in scriptural context, and he asks us the same thing today. He asks each of us to pray for the desires of our hearts. It may surprise you how difficult it is to know what the desires of your heart really are. Think about it. Think about it right now. What is the deepest desire of your heart? Ask yourself, for Christ is here, now, waiting for you to ask him for whatever that dearly held desire might be. I believe that our hearts' desires are the best compass we have to know the direction we should each travel, the step each of us must take out of this present moment.

Sometimes the Lord grants us our hearts' desires even when we do not know what it is we really want. When I was expecting my son, I decided that my heart's desire was for him to be made normal—whatever that means. After he was born, I prayed for that change to occur, and then I'd watch the baby to see what would happen. Why not? I believe in miracles. My son remained the same, but what I came to understand by praying for the desires of my heart was that a change in him was not what I really wanted. What I wanted was a freedom from the pain I was experiencing as a result of his disability—a pain that was caused by my own way of seeing, not by my son's condition. God answered my prayers with a miracle, but it was not a miracle that "healed" my child. It was a miracle that healed me, so that I am now able to accept my son, with joy, exactly as he is. That was the true desire of my heart, and it was granted.

Life's situations aren't always so dramatic. One thing that stalls my progress as I try to get through life is a denial of the truth about the more mundane things. For example, through all my years of graduate school and working and having children, I carefully trained myself to ignore my body's need for sleep. I've gone as long as five days at a stretch without sleep, and for one memorable year (which I can't remember at all) I slept less than three hours a night. I don't think that's good—in fact, I think it's a sin. But still there are times when I find myself thinking that I have gone spiritually dead, that the heavens have turned to brass, that God no longer loves me, that my prayers will never be heard, and that I might as well go straight to Outer Darkness without passing "GO" or collecting two hundred dollars. More often than not, when I sit down and take a good look at the truth, I discover that I am simply tired. If I search further for the desires of my heart, the first thing that springs to my mind is that I want to go to an island on the coast of Mexico where no one will ever bother me for the rest of my life. But, as I search deeper, I usually find that what I need is a nap. Don't laugh. When the truth and the desires of my heart tell me that what I need most for my spiritual development is a nap, no amount of fasting, prayer, and scripture reading are going to help one bit until I take a nap! So go ahead! Take a nap when you need one—knowing that the Lord is deeply concerned about your desires even on that level.

I am constantly amazed and astonished by evidence that he cares so much about the most trivial details of my life. He cares more than I do. I have experienced the miracle of his love time and time again when I have had the honesty to accept where I am in my spiritual development and asked him to take me where I want to go. The infinite journey does indeed start from beneath our feet, and it stretches out from beneath each of our souls as well, from this present into an endless future. I have a testimony that if we ask our God to help us in our respective journeys, he will guide us to our destinations and help us find joy in every step along the way.

QUESTIONS AND RESPONSES

Q. One sister writes that she had a loss of self-esteem when she miscarried for the third time. She had six children and her self-worth was based on her ability to be a mother and bear children. For her the miscarriage was more than a loss of a child, it was the loss of self. She asks, "What did you find was the real base of your self-worth?"

Martha: For me, it was discovering that there was something more to my son than the things by which the world measured his success. I find that every day—I saw it this morning. There is a moment of pain sometimes when I clearly see that he will never achieve in the same way other children achieve, and then there is a sudden realization that there is something else, something more. My son is like a magical vehicle, a car or a train. It looks battered and beaten on the outside, but when you climb inside you learn that it can take you places that you did not know existed. He is a very spiritual being, and I discovered through him that there was a world of the spirit, that there is a kind of communion that goes on beyond the physical realm and there are loving beings caring for me in that nonphysical world. My experiences with my son remind me of the existence of spirits and of my own spirit. When I remember to take that spiritual perspective, it suddenly doesn't matter whether or not I have a degree from Harvard. The value of my being is spiritual and eternal. It has nothing to do with any achievement. That realization is the basis of all self-esteem.

Q. "One of the most painful experiences of my adulthood is dealing with the criticisms of other women while serving in a high-profile church calling. In all honesty, this experience has left me wounded and wary."

Martha: A lot of people who are not in high-profile church callings might also identify with this question, but it is true that as you climb the ladder of prestige and leadership in any social group, the pressures become greater. You are seen as a figurehead, and criticisms are almost inevitable. It can be devastating to deal with the fact that no two people are going to want exactly the same thing of you and that you may therefore be criticized for whatever you do.

It might help you to remember that Christ was not an accepted part of the church hierarchy when he lived in Jerusalem. The Jews of that time had a church hierarchy whose leaders were pharisees and scribes — words we now associate with hypocrisy and unrighteous behaviors, but which meant high church and social status in Jerusalem (there, as in many of our Utah communities the church and society were pretty closely interlinked). At any rate, these were the individuals who had made good by looking good. They didn't get much criticism. They got very, very little. Christ, by contrast, was the true head of the Church — and he got criticism from just about everywhere. Jesus simply did what he knew was right and in accordance with the will of the Father. He made no bones about it. That drove a lot of people absolutely crazy. Christ was nailed to a cross for doing nothing other than championing the will of the Father, and the people who crucified him were those who never risked criticism by taking a stance that differed from the prevailing political or social trends.

All I can say to someone who is hurting because of the criticism of others is something I heard from a very wise woman when I was deliberating over a decision of my own. I was worried that people might think ill of me or criticize me for my decision. This woman pointed out that when I stand before my Heavenly Father in the last day, the people whose criticism I feared are not going to be there with me. Only one person will be with me, and that is the God who has been telling me throughout my life which way I should turn. In moments of confusion, the only honest thing you can do is to be true to yourself, to what you feel in your heart is God's will for you. And if you are always true to that, I promise you—I guarantee you—you will be criticized. And you will feel alone, and you will feel abandoned, and you will feel betrayed, but when you have stood in that place for a while and learned to deal with those difficult feelings, you will be able to open your eyes to something else. You will find that you are not as alone as you thought: the God of love is standing with you, and he knows that although you may not have chosen the perfect path, you chose what you thought was best instead of simply reacting to the criticisms of others. That is true whether you are a mother, a daughter, a wife, on the city council, or whatever. Responding to the desires of others is often an easier way than responding to the truth which is within you, but the light of Christ can tell you which way to go and you will find that that light has not betrayed you in the end. Stick to that.

Q. "What is mighty prayer as mentioned in the scriptures? How does today's woman have mighty prayer?"

Francine: Many persons would be happy to supply you with recipes and legalistic definitions of mighty prayer. I'd like to respond by telling some stories.

When I first read the book of Enos, I thought, He prayed all day and all night. How could he keep going without saying the same thing over and over? What was he thinking so long? How could he keep on without going to sleep? Was he kneeling all that time? How could his muscles stand the strain?

I was a teenager, and I had a lot of questions. All day and all night seemed a very long time to pray. Then, when I was trying to decide whether to marry my husband, I prayed for one and a half years, and the prayer was intertwined with all else in my life.

President David O. McKay, one day when he was young, was riding his horse on a steep hill. He was certain that God was good and God loved him, but what he didn't know for sure was if the gospel the Church teaches is true. So he got off his horse and knelt down and prayed. Then he got back on his horse and rode away, knowing that he was exactly the same boy as when he got off his horse. Only many years later, as an adult, after he'd become a mission president, did he receive the kind of revelation from God that he had hoped for many years earlier.[3]

A woman in Connecticut many years ago was contacted by the missionaries, and she believed what they told her. She had a son who was a track star. He had a scholarship to a major university on the basis of his track performance. The woman was black, and when she went for her baptism interview with the mission president, he found that nobody had told her that blacks could not hold the priesthood. When he explained that to her, she wasn't sure if she wanted to join a church that wouldn't allow her son, her fine good son, to be a full participant. The mission president advised her to go home and pray about it. She and her son knelt down by the sofa and prayed, and prayed, and prayed. They prayed long into the night, and finally the son fell asleep with his head against the edge of the couch. She kept praying. Long long hours after she'd begun, she heard a voice that said to her, "Set it aside. It will be taken care of." She and her son were baptized.

One night in the Missionary Training Center, a young Provo woman longed greatly for a revelation about the truthfulness of the gospel. She believed in God but wanted the kind of testimony she hoped she could help converts to obtain. She needed to be alone, which is not easy in the MTC. She looked, and looked, and looked, and finally found a janitor's closet on the first floor where she could have privacy. She knelt down and prayed. She did not get an answer. Her desire was great; her soul was intent. She wanted to know. She finally went back up to bed and decided that she already knew the gospel was true.

There are as many stories as there are persons who have prayed. They suggest the difficulty of any precise definitions of mighty prayer, of saying this is a mighty prayer and these others are not. Prayers are individual reaches from individual humans to God. Solomon said that only God knows the heart of a human, and prayers are matters of the heart.

If you really want to know, if you're willing to continue praying as long as it takes . . .

Martha: Let me put something in here. I don't think it's just duration.

Francine: No, I was not going to say that either, but go ahead.

Martha: There is a point at which I have felt the Lord is free to respond to my prayers, however long they may be. That is the moment at which I trust him to answer. When I open my heart to an assurance that I will get an answer, that this will be taken care of—just as the voice told the woman—the answer itself seems to follow very easily. There have been times when I have prayed all day and all night, and it was at the moment when I finally gave up and said, "I know you're there anyway" that I felt deeply that my prayer had been answered. I think the scripture that says that the Lord works in great ways that seem small to the understanding of men may apply to mighty prayer as well.

Francine: I agree.

Q. Here's another question about prayer from a woman who prayed to know what counselors to ask for. She felt she received true inspiration about the counselors she should have, but then the bishop didn't give them to her, and she began to wonder about her inspiration.

Francine: I've had such an experience myself. I've felt very strongly at times that my prayer for inspiration was clearly answered, and that it came after prayer with all my soul, all my intent, all my focus, all my certainty that God would answer. And yet others in charge did not act upon the same inspiration. I've had to acknowledge that however real my prayer and my answer, I do not direct the whole universe to proceed as I might like it to do.

I like our account of the sons of Mosiah wanting to go to the Lamanites and their father praying to God to see if they should go. The answer was yes, let them go to the Lamanites "because many will hear their voices and gain eternal life and I will deliver your sons from the Lamanites." The sons suffered much, but I remember reading and thinking, "What a promise. If I knew I would be delivered, I'd dare anything. If I knew that God would deliver me, I could stand anything." And then I thought, "I do have that promise." I'll more than survive anything, even if I can't control all I experience. That's what the mission of Jesus was about.

Q. "Please address the problem of dealing with the apparent contradictions in the rules, for example, Adam and Eve."

Francine: I rejoice in the agency God has given prophets, translators, writers, and readers who function "according to their own language and understanding." Consider what our scriptures are: records of many men in many circumstances writing for many persons in many contexts over thousands of years. Remember all the human translations between what God gives and what we read, not just translations from one language to another, but from one culture to another, one time to another, many persons to many others.

If we had no agency, which is the ability to create reality, then there would be no interpretations or contradictions, and we would not struggle to make sense of them. Instead, we might be directly imprinted by a controller. I prefer agency, the agency that makes life so *adult* and sometimes painful a process.

One of our tasks as human beings is to sort out differences and choose what to do. That is a very dangerous process, because we are liable to error. But it seems to me that God does not intentionally deceive. God does not intentionally confuse. God does allow confusion to be created. We are invited to face it honestly and take his help.

Martha: We've had the lion's share of time in starting this conversation, but it really didn't begin here, and it certainly doesn't end here. We hope you'll continue it with each other as you go through life. Francine and I both hope that you can take whatever we've said—the themes of prayer, surrender, searching, acknowledging, ignorance, and so on—and measure our comments against the light of truth in your own soul. Then, discard whatever makes no sense to you, and keep only what sounds right. That applies in any situation: listen to everything, but follow what is in your heart. Follow it regardless of what we have said, regardless of what anybody says. It will lead you along the path to spiritual development and it will lead you into joy.

NOTES

1. See Matthew 18:1–4. Jesus speaks of becoming humble as a child is humble, not of staying as ignorant, inexperienced, and limited as a child.
2. C. S. Lewis, *The Great Divorce* (New York: Collier Books, 1946), p. 68.
3. David O. McKay, *Cherished Experiences,* comp. Clare Middlemiss (Salt Lake City: Deseret Book Co., 1955), p. 16.

Staying Together
Despite Not Praying Together:
Families Dealing with Inactivity

EDWARD L. KIMBALL

Many Latter-day Saint families include members who are no longer as active or involved with the Church as they once were. Differences and disagreements between those who are active and those who are not can strain family relationships. As active members hoping to reconcile differences, we may seek advice from others. But since every situation and relationship is different, the solicited advice may not fit our situation. More important than any specific advice we receive may be the simple awareness that we have lots of company. The very universality of our problems can reassure us that inactivity and failures to bridge differences within the family are not necessarily the fault of any one person. We need not think we have done something wrong or that if we had only done something different or been more deserving, all would have been well. General Authorities have inactive family members; so do our bishops and our neighbors, as well as you and I.

I

Although I have not yet had to face the conflict and heartache of a child or spouse choosing a different path, I do have a brother who, although active in the Church for many years, has hardly been inside an LDS chapel in the past thirty years except to attend our parents' funerals. I have some sense of the anguish our parents felt at that fact.

Edward L. Kimball has taught as professor of law at Brigham Young University's J. Reuben Clark Law School since its beginning in 1973, with special interest in criminal justice administration and professional ethics. He is the coauthor of biographies of his parents, Spencer W. and Camilla Eyring Kimball. He is married to Evelyn Bee Madsen and serves as a Sunday School teacher.

They would have done anything in the world to bring my brother back to activity, yet they could do nothing except love and wait. And sometimes the most difficult thing of all to do is nothing.

I know that my parents tried to exercise restraint, and consciously they may have known that to nag would only raise barriers. But the truth is that when they were with my brother, they could not always refrain from trying just one more time to "get through" to him. I recall once hearing our father say, "Son, haven't you eaten husks long enough?" That reference to the prodigal son could hardly do other than alienate. (Luke 15:16.) A person willing to recognize himself as a prodigal son would already be on his way to a welcome homecoming. Because my brother does not think of himself as a prodigal, our father's characterization was simply one more source of estrangement.

Family members who are active Church members often feel they are in a Catch-22. If they let go and accept the inactive member as he or she is, they feel they have relinquished responsibility, condoned the loss of faith or faithfulness, and failed to pass on what is of greatest worth. But if they continue pushing, they run the risk of driving a wedge even deeper. The inactive family member may well perceive actions or words as concerns only for appearances or as motivated by guilt. Worst of all, the inactive person will feel criticized and rejected.

The scriptures pointedly tell us that parents are to teach their children "the doctrine of repentance, faith in Christ the Son of the living God, and of baptism and the gift of the Holy Ghost by the laying on of the hands . . . and they shall also teach their children to pray, and to walk uprightly before the Lord." (D&C 68:25, 28.) Parents can properly expect their young children to participate in Church activities. But children have their own agency, and at some point (sooner than many parents might choose), it is either impossible or inadvisable to require Church participation. At that age, which varies from child to child, the admonition of Doctrine and Covenants 121:41–42 fits perfectly: "No power or influence can or ought to be maintained by virtue of the priesthood [or, I would suggest, by virtue of parenthood], only by persuasion, by long-suffering, by gentleness and meekness, and by love unfeigned; by kindness, and pure knowledge."

I think my parents would have wanted to quote from the next verse as well: "reproving betimes with sharpness." Although a challenge or reproof may at times be appropriate, the scripture specifies two crucial qualifications—the challenge should come "betimes," that is, promptly, and the Holy Ghost must inspire it. Too often personal desire inspires our reproof, not the Holy Spirit's whispering. Despite these considerations, there is often great pressure on parents, both from inside and outside ourselves, to pass on our values. Dealings with a child who rejects what is meaningful and dear to you can be extremely difficult.

We sometimes perceive distancing from the Church as distancing from family, but the two are only sometimes linked together. My brother, for example, may be the most intent among my family members on maintaining close relationships. When we talk of a family reunion, he is the strongest supporter. When I am at his table, he invites me to offer prayer. He does not reject me because of my activity in the Church any more than I reject him for his inactivity. He is willing to allow me to be religious, just as he expects me to let him be nonreligious. He has not changed from being a good and honorable person and my friend; he simply does not now have a conviction of the truthfulness of the LDS gospel.

Differences in Church activity need not result in distance between family members; distance more often results from the ways we react to those differences.

II

President Spencer W. Kimball once compared the influence of a child's home life to ocean currents. He noted that icebergs calved in Greenland inevitably move south, despite being pushed to and fro by the winds, waves, and tides. The Labrador Current, beneath the surface, carries the icebergs ultimately to the warmer Atlantic waters, where they melt. Similarly, he said, "I have sometimes seen children of good families rebel, resist, stray, sin, and even actually fight God. In this they bring sorrow to their parents, who have done their best to set in movement a current and to teach and live as examples. But I have repeatedly seen many of these same children, after years of wandering, mellow, realize what they have been missing, repent, and make great contribution to the spiritual life of their community. The reason I believe this can take place is that, despite all the adverse winds to which these people have been subjected, they have been influenced still more, and much more than they realized, by the current of life in the homes in which they were reared. . . . There is no guarantee, of course. . . . The children have their free agency."[1]

Overall a hopeful statement, his analogy suggests a likelihood of change and the reassuring probability that parents have done their part even when children leave the Church. The Prophet Joseph delivered an even stronger statement of the ultimate power of parental influence at the funeral for Judge Elias Higbee, in 1843: "The servants of God are sealed in their foreheads, which signifies sealing the blessing upon their heads, meaning the everlasting covenant, thereby making their calling and election sure. When a seal is put upon the father and mother, it secures their posterity, so that they cannot be lost, but will be saved by virtue of the covenant of their father and mother."[2] Joseph Smith seems to be referring to those parents who, through their extraordinary faithfulness, have had their calling and election made sure.

In 1929 Orson F. Whitney interpreted this teaching at general conference: "The Prophet Joseph Smith declared—and he never taught more comforting doctrine—that the eternal sealings of faithful parents and the divine promises made to them for valiant service in the Cause of Truth, would save not only themselves, but likewise their posterity. Though some of the sheep may wander, the eye of the Shepherd is upon them, and sooner or later they will feel the tentacles of Divine Providence reaching out after them and drawing them back to the fold. Either in this life or in the life to come, they will return." Rather than badgering them back to the faith, he instructs, "Pray for your careless and disobedient children; hold onto them with your faith. Hope on, trust on, till you see the salvation of God."[3]

The idea that the faithfulness of the parents will save their children is comforting, but it is, after all, in tension with principles of agency and individual responsibility. We are taught that we will not be punished for our parents' sins, nor will we be saved by our parents' righteousness. Alma the Elder's prayers brought an angel to confront his son, but it was still for young Alma to change his life.

In *Doctrines of Salvation*, Joseph Fielding Smith reconciled the two concepts of children's being sealed to their parents and their being "saved": "All children born under the covenant belong to their parents in eternity, but that does not mean that they, because of that birthright, will inherit celestial glory. The faith and faithfulness of fathers and mothers will not save disobedient children.

"Salvation is an individual matter. . . . But children born under the covenant, who drift away, are still the children of their parents; and the parents have a claim upon them; and if the children have not sinned away all their rights, the parents may be able to bring them through repentance, into the celestial kingdom, but not to receive the exaltation. Of course, if children sin too grievously, they will have to enter the telestial kingdom, or they may even become sons of perdition."[4]

Nonetheless, parents may derive comfort from the idea that consistent faithfulness in their own lives will benefit their children, both as an example and through the long-term power of the sealing ordinance. It may be, then, that parents can contribute most to the welfare of their children by perfecting their own lives, including their capacity to love as Christ loved. Thereby they put in motion a current that can affect other lives. It is not for us to judge—we are to leave that to God, who has greater understanding of all of us and our motives.

III

Inactivity in the Church has various causes. Sometimes someone who is perceived as representing the Church may offend or act in an unchristian way that precipitates resentment and doubt. Or loss of faith may come from disbelief in doctrine, whether rightly or wrongly understood. For some individuals, inactivity is a well-informed and carefully considered decision. Others may become inactive over disbelief, never having really grappled with doctrine. Some young adults never move from a juvenile understanding of the gospel to a more robust and mature understanding that they can match against the "philosophies of men."

Perceived inadequacies of the Church organization may also precipitate inactivity. Unmarried people often feel left out, or leadership positions may seem disproportionately occupied by professional or white-collar workers. In such circumstances, some members find their involvement unrewarding. Other inactive members are simply following friends whose regard and values weigh more heavily than those of family members actively involved in the Church. Habits that make the person uncomfortable in the Church setting are another cause of inactivity. Whether we mean to create such discomfort or not, a nonconforming person will feel ill at ease in a Church where conformity is highly valued. A barrier will be there—almost unavoidably.

But whatever may cause these winds and waves and tides that push our loved ones away from the Church, some of our reactions will hurt and others will help.[5]

Scolding hurts. Raising our voices only increases resistance, particularly in our children, whatever their age. Feelings of guilt and embarrassment can cause the scolder to overstate and overreact, which easily results in anger and antagonism in the inactive family member, starting a vicious cycle that can destroy love and true communication.

More subtle than scolding about behavior but just as damaging are critical attitudes. These are quickly perceived and instantly create barriers. You may legitimately describe your *own* feelings, but you can expect resistance to your telling others how *they* feel or should feel. Elementary psychology tells us that less resistance will result from saying, "I feel hurt when you reject my values" than from saying "You are a rebellious child. You have rejected proper values." The inactive family member may still respond to your describing your hurt feelings with "You are trying to shame me and make me feel guilty" or "You should not feel hurt. My beliefs are my business. They have nothing to do with you." But at least a possible foundation of communication will be established for a discussion and ultimate understanding. When we start challenging others' feelings or labeling them as rebels, prodigals, and so on, the labeled person's only possible response may be to walk away.

Inconsistency hurts. If we would let a friend who uses a pipe smoke in our home, we should not be more stringent with our own adult child. But if our family policy is to ask all visitors to smoke outside, we should be able to apply the same constraints to a family member. The principle of consistency also applies to our attitudes about our own Church involvement. We may be tempted always to cast Church activity in a positive light in the presence of the inactive member. However, we should be honest about our feelings and beliefs. If we have personal questions about Church doctrine or history, if we see difficulties in the way a program in our ward is functioning, if we struggle with a calling, we ought not pretend that everything is perfect. We might add, "Nevertheless, I believe the Church is true," or "Nevertheless, I believe attending church is important." Even small deceptions create barriers. Family members will quickly sense hypocrisy or pretense and ascribe it to a hidden motive to manipulate them back into the fold.

In most cases we should also be honest and open about our positive feelings and our activity in the Church—and, in the right setting, about our own spiritual experiences. If less active family members object to our "always talking about Church things," we may need to explain without embarrassment that while we will not try to force gospel discussion, the Church is an important part of our lives. We are not trying to irritate, but we also are entitled to live our life without artificial constraints. We should clarify at some point that our references to church are not intended as subtle jabs. But if we profess that, we must be certain it is true.

Love and approval help. We should love and base our love on understanding. Even though loving others does not require agreeing with whatever they do, unconditional love by definition does not depend on Church activity. No matter how much we profess our love, if we don't show sensitivity, respect, and understanding, that love cannot flourish. I deeply value my friendship with my brother even though our choices have led us in different directions.

It is important to concentrate on the good. We should compliment qualities and conduct we admire—but genuinely, not manipulatively. Honest appreciation strengthens relationships. There will always be strengths, even if there will also be behavior we find troubling. We are entitled to make clear our own values, but we are mistaken if we assume that inactive members have no values of their own. Respect needs to flow both ways.

Communication helps. We should keep the lines open. The proverbial saying, "If you can't say anything nice, don't say anything at all," will undermine communication if applied in reverse. When relationships are tense, others may assume that if you don't say anything, it is because you have nothing nice to say. Silence is often erroneously understood as evidence of disapproval. Inactive family members are often sensitive to criticism and will find it in our silence. With them it is better to express our feelings, even disagreement, while reaffirming our continuing affection, no matter what.

Communication is desirable for many reasons. Consider what would happen were the inactive family member to become interested, in any degree, in increasing involvement with the Church. After a person has been away for a while, there is great hesitancy to return. "What will people think? What will they say? I don't know anyone any more. What if I am called on to pray in a Sunday School class?" It would be ideal if their relationship with us could provide a bridge for the first, often difficult steps.

God is concerned with the welfare of all his children. It is therefore appropriate both to pray for others in our family and to pray that God will let us know what we should do to bless their lives. That may mean backing off and keeping quiet. It may mean giving up our expectations. It may mean we are responsible in the final analysis only for our own salvation. Coercing good was Satan's proposal, a plan our Heavenly Father rejected unconditionally.

In all aspects of our lives, we encounter things we can change and things we cannot. Wise people learn the difference. We cannot control another person's conscience, nor should we seek to. Agency is precious, and coercion is contrary to God's plan. At most we offer persuasion and love unfeigned; we do not coerce.

Perhaps, after all is said, three considerations are more basic than any others: maintaining our own standards, showing love unchanged by inactivity, and praying for patience and wisdom. Example, love, and prayer can be our contributions to the undercurrent that may bring loved ones to the warmer waters where icebergs slowly melt.

NOTES

1. *The Teachings of Spencer W. Kimball,* ed. Edward L. Kimball (Salt Lake City: Bookcraft, 1982), p. 335.

2. Joseph Smith, *Teachings of the Prophet Joseph Smith,* sel. Joseph Fielding Smith (Salt Lake City: Deseret News Press, 1938), p. 321; Joseph Smith, *History of the Church of Jesus Christ of Latter-day Saints,* 7 vols., 2d ed. rev., edited by B. H. Roberts (Salt Lake City: Deseret Book Co., 1978), 5:530. Compare Doctrine and Covenants 132:26.

3. Orson F. Whitney, in Conference Report, Apr. 1929, p. 110. Whitney also goes on to note, "They will have to pay their debt to justice; they will suffer for their sins; and may tread a thorny path; but if it leads them at last, like the penitent Prodigal, to a loving and forgiving father's heart and home, the painful experience will not have been in vain."

4. Joseph Fielding Smith, *Doctrines of Salvation,* comp. Bruce R. McConkie, 3 vols. (Salt Lake City: Bookcraft, 1955), 2:91.

5. For suggestions, see Nadeoui A. Eden, "I Have a Question," *Ensign,* Feb. 1992, p. 53.

Forgiving One Another

CAROL L. CLARK

My personal odyssey toward understanding forgiveness began when I was in my early thirties. One day in May I sat in a lawyer's office with hate in my heart. I had been pushed into this hate by a series of vile acts, and at that point dark feelings unlike anything I had experienced before consumed me. A man had wronged me, and I had decided to take the gloves off and do to him what he had done to me, to the degree he'd done it to me. I had mentally prepared to tell my lawyer to make this man's life as miserable as he had made mine. I wanted to extract from him his money, his energy, his time, and most of all, his facade. I wanted him to suffer, as he had made me suffer.

While I sat waiting to deliver my well-calculated message to the lawyer, I was researching for a church assignment. As odd as that seems to me now, it was logical at the time. Surrounded by legal books, I was reading my own book: the New Testament. I perused several passages and took notes. Then I read: "And be ye kind one to another, tenderhearted, forgiving one another, even as God for Christ's sake hath forgiven you." (Ephesians 4:32.)

No special light illuminated that scripture. No angel descended. Yet I could never verbalize the spiritual power of that message to my heart. It was as if all the teachings of the gospel came together into one great whole, and in that instant I could see through a glass clearly, rather than through a glass darkly. I was affected to my very core by those words.

My feelings for this man did not change. What he had done to me did not change. But I changed. In that moment of instant awareness, I

Carol L. Clark has served as a member of the Relief Society General Board and as administrative assistant to the general presidency of the Relief Society. She has held prominent positions in business, education, and government and has written and edited several books, including A Singular Life *and* Knit Together in Love.

knew that the gospel called me to something higher, better, and finer than I had ever previously been called to. For the first time in my life, I felt the Savior could save me.

I did not give my speech to the lawyer. My spiritual insight, however, did not make my life better—it got worse. The man persisted in making my life exceedingly difficult. At a particularly low point, I remember, my mother said, "We'll forgive him." Her words reminded me once more of a loftier purpose.

Although I am not easily moved to anger, I am the kind of woman who holds a swell grudge. I am not a water-off-a-duck's-back person. Wrongs soak into my feathers and ruffle them thoroughly. So to be greatly wronged and to feel I must forgive the perpetrator was a spiritual mountain of great magnitude to climb.

My experience in the lawyer's office was the first step; my mother's words of promise the second. My own integrity and the light of the gospel beckoned me to higher ground. I knew intellectually and in my heart I needed to forgive, but I had little idea at times if I could reach a summit that seemed so far away. My negative feelings, combined with difficulties I had yet to endure, led me to rely on five spiritual tools:

Prayer. I prayed several times a day that the Lord would bless me to forgive this man. At first I couldn't even say the words—forgiveness was only a vague thought in my mind. But I knew that it was the right goal. I also knew that I wouldn't easily recover from the blow I'd been dealt. Throughout the process of forgiveness, it never crossed my mind that I should forgive him sooner than I was able. I just knew that I should keep my eye on my goal. My prayers reflected that, even though they came from a heavy, broken heart. I have never felt greater moments of spiritual distance from or closeness to the Lord than I felt during my many prayers. I kept praying.

Goals. Forgiveness was part of a broader goal—that of total health. I had a severe case of pneumonia during this time, and I felt so awful physically that it seemed my body and spirit were working in tandem. For a season, the whole of me could not function fast or for long. Almost unconsciously I seemed to set a reasonable pace for myself. I didn't expect to be able to scale my spiritual and emotional mountain overnight. I just kept moving toward it, knowing the goal was worthy.

Scriptures. I read every scripture in the Topical Guide about forgiveness. I read each one many times. At first they didn't mean anything to me. But I kept at it. And at it. And at it. Eventually, phrases made sense.

The most helpful concept I found was in Doctrine and Covenants 64:10–11: "I, the Lord, will forgive whom I will forgive, but of you it is required to forgive all men. And ye ought to say in your hearts—let God judge between me and thee, and reward thee according to thy deeds." These verses and others helped me focus on my responsibility and let me leave other matters to higher powers. They alleviated some of the unrest in my soul, as I sorted out what I had to do and what I didn't have to worry about. I took profound comfort in the idea that my part was to forgive. The Lord would make the judgment.

Other scriptures helped me sort through difficult emotions and stop dwelling on my misery, wondering why this man was getting away with so much. During the months when more and more problems engulfed me, I reread Nephi's account of his persistent trouble with his brothers: "I . . . did cry much unto the Lord my God, because of the anger of my brethren. But behold, their anger did increase against me." (2 Nephi 5:1–2.) I unsuccessfully tried to resolve a lawsuit peacefully with this man. Then I remembered Alma who "labored much in the spirit, wrestling with God in mighty prayer, that he would pour out his Spirit upon the people who were in the city. . . . Nevertheless, they hardened their hearts." (Alma 8:10–11.) These stories provided me with superb examples. They assured me that others had endured to the end and had overcome difficulties similar to those I was encountering.

Support. My wonderful parents stood steadily by me, and I felt incredibly blessed. They let me talk and talk and talk about all I felt because they understood I solve problems best when I can verbalize ideas and feelings. Sometimes I went on for hours, outlining every detail of my experience and reviewing sections of it repeatedly. Quite literally, I talked things out with them.

Friends stood by me too. They prayed and fasted with me on several occasions. Even when they were halfway around the world, I felt a peace and support as a result of their spiritual efforts in my behalf.

Steadfastness. The scriptures talk about being rooted and grounded, firm and steadfast. In my process of forgiving another, I studied the Master Teacher and tried to follow him. I did not know how the process worked all the time. I just kept trying. Even when I didn't feel much besides pain, I wanted to forgive, and I did all I knew how to do. And the Lord helped me.

One day three years after I started praying daily about this matter, I just felt better. During one ordinary day, I simply became aware of an ease in my heart. I knelt in prayer to thank the Lord for being able to say in my soul what I had longed to say—I forgive him.

I don't know if three years is a little or a lot of time to be able to forgive. I don't think it matters. What matters is that I forgave him. I still have memories and feelings about this episode of my life—but I forgave him. Sometimes even now I put his name in the temple, hoping that he might be blessed and that I might remember the significance of the covenants I have made.

The process of forgiveness taught me. It has softened my heart and ground off some rough edges. I've forgiven others since for much lesser wrongs. No matter how slight the offense, I still find that for me the process requires a heartfelt effort. I am the same person, naturally inclined to hold a grudge, but now I know more about myself and know how refreshing forgiveness is. To be able to say, "I forgive him," is worth every ounce of determination and every hard-working prayer.

When I was a child, I thought being able to forgive was like puberty—something that just happened to you. I was wrong. Forgiveness is a high-level spiritual skill that demands great effort, yet pays large peaceful rewards. It is one major way to understand the Atonement. Never have I felt the Atonement more personally than when I worked for years to forgive someone who had wounded me to my very core. During that period of my life, few days went by that I didn't thank the Lord for the successful mission of his Only Begotten Son.

One of the first things Paul said after he was called as a missionary was, "Through this man [Jesus Christ] is preached . . . forgiveness of sins." (Acts 13:38.) For years that scripture meant little to me. Now I know that both through forgiving another and through asking for forgiveness we can find our way toward the sublime heights of spiritual maturity.

Come into the Fold of God

MARIE CORNWALL

Mosiah 18 teaches us about our baptismal covenants in a way that is not as clearly stated elsewhere in the scriptures. Alma, who had been a wicked priest of King Noah but had repented and followed the teachings of Abinadi, spoke about baptism to the people gathered at the Waters of Mormon: "And now, as ye are desirous to come into the fold of God, and to be called his people, and are willing to bear one another's burdens, that they may be light; yea, and are willing to mourn with those that mourn; yea, and comfort those that stand in need of comfort, and to stand as witnesses of God at all times and in all things . . . — now I say unto you, if this be the desire of your hearts, what have you against being baptized in the name of the Lord?" (Mosiah 18:8–10.)

From this passage of scripture we learn that when we enter into the fold of God, we covenant both with God to obey his commandments and to recognize and take upon ourselves the name of Jesus Christ and also with the community. That community can be as small as our local wards or our neighborhoods, but it can also be as large as the world community, the community beyond our community of believers. Mosiah 18:8–10 requires that we remain connected to the world; we are promising God not only to keep his commandments but to comfort and to mourn with and witness to others, whether or not they have made similar promises — no matter where they are in life or what they are doing.

Several verses later it is recorded that Alma "commanded them that there should be no contention one with another, but that they should look forward with one eye, having one faith and one baptism, having their hearts knit together in unity and in love one towards another."

Marie Cornwall, an associate professor of sociology at Brigham Young University, is director of the Women's Research Institute at that university. She teaches Gospel Doctrine in the Sunday School of her Salt Lake City ward.

(V. 21.) And then in verse 29, "And this he said unto them, having been commanded of God; and they did walk uprightly before God, imparting to one another both temporally and spiritually according to their needs and their wants." These verses broaden our understanding of what it means to be a Christian. Our responsibility is not only to God but also to individuals all around us—women sitting next to us in church or next to us on the bus, or women in our local homeless shelter or crisis center, or women we're assigned to visit teach. We made a covenant with these people to mourn with them and to comfort them—before we ever met them—when we entered into those baptismal waters.

Further understanding of our baptismal covenants can be found in Acts 4:32. We learn that the Saints of Christ's church in Jerusalem "were of one heart and of one soul: neither said any of them that ought of the things which he possessed was his own; but they had all things common." These people were of one heart and one soul, and having all things in common was one way in which they maintained that unity.

Another scriptural account—4 Nephi—tells of a people who created a community where all felt as one. They also had all things in common. It was a community, we read, where "there was no contention among all the people, . . . [where] there were no envyings, nor strifes, nor tumults, nor whoredoms, nor lyings, nor murders, nor any manner of lasciviousness; and surely there could not be a happier people among all the people who had been created by the hand of God. There were no robbers, nor murderers, neither were there any Lamanites, nor any manner of -ites; but they were in one, the children of Christ, and heirs to the kingdom of God." (4 Nephi 1:13, 16–17)

Fourth Nephi records hundreds of years of history in a few verses. We learn, however, that there is a point at which the community became divided. "And from that time forth they did have their goods and their substance no more common among them. And they began to be divided into classes." (Vv. 25–26.)

In Doctrine and Covenants 78:5–6 we read, "That you may be equal in the bonds of heavenly things, yea, and earthly things also, for the obtaining of heavenly things; for if ye are not equal in earthly things ye cannot be equal in obtaining heavenly things." And in Doctrine and Covenants 70:14 we find, "Nevertheless, in your temporal things you shall be equal, and this not grudgingly, otherwise the abundance of the manifestations of the Spirit shall be withheld."

At present our Church leaders are not encouraging us to live in common, and I suspect many of us are glad in our deepest, darkest hearts. But I believe firmly that at some point in the future we are going to have to live in this way. In the meantime, what can we do to prepare ourselves to have all things in common? What kinds of activities will prepare us to live in the community that God envisions? Perhaps recognizing and struggling with the many ways we are divided will help us prepare to live together in unity and equality. In addition to economic inequality, we divide ourselves by race, religion, level of education, and by marital status. How do we reach across these divisions to create a community that God tells us is not only possible but preferable to what we now experience?

Elaine L. Jack, Relief Society general president, has issued a call for unity. She has said, "Our individual lives, our circumstances, and our challenges are as diverse as the countries and cultures we come from. Yet our commitment is the same. Today, we can all rejoice in being women of The Church of Jesus Christ of Latter-day Saints. We are united in devotion to our Father in Heaven and in our desire to touch the lives of others. We serve as partners with our brethren in building the kingdom of God. . . . We are bonded as we try to understand what the Lord has to say to us, what He will make of us. We speak in different tongues, yet we are a family who can still be of one heart."[1]

Let me offer several examples of people who have attempted to go beyond the social categories that divide us. The first example is my neighbor in Salt Lake City. I live across the street from Fred and Rochelle Wenger. Fred is the rabbi of the Jewish synagogue in Salt Lake City. When I moved into my home a couple of years ago, he, as a good neighbor, came over to introduce himself and to find out about me. I told him a little of myself, and at one point he said, "I want you to know I wouldn't normally ask this, but I've lived in Salt Lake City long enough to know that this is what you ask—are you active LDS?" I nodded and explained that I taught at Brigham Young University. He paused for a moment and responded, "Well, then, let me welcome you into the Monument Park Third Ward. Your bishop is Bishop Morris Linton, a very good man; I'm sure you'll like him. I can give you his phone number if you'd like."

That isn't the end of the story. About six months later, I was walking down our street. He and his wife were sitting on their front porch. "Where were you last night?" he called out to me. "Where was I supposed to be?" I asked. He said, "There was a ward party last night. Why weren't you there?" I said, "I guess I missed it. I must have forgotten about it." In a concerned tone, he questioned, "You're not going inactive, are you?" Fred and Rochelle have created an image for me of people willing to extend themselves beyond some of the social boundaries created by difference and to create a sense of community. In watching over me, he witnessed the importance of going to ward parties, of being part of a community, and of not allowing religious difference to interfere with the creation of community.

Let me give you another example of how we might move beyond social categories that divide us. Hattie Soil is a Relief Society president in the Hyde Park Ward in Chicago. She is originally from Memphis, Tennessee, and knows about growing up in poverty. She has written about her experience as a black member of the Church trying to bond with white members and create a unity of heart. She says, "When my family and I first joined the Church a number of years ago, our branch was composed of students from the University of Chicago. My husband and I used to sit in amazement as we listened to their stories of hardship. Their idea of a hard time was struggling with their studies or living in an area other than what they were used to. My husband and I, with three young sons, often wondered what these university students would do if they had to struggle for their next meal or worry about their children surviving from day to day in a gang-infested neighborhood or in the Chicago public school system. It was years before I began to realize that their problems were just as serious to them as mine were to me. When I received that enlightenment, I was on the road to understanding others."[2] Hattie explains that understanding others is a possibility only "after we acknowledge our own experiences and backgrounds." Knowing ourselves precedes reaching out to others.

Religion, race, and social class are probably the most dominant dividers in our society. It will be very difficult for us to move beyond those differences, but I strongly believe that we must. Somehow we must learn to respond to people who are different from us, and respond in a way that is respectful and recognizes their value and equality with us.

I want to diverge here briefly. As a social scientist, I always look at things from an empirical point of view—what do the data tell me? Let me share some data with you as I introduce what I think is a very difficult problem in LDS communities within the United States, and particularly in the intermountain area.

If I were to ask LDS women individually, "Do you work?" I would get a variety of answers. Some would bristle and say, "Of course I work — I am a homemaker with children to care for." Others would supply an occupation or job title. Language is one of the ways in which we divide ourselves. It is, of course, a very different question from "Do you work?" to ask "Are you employed?" or "Do you earn a wage?" All women work, and I believe in the importance of all the different ways in which women work. The fact that we are not always careful about the language we use to distinguish between one type of work and another suggests the tension that exists within our communities over what women do.

To understand these tensions, I think we ought to examine a significant social change that has occurred in the past three or four decades. From 1950 to 1990, the number of women in the labor force almost tripled in the United States. This statistic is for married women, living with their husband. My family illustrates this change. When my mother gave birth to her third child in 1949, only one woman in five was in the labor force. My younger sister, a second-year law student about the same age now as my mother was then, gave birth recently to her third child. Three out of five of my sister's married peers are in the labor force.

What has brought about this change? During the 1970s, when women were entering the labor force in record numbers, social scientists attempted to explain why. James Coleman, a noted sociologist, described the phenomenon this way: "Women who were not in the labor force . . . found themselves left behind. . . . They were left in a social backwater, with children as their principal social companions. The household, which was once a locus of intense relations, now became psychologically barren. . . . In recent years this psychological deprivation has, I suspect, been the major factor leading to the massive influx of women into the labor force."[3] This is not a very accurate nor helpful description of women's experience. Boredom, association with children, and psychological deprivation are not the forces behind women's participation as wage earners. When we carefully examine the societal changes taking place, we understand that women left home to participate in the labor force as the economic structure changed. Women living in the United States today live in a society where the production of goods and services takes place outside the home, not in the home or on the farm. Women joined the labor force not because they were fleeing "psychological deprivation," but because the economic structure changed.

Let's look at what has happened to average family incomes in the United States during the last forty or so years. From 1945 until about 1970, average family income in the United States climbed steadily. Every year the median income for families increased. But since 1970, family income has not continued to increase. In fact, the only reason that average family income has not actually declined is that women joined the labor force to supplement their husband's income. Moreover, the average income for households headed by females has always been much lower compared to the average income for married couples, and that difference has actually increased over the years. I point out this fact because the number of households headed by females has also increased.

Kathleen Gerson, author of *Hard Choices: How Women Decide about Work, Career, and Motherhood*, has suggested that women move into the labor force both because of opportunity (the economy of the United States grew and needed more workers) and because of economic pressures to supplement a husband's income or to provide for their own support.[4]

Now let's look at the number of young mothers in the labor force. Between 1975 and 1989 the number of women in the labor force who had had a child in the last year rose from slightly more than 30 percent to slightly more than 51 percent. That is a dramatic change in only fourteen years. LDS culture values children highly and strongly emphasizes that women should be in the home, especially when there are young children in the family. And yet, LDS women living in the United States are employed at the same rates as women in the general population.

Consider the effects of that change. In a very short time, women's behavior shifted from a clearly identifiable standard for making choices about employment (most new mothers stay home with their children) to a not so clear standard (some new mothers stay home with their children; others are employed). Clearly, from a sociologist's perspective, when seven of ten women make the same choice, identifying the "correct," or socially acceptable choice, is easy. But when the percentage is fifty-fifty, the "correct" choice is not so clear. Sociologists would say that we are in a period of normlessness. There is no norm, no one right way. Furthermore, it may be that our society still values women's staying home to care for their young children, but because of economic need very few women are actually able to make that choice. In a period of rapid social change, the existence of a gap between societal values and the choices women actually make creates a lot of dissonance and ambivalence for women making these choices. One woman's choice becomes another woman's indictment.

Other statistics demonstrate further change. Since 1975, there has been a dramatic increase in the number of women obtaining graduate degrees in law, dentistry, and medicine. Half of all Ph.D's in the social sciences these days are being given to women. These degrees reflect what happened in the seventies and eighties. Women recognized that if they were going to be in the labor force, they needed an education to make a good wage, and so they began to pursue advanced degrees.

Nationally, women make seventy-two cents for every dollar a man makes. This figure has increased ten cents in the last decade. In the state of Utah, that ratio is fifty-four cents to every dollar.[5] Part of the discrepancy results from the strong LDS ideal for women to stay at home, which means that although as many Mormon women work, they are more likely to work part-time. Many employers prefer to fill jobs with women who work part-time: such employees can be paid less money and they don't have to be paid benefits.

Kathleen Gerson's examination of how women make family and career choices describes the forces in United States society that discourage women from making choices toward domesticity. Gerson says that most women she studied fully expected to live a domestic life — to be at home, supported by a husband, and caring for children. But, she found, by their late thirties and early forties, only a minority of the women were able to have that kind of life. She identifies four societal characteristics that encourage women to choose a domestic life-style: First, a family system characterized by permanent, stable marriages. Second, a household economy founded on one paycheck, a "family wage." Third, limited work opportunities for women. Fourth, behavioral similarity among women, that is, most women are able to choose a domestic life and do so.[6]

These four characteristics do not describe current United States society. Divorce is prevalent, even among Latter-day Saints. Real economic growth has not occurred for more than two decades; new jobs are primarily in the lower wage categories, in the service sector — fast food service and retail sales, for example. At the same time, there are fewer jobs in manufacturing. And finally, women have career and job opportunities and choices.

Accompanying this dramatic social change, Gerson notes a rising division among women: "The deepening divisions among women and between traditional and nontraditional households . . . are as significant as the conflicts between men and women. The contradictory nature of change ensures that differently situated women will disagree about where their best interests lie.

"Domestic women, whose interests remain lodged in traditional family forms, understandably fear the erosion of the protections offered by traditional arrangements. . . . Nondomestic paths for women, however, are too long in the making and too deeply rooted to dissolve in the face of this opposition. They also guarantee that women's demands for equality will continue. These demands stem as much from new forms of female economic and social vulnerability as from a more general desire for liberation. Divisions between those who embrace new patterns and those who oppose them will thus continue to generate intense political conflict over women's, men's, and children's proper places in the social order."[7]

Gerson suggests, and I concur, that the feminist movement did not by itself create the societal shifts we have seen; rather, economic changes have been the prime mover. The resulting changes in women's lives will continue to create intense conflict between those women who by choice or circumstance make different decisions. I see that conflict in our local wards—divisions between women created by differences in labor force participation, marital status, and motherhood. Why do we let these differences divide us?

Thinking of differences that divide us, let me share with you some recently collected data about LDS women and their television-watching habits. Dan Stout, an instructor in the Brigham Young University communications department, conducted a survey among LDS women in three regions of the country. He found some very similar attitudes among LDS women. Almost all agree that there is too much sex and violence on television. Almost all report they generally don't hold the remote control when watching television with their husband.

But in other respects, these LDS women displayed very different attitudes about television. Statistical analysis revealed three significant response differences. The first group, about 46 percent, seldom watch television. It isn't part of their routine, and isn't a source of entertainment for them. Television is almost irrelevant in their lives. The second group, about a third, watch TV to get away from it all, to get away from tension.

They use it as a source of entertainment, or they have it on during the day for company, for noise in the house—but about half this second group report that they feel guilty when they watch. The final group, about one in five, look forward to watching. Television is part of their daily routine, gives them something to talk about with their friends, is a significant source of entertainment, and they don't feel guilty about watching TV.

My point is, LDS women do not all respond in the same way to television. But those differences in television watching don't divide us in the same way that other differences—like labor force participation—seem to. One reason, of course, is the tremendous value we place on families and children. In the past, our leaders have instructed us in our family duties, encouraging women to marry and have children and discouraging women from entering the labor force. We have also received instruction from our leaders about scripture study, personal prayer, and paying our tithing. Just last week, I heard of another woman who, in the process of seeking employment, was asked by a well-meaning Latter-day Saint and potential employer, "How can you justify working when you have young children at home?" This question, aside from being against the law, seems all the more inappropriate when we realize that the potential employer would never have thought to ask, "Do you read your scriptures? Do you have personal prayer every night? Do you gather your family together for family home evening?" A woman's choices about prayer and tithing are in the private realm and are private behaviors, but a woman's decisions regarding employment, marriage, or number of children are private decisions that result in very public behavior. Let us be careful that we do not judge or impose personal values on the agency of others.

Another factor adds to the tension between women. We all grow up thinking that there is a set pattern to life—young adulthood, education, romance, marriage, children, etc. But life just does not flow in such neat patterns for most women. We see, for example, many women returning to school after their children are grown, entering careers at age forty or fifty. We must be cognizant of the many patterns a person's life can take.

My own experience was very different from that of many of my friends. During my twenties I worked full-time, served a mission, and then entered graduate school. The women around me were getting married and giving birth. It seemed to me that their lives were more valued by my community than was mine. I struggled with being different, was sometimes angry and often envious of these women whose lives seemed so perfect. Years later, after I had received my Ph.D. and been appointed to a faculty position at BYU, I found that women who could and had made the valued choices of marriage and children were sometimes angry and envious of me.

How do we reach across the aisle to one another? First, as Hattie Soil has suggested, we need to examine our own backgrounds and experiences, we need to know ourselves, and then we need to open ourselves up to others and to their different experiences. We can build the kingdom of God by building ourselves as we build a community of women. That means that we must support our sisters as they confront real problems: abuse in all its forms, sexual harassment, rape, such economic problems as poverty and wage discrimination, the lack of good child care. Let us open our hearts to mourn with these women. To comfort them. To witness to them not only of God's love but of their individual worth in our community.

NOTES

1. Elaine L. Jack, "Charity Never Faileth," *Ensign*, May 1992, pp. 90–91.

2. Hattie M. Soil, "A View from the Inner City," *Women Steadfast in Christ*, ed. Dawn Hall Anderson and Marie Cornwall (Salt Lake City: Deseret Book Co., 1992), p. 282.

3. James Coleman, *The Asymmetric Society* (Syracuse, N. Y.: Syracuse University Press, 1982), p. 130.

4. Kathleen Gerson, *Hard Choices: How Women Decide about Work, Career, and Motherhood* (Berkeley: University of California Press, 1985).

5. Nancy Amidei, "The Feminization of Poverty—How Does It Look in Utah?" Belle S. Spafford Conference Report, University of Utah Graduate School of Social Work, Salt Lake City, Utah, 7 June 1991.

6. Gerson, p. 204.

7. Gerson, p. 223.

Inside the World of Islam

DONNA LEE BOWEN

Much of the world's history reflects the human fear of differences, be they in appearance, in actions, or in thought. For reasons that historians have never sorted out satisfactorily, religious faith has divided peoples across time and lands rather than united them. War after war has resulted from religious differences. Today, after the dissolution of the Eastern bloc, we notice that the old Marxist or Communist enemy has been replaced with a new one. The media publicizes the emergence of a new adversary to the West on the world scene: Islam.

Westerners have misunderstood Islam since early contacts between Muslims and Christians in the seventh century after Christ. (Believers in Islam are called Muslims.) That misunderstanding has often led to fear. In recent years, Islam has been identified not only with fanaticism and fundamentalism but also with terrorism. Islam is associated more with "holy war" than with the teachings of its religion.

One simple fact accounts for much of this gap in understanding. Few Westerners know Muslims personally or have any experience with Islam. Too often their knowledge of Islam comes from screaming newspaper headlines or the evening news. The lives ordinary Muslims live seem remote and unfathomable. It was this same readiness to stereotype and distrust that led to the medieval superstition that Jews were demons and devils. I have spent years living and working in the Middle East and know many Muslims as well as I know my Mormon neighbors. The everyday reality that we experience together as believers in God flies in the face of media perceptions of Muslims and gives us more common ground than many believe.

Donna Lee Bowen has lived in several Muslim countries: Egypt, Iran, Tunisia, and Morocco. An associate professor of political science and Middle Eastern studies and associate director of the Women's Research Institute at Brigham Young University, she has coedited the book Everyday Life in the Muslim Middle East. *The mother of three daughters, Donna Lee is married to James R. Barnes. She is a Sunday School teacher.*

Last April I traveled to Morocco, arriving in Casablanca early in the morning. There I boarded another plane to fly to Tangier, a half hour away. As I made my way to my seat, I noticed that everyone was dressed in white—the men in white robes, the women swathed in white from head to toe and wearing very different headdresses from their usual garb, a white scarf that completely framed their face. Wondering what was up, I made sure that I sat down next to one of the couples, a husband and wife who looked approachable. We began chatting, and I learned that they had just come from Mecca in Saudi Arabia, where they had made the lesser pilgrimage, the *umra*. As we talked, they mentioned that they were from Tetouan, a town in northern Morocco. About a decade ago I had worked with a gentleman from Tetouan, and so I inquired about him. My new friends replied, "Mustafa Daoud? He is here on the plane with us," and the wife took me by the hand and led me to the front of the plane calling out, "Mustafa, here's a friend of yours." Because we were both ten years older than the last time we met, we had not recognized each other. I sat with him and his wife and spent the flight catching up and talking religion.

Dr. Mustafa Daoud, son of a well-known religious scholar, is an obstetrician-gynecologist whose great love in life is delivering healthy babies. When we first met, he was the director of the Moroccan national family planning program. I can say without prejudice that this talented and judicious man was the best director they had had up to that point. After I left, I heard that he had tired of public life and had returned to Tetouan to pursue a private practice in medicine. As we talked, I asked about the pilgrimage that he had been on. His face lit up, his wife's face lit up, and they said, "It was absolutely marvelous. This is not the first time we've gone. We've gone before, probably three, four times. We've made the greater pilgrimage, the *hajj*. You cannot imagine the power of standing in Mecca shoulder to shoulder with literally two million Muslims. We felt the strength of our community as we gathered, as we participated in the community of believers there, praying and kneeling together to acknowledge the greatness of God."

As I listened to my friend Mustafa, I felt that nothing separated us. As we talked about our God, as we talked about our societies, as we talked about the way we saw the world, we communicated perfectly because our concerns as believers in God were so similar.

Riffat Hassan is a Pakistani Muslim woman with whom I also share this same sense of friendship united in respect for the power of religion and the word of God. She is the director of the religious studies program at the University of Louisville. She has studied Christianity and Judaism, as well as her major field of Islamic religion, and holds United States citizenship after living in the United States for around two decades. What follows is a dialogue between Riffat and me, an LDS woman from Bountiful, Utah, who has studied Islam and Muslim societies over the past twenty-five years. Our dialogue focuses on some of the concerns shared by both Muslims and Mormons.

Riffat: We are living in very difficult times. We are living in a world that has changed radically, even in the last couple of years. If you look at the world in terms of blocs that we've become used to since the Second World War, you cannot help but notice that the two largest blocs left in the world now are the West, which you could understand as being largely Judeo-Christian (or from another perspective, largely secular), and the world of Islam. More than one billion Muslims now live in many countries and in a large number of cultures in the world. It is absolutely imperative that the peoples of these two blocs learn to understand each other, because whether they like each other or not, they are going to have to deal with each other. In the next few decades the bridge building between these two worlds, which seem currently to regard each other with great antagonism and hostility, needs to be accomplished, the tensions need to be resolved. For this reason it is very important for Americans, for all Americans, to understand Islam.

There are many reasons for the negative stereotyping. It is not a new development. It didn't start in 1973 with the Arab oil embargo or in 1979 with the Iranian revolution or in 1989 with the outcry over Salman Rushdie's book or in 1991 with the Gulf War. It goes back all the way to the seventh century when Islam appeared in the West and through the centuries to Dante, the great poet of medieval Christendom, who remarked that Islam was the great divider that split the world of Christendom.

So Islam has always been seen in the West as not only the other but also as the adversary. That view persists, which is why I think it is important to establish at the very outset that this historical conflict has not been between Islam and Christianity as religions — or even between Islam and Judaism as competing faiths — but has been a political conflict between the world of Islam and the world of Christendom. It's been a clash between two empires. The religions themselves are very similar. Christians claim to be the true Israel, continuing the Hebrew tradition;

Muslims make the same claim vis-à-vis the Jewish tradition and the Christian tradition. Islam claims to be a continuation of the same prophetic tradition. Therefore, part of my heritage as a Muslim is the message of all the prophets of the Jews and the Christians, because unless I accept the message of Judaism and Christianity as authentic, my Islam is incomplete. So, to my way of thinking, in some fundamental ways no basic difference or division exists amongst the three religions that Muslims call the religions of the book. The Quran refers to the Jews, the Christians, and the Muslims as people of the book. We have a lot of things in common. This commonality makes it imperative to understand both the historical reasons for the misunderstandings that currently exist and for the problems we together face as a global community.

Donna Lee: Firm believers of any religion have trouble believing that adherents to other religions have similar feelings about their faith. I was no different. While I was in graduate school, I found to my surprise that I could speak with great ease about my religious beliefs to Muslims, Jews, Roman Catholics, or Hindus, even though our core beliefs differed. I had far more trouble speaking to Mormons or Jews or Muslims who were not believers in their faiths.

My friend, colleague at BYU, and home teacher Dil Parkinson tells a wonderful story about his experiences in Cairo. He spent several years in Egypt doing social linguistic research, which meant living twenty-four hours a day in people's homes, in coffee houses, in factories, in schools, going to weddings, going to funerals—basically being part of ordinary Egyptians' lives. He became acutely aware of how they lived life, of the religious rituals that punctuated their lives, such as the five daily prayers, and the verbal expressions, proverbs, and greetings that are colored by Islam. In short, he became aware of how deeply Islam suffused their understanding of life.

As is the problem for many researchers, suspicions arose that Dil was possibly a spy, however unlikely, for United States interests. Some intensely patriotic Egyptians, seeking to serve their country and religion by uncovering Dil's espionage, became very interested in him. To better sniff out any imperialist plots to undermine Islam, they pretended friendship and soon were inviting him to their homes. As time passed, they got to know him and he them, their fears were dispelled, and real friendship developed. What touched Dil most is that, at the end, they sincerely tried to convert him to Islam. That's a new experience for

Latter-day Saints, who are used to trying to convert other people and who generally believe that members of other religions aren't as attached to their religion as we are to ours. Proselyting religions tend to view conversion as a one-way street headed their way. Dil's friends felt so strongly about Islam that, once they accepted and liked him, they wanted him to become a Muslim so that he could be saved.

Riffat: When people ask me, "What does it mean to be a Muslim?" I explain that being a Muslim means living in accordance with the will and pleasure of God. How does one do that? First, it requires knowing what God wants of us, how God wants us to live our lives. The revelation that lays out God's expectations was given to the Muslims through the Quran and through the teaching of the Prophet Muhammad. The major, or highest, source of knowledge is revelation, which for Muslims is the Quran; but Muslims also believe in previous scriptures, so theoretically Muslims believe also in the biblical text.

To me the essence of trying to be a Muslim, trying to live in accordance with the will and pleasure of God is contained in the word *jihad.* People usually think *jihad* means war. But the word *jihad,* from the root word *jahada,* means literally "to make an effort, to strive, to exert." Islam is a religion of great self-effort; it's not easy to live in accordance with the will and pleasure of God, particularly in today's world where there are so many distractions and temptations. The word *jihad* in Islam is understood in two senses: the greater jihad, and the lesser jihad. The greater jihad is striving with oneself against one's own weakness, one's own arrogance, one's own ignorance, one's own selfishness, and so on. All humans are fallible. We have so many shortcomings. The greater jihad, an ongoing, continuous process, is our struggle against them. The lesser jihad is the struggle against external odds, external events or persons that obstruct justice.

Donna Lee: The more I study Islam, the more I respect the way your religious practices develop both spiritual depth and community spirit. To use LDS terms, your jihad combines both spirituality and action. The five pillars of Islam—those five practices that Muslims are expected to perform (the profession of the creed, prayer, tithes, fasting, and the pilgrimage to Mecca)—operate on two levels at once. For example, prayer, in which an individual communicates with Deity, may be performed in the mosque standing shoulder to shoulder in a great show of community solidarity and equality, or it may be performed at home alone—as many women choose to, when their duties allow a break.

Riffat: In the prayer, the men and the women pray in separate groups, but rich and poor, young and old, stand side by side. At one point in the prayer, they drop to their knees and touch their foreheads to the ground while repeating "God is great." Both their physical movements and the language of prayer symbolize the equality of humankind as well as humility before God. During the month of Ramadan, Muslims fast to cleanse their bodies, to emphasize the reality of the blessings God grants to humankind, to feel the hunger experienced by the poor among them, and to obey the dictates of God. All give extra alms to the poor, and no one is ever turned away from *iftar*, the meal at sunset breaking the fast. In some Muslim lands, all Muslims, rich and poor, break the fast with the same food, often a soup, symbolizing the unity of Islam worldwide.

Donna Lee: The United States and Western Europe have seen a great deal of propaganda on the place of women in Islam. The film *Not Without My Daughter* horrified many Western women by suggesting that women have no rights whatsoever in Islamic countries. Since we have no access to other views, films like this one are taken as reality, describing the social norm rather than dramatizing a tragic family breakdown. Is there cause for our alarm? I myself know from living in Islamic countries that in those countries Western wives of Muslims may have fewer rights than their husbands or their Muslim in-laws. I also have seen among my acquaintances, however, strong marriages between Christians and Muslims. These families often are more committed to family, children, and religious values than many of my American Christian friends.

What is the position of women in Islamic society? To what extent does Islam assign a lesser place to women? Or, is the situation of Muslim women more a result of custom or political expedience?

Riffat: The gap between theory and practice in Islam is in this case extremely wide. I have spent about sixteen or seventeen years of my life working on the Quranic passages relating to women, and on the basis of all my research, I am personally convinced that the Quran does not discriminate against women.

The Judeo-Christian creation story stipulates that Eve was created from Adam's rib. Many Christians use this text to suggest that women are inferior to men. In the Quran, there is no story of an Eve being taken from an Adam's rib — so there is no implied but unstated inequality. Actually, many Muslims will agree with me on this question of equality, based on their study of the Quran, but then they turn around and say, "Yes, standing in the sight of God they are equal, but in terms of each other they are not equal." What has happened is that a hierarchy has been created—a problem that crops up in patriarchal religions: no matter where you start, you end up with a hierarchy.

So what do we mean by equal in Islam? In Islam there is a division of functions. Some functions are allocated to men and others to women. For example, there is one function that only women can perform— bearing children. Men cannot do that thus far. The Quran attaches the greatest importance to bearing and raising children. Without any exception, the mother is the most respected person in Islamic society. I have great difficulty explaining that to American feminists. They don't understand it. The overall emphasis of the Quran—if rightly interpreted (which it hasn't been for fourteen hundred years, but we are getting started now)—is on justice. To have a healthy and sane society, you have got to have justice. So while women are performing this very important function of bearing and raising children, they should not also be obligated to earn a living. The Quran speaks of this very wholesome division of functions within society. It is a common link between me and you because the Latter-day Saints also believe that this division is a very important message to articulate in our society. I call myself a feminist, but to me feminism has to do with every human being having the right to develop his or her human potential. It isn't women saying "I want to be the same as a man," because the man then becomes the model, and he is always going to be ahead of us—more a man than we can be or want to be. That isn't my kind of feminism. In America I am told that women want the right to work, and I say, "Right, you want the right to work—and to work yourself to death." I am a single mother; I have raised my child since she was three months old. That has taken a lot of courage, but let's not romanticize the situation, because it is inherently unfair. God wants children to have two parents, and where women are forced into being single parents, something is wrong. When I go to bed after working sixteen or eighteen hours a day (the minimum that I have to work just to survive), my thought as I drop off to sleep at night isn't, "Look what a liberated woman I am!" Rather, I feel entirely enslaved and dehumanized by an unfair system. We need to rethink our models of liberation. I am not in favor of reinstituting a male hierarchy—or any hierarchy—because that is also wrong. But I think we have to emphasize justice, which is at the heart of religion. God is just, and he wants us to have justice in our lives. A lot of what we call feminist striving is not what I would call justice. I think this striving has to do with power, and that is another issue, another game.

Donna Lee: In this area, Mormons and Muslims would strongly agree. Several months ago a Relief Society lesson stressed the importance of recognizing the seasons of a life—that we have various times of life to accomplish our various goals and that patience and judiciousness will be our friend in doing so. Many Latter-day Saint women are also concerned with historical and present injustice, what we term "unrighteous dominion." At the same time, pragmatic women recognize a functional need for a division of labor between husband and wife. And fatigue makes many of us realize that we are not superwomen and cannot do everything at once, however much we think we should be able to do so. But reconciling all this within a range of religious precepts and practical scheduling is difficult. And, Riffat, no one has yet really begun to work on the ways Latter-day Saint men are discriminated against, given our present imperfect social system.

Riffat: I find it interesting that certain words that I find positive my American students regard as "bad," words such as *traditional*. They see me wearing traditional Pakistani dress, and they think that is terrible. They think of tradition as a negative force. I have them read Salman Rushdie's *Shame,* which is a very hard-hitting critique of relationships between men and women in closed societies. They say over and over that these Muslim women are so oppressed. I say, "Whose perception is that? Yours, or their perception of themselves? Do they perceive themselves as being oppressed?" They would also say to you, Donna Lee, that Latter-day Saint women are very oppressed. But, whose perception is that? That is what we have to ask. If a woman is happy and fulfilled in doing whatever she is doing, then do the people outside that tradition have the right to judge her, to tell her she is oppressed and make her feel devalued?

The feminist movement is warped two ways. On the one hand, the feminist movement elevated the housewife to a homemaker, but then on the other hand, it made women feel that being a homemaker and staying at home was a cop-out. A lot of women within the Muslim and the Mormon societies have made a self-conscious decision that they are not oppressed. They are not being forced to be at home. They are as liberated as a woman who chooses to go to work. That choice should be respected. I get upset when a woman says, "I am only a housewife."

Women have internalized this negative message, and we need to get rid of it. It is a great privilege to have the opportunity to be at home. With all my heart I wish that I had had more time to spend with my daughter when she was growing up. That is a great privilege. One problem with living in America is that unless you get paid, American society does not value what you do. We need to change that idea too.

Another parallel I see between Mormons and Muslims is that both are traditional societies with a notion of the proper order of things: for example, each divides the world into two spaces, public space and private space, or the domain of the home and the domain of the world. That division does not need to mean that women are confined to private space and men can have the public space. Even though most women in the world would like to be married and have children, they do not wish to create a separate domain for women. Most women would like to have more opportunity to be educated and to fulfill themselves in work according to their talents. That relates to the matter of justice. God has given all of us different talents. If God gives us a certain potential and a certain capability, it is to be used in a constructive fashion. Both Muslim women and Mormon women believe that.

Donna Lee: If women are held in such esteem by Islam, why are children taken away from them and men given custody of children over the age of seven (for boys) and nine (for girls)? Why do we have the high incidence of wife beating in Muslim countries? Is there something in Islam that speaks to violence? Are Muslims' minds turned towards revenge? What we see of Islam in the popular media causes us to associate violence with Islam. Why is that?

Riffat: This is a twenty-part question that is very complicated. The very meaning of the word *Islam* is peace. So, to say that Islam is a religion of violence is a contradiction of the word itself. That misunderstanding, however, is widespread. I have heard or read again and again, "Islam was spread by the sword," but it really was not. It was spread by mystics, missionaries, and traders. Although like other people Muslims have fought many wars, Islam was not spread by the sword. Since the Salman Rushdie crisis in England, much militancy has been associated with the Muslims, especially young ones. Before that, young religious Muslims were seen as law-abiding good citizens. What happened? Salman Rushdie's book talks about revered Islamic personages — the Prophet Muhammad, the wives of the prophet, and others — in the worst possible way. He compares the prophet and his wives to a brothel with prostitutes, and Muhammad to a false prophet. That so offended the Muslims that they were not willing to accept the British political value of freedom of speech and expression. They felt that there must be limits placed on free speech to respect religious sensibilities. Ironically, there is in England a law against blasphemy that applies to Christianity—but not to other faiths. These young Muslims have established a Muslim Parliament in Britain because they feel our entire culture is being undermined by the values of a government that considers us backward and alien.

I lived as a student in England for eight years. Most of the Muslims living there are very conservative, blue-collar workers. The wives are mostly veiled, and they don't believe in educating daughters. That is the culture that they bring with them. Often Westerners use our cultural values against us to show that Muslims are backward and barbarous people. But our values are examined out of context.

Muslims are greatly challenged by modernity. We weigh Western practices. On the one hand, the West gives us electricity, health care, and better roads, but westernization also brings pornography, secular values, and moral permissiveness. So Muslims fear westernization, and not without cause. If you ask an average Muslim to name one symbol of westernization, they will say "an emancipated Muslim woman," meaning sexual permissiveness and loss of faith, not enlightenment or liberation. Yet nothing in the Quran says that Muslim women should stay at home, not be seen outside, or wear a veil, so making these customary practices into religious values is a mistake. These are, as you suggest, customs, not Islamic beliefs. Also, the Muslims are very conservative, and we cannot separate the issue of gender from race and class. Thus, on the one hand, Muslims want their wives to stay indoors and be veiled but, on the other hand, upper-class women have some opportunities few Western women do. For example, in only the last two years, two Muslim countries have had women as prime ministers, Pakistan and Bangladesh. So we have in Muslim countries all these contradictions—tensions between custom and doctrine.

Donna Lee: Riffat, we have spoken about the divisions between Muslims and Christians and the misunderstanding that permeates much of the political and religious climate. If we are to grow closer rather than farther away, what bridges can you identify for us so that we may cross over into your world?

Riffat: That is a marvelous question. We need to see each other as human beings and as people of faith faced with similar problems. If we believe that there is one God and this God is the God of love and of justice and of mercy and this God cares for all creatures, then what better ground do we have to come together than that? We must use our faith to come together and talk to one another face to face. When we don't see each other, we remain faceless, and we remain the other whom we don't know and can't trust. Dialogue is a slow process, but if people of faith talk together, perhaps we have a chance.

When I first came to this country I felt like a mutilated woman. I have been in a state of struggle against patriarchy from day one. I came from a family where my father was a very good man and very conservative. He believed that girls should be married at age sixteen to whomever was picked out for them. That is what my two older sisters did. I fought it. I became the deviant because I wanted to study. Everything I did my father thought was all wrong. I wasn't doing anything immoral, but just because I wasn't agreeing to be married at age sixteen, I became an outcast.

So I have my own contradictions and conflict with Islamic customs. I have had to remain outside and fight and fight, and I am still fighting. Whenever I run into two or three Muslim men, I know they will start badgering me. The process goes on, and I am very weary of it. I am not at all an integrated person, though I may have fooled you a little bit. My daughter who is eighteen is far more together than I am ever going to be, because she was never ripped apart the way I was and the way I still am in some ways.

What caused me to become healthy and whole to whatever extent I am is through my dialogue not with Muslims but with Jews and Christians. These are the people who gave me back my faith and my person and my wholeness. I know that dialogue works because it worked for me. While at the BYU-Relief Society women's conference, I attended a session on healing and forgiveness. It was marvelous to hear those women's words on forgiveness. Their faith came through so strongly. Faith is one indivisible substance we share, and the faith in all of us unites rather than divides us. What might divide us is historical actions or doctrines and dogma. It is not our faith that can divide us. If we have that faith in our common humanity and in our one God, then we can heal the world. That is the bridge I would like to build.

Donna Lee: On 15 February 1978, the First Presidency of The Church of Jesus Christ of Latter-day Saints issued the following statement:

Based upon ancient and modern revelation, The Church of Jesus Christ of Latter-day Saints gladly teaches and declares the Christian doctrine that all men and women are brothers and sisters, not only by blood relationship from common mortal progenitors but also as literal spirit children of an Eternal Father.

The great religious leaders of the world such as Mohammed, Confucius, and the Reformers, as well as philosophers including Socrates, Plato, and others, received a portion of God's light. Moral truths were given to them by God to enlighten whole nations and to bring a higher level of understanding to individuals.

The Hebrew prophets prepared the way for the coming of Jesus Christ, the promised Messiah, who should provide salvation for all mankind who believe in the gospel.

Consistent with these truths, we believe that God has given and will give to all peoples sufficient knowledge to help them on their way to eternal salvation, either in this life or in the life to come.

We also declare that the gospel of Jesus Christ, restored to his Church in our day, provides the only way to a mortal life of happiness and a fullness of joy forever. For those who have not received this gospel, the opportunity will come to them in the life hereafter if not in this life.

Our message therefore is one of special love and concern for the eternal welfare of all men and women, regardless of religious belief, race, or nationality, knowing that we are truly brothers and sisters because we are sons and daughters of the same Eternal Father.

Coming Up on the
Rough Side of the Mountain

BETTY STEVENSON

I grew up in the early 1950s in an unincorporated, country area of Contra Costa County, California. In 1976 I moved to East Oakland and was living there in 1981 when the missionaries came. I would be putting it nicely if I said they were welcome. When they came to my house the first time, I was not at home. I was busy wheeling and dealing, drugs mostly. But they were persistent. I was truly living in darkness. It takes a lot of darkness before you can recognize the light when it comes. At least that was my experience. One day I came home and found a card they had left that said, "Does it meet the test?"

My family is Baptist. During my childhood, my mother worked very diligently in church, but for me that is where religion ended. We went on Sunday, listened, and if we could, we children were supposed to get something out of it. But I couldn't. I never did understand all of the yelling and hollering. I always felt like something was wrong with me because I didn't feel like doing that. If you didn't feel this spirit that made you whoop and holler, then you were put into a category. I was in that category from day one. It was sort of like I knew I was going to hell and didn't really care. I figured that I might as well have a good time on the way, and we would at least have a family reunion, because I knew I wasn't going alone. I saw what the grown-ups around me said and did. I saw and heard the lies, the unfaithfulness, the cruelty. I saw no evidence of goals I could achieve, and I picked up on all the wrong examples. At an early age, I turned my back not only on my family but on my race and religion as well.

....

Betty Stevenson, a convert to the Church, is the single mother of two children and the foster parent of six, ranging in age from three years to twenty-one. She has given firesides and workshops for youth, single adults, and missionaries on her experiences as a black convert to the LDS Church. She serves as a ward Relief Society president.

Nothing was sacred in our mostly black neighborhood. I grew up with continual arguing and fighting. When I got tired of listening to it at home, I could always go to the neighbors and hear them get down on their kids or beat their wives. I didn't even have grandparents to nurture me. Nor did I have the community that most of you were born into — a place where you help each other. Friendship didn't really mean anything. People did not take care of the down and out — maybe because everyone was down in one way or another.

As a kid I thought that was more reason to stick together. Somehow I knew it was right to help those who could not help themselves. I have always believed that there was something good, but I couldn't ever describe it or explain the feeling. There wasn't anything I could tell people. But I believed in something that was deep inside of me. In spite of being as bad as I was, I felt compassion for children, old people, and people who couldn't help themselves. I remember an old bum we called Peewee who just hung around the neighborhood. No one wanted Peewee around. He wasn't allowed in anyone's home. I remember stealing food and giving it to him on the sly. I can remember the day they found Peewee dead in the back seat of a car he had crawled into across the street from my house. No one cared. People didn't seem to care what happened to each other. I did not grow up feeling wanted.

By the time the missionaries came to my door that February in 1981, I was almost forty and I didn't want to hear anything they had to say. I had no faith in people, and I had little belief in God. When I peeped out the window and saw two clean white boys at my door looking and sounding official, I thought they were police. I wasn't about to let them in. But, while I was hiding from them I heard a thought to go and open the door. Well, you may think this was a dramatic witness, but for me it wasn't. I was loaded — on drugs or drunk — most of the time, and I always heard voices. This was, however, the first time in my life that I stopped and listened again.

All the while these young men were standing outside my door. They wouldn't go away until I came and answered. When I let them in, they didn't come in condemning me. I didn't feel as though they were looking down at me. As a matter of fact, I was quite surprised because they said they could feel the spirit of God in my house. That was the last thing I wanted in my house, and religion was the last thing I wanted in my life. My relatives were Baptists, Jehovah's Witnesses, Methodists, and Seventh-Day Adventists, and I didn't want anything to do with any of them. But these young men came with the Spirit. Even in my condition I could feel that. I often hear people say that the Lord's Spirit cannot dwell in unclean temples. If that is true, there is no way that I could have heard, felt, or seen anything that day. But I did, and I told the missionaries that.

Then they told me about Joseph Smith. Now, we were doing pretty well together as long as they talked about God. But when they started talking about this white boy who had found gold plates and talked to a dead angel, I wanted them to get out. They gave me a Book of Mormon when they left, but I only flipped through it and put it down. Eventually, about a month later, I picked it up and read the first few verses of the first chapter: "I, Nephi, having been born of goodly parents." Those words burned deeply in my heart, and I cried, and I still cry whenever I hear them. Those words were meant for me. I didn't have goodly parents. Or at least I didn't think I did. I have since come to realize that they weren't as bad as I thought they were. As a matter of fact, what I heard from them set the foundation for me that enabled me to understand when the missionaries came.

I went to church with the missionaries and learned that I have a Mother and a Father in Heaven that love me, the mother and father of my spirit. My understanding jumped from my earthly parents to a heavenly realm. That understanding kept me coming to church because many of my experiences were negative. People tolerated me, but I could tell by their coldness and their looks that they did not want me there. People would say and do things in total opposition to what I was learning and feeling. Once a sister phoned to tell me she hoped I wouldn't bring any of my friends to church. Now I am grateful for those people and the ugly things they said because they made me think. I had to go home and deal with what I truly believed. The sister who phoned didn't understand my reason for being at church. I came to church to learn and to grow . . . to change. I'm still here for the same reason.

I learned that if I would humble myself before God, he would make these weak parts of me become strengths to me. (Ether 12:27.) And I had plenty of weakness. At that point I was dealing with a six-year addiction to heroin. The amount I was using would have brought in about four hundred dollars a day if I had sold it. I smoked cigarettes, marijuana, and was even hooked on nasal spray. I had served time in prison. I was not very teachable. I went to church to upset people. In Sunday School class, I deliberately asked questions that I knew nobody could answer. I didn't care about upsetting or shocking people. The more shocked they were, the better I felt. In Relief Society, when I stood up and expressed how I really felt, there were people who didn't want to hear it. I saw a lot of sisters holding their hearts and rolling their eyes.

At the time the Oakland Stake was working hard to help Cambodian and Laotian refugees, teaching them how to ride the buses and speak the language. It was an all-out effort. I remember missionaries running across my feet to get to a Cambodian. I would stand there and wonder, where do I belong in all of this? What in the world am I doing here? I was at a disadvantage because I spoke English and was born and raised in this country, but I was a refugee just as sure as if I had just gotten off a boat. I spoke street language, gangster language. When I first started talking to my bishop like this, I could see he felt it wasn't really proper. But I talked the way I talked, and I said what I said, and I called things what I called them. And then I would go home and pray to God for a new vocabulary because I didn't want to kill anybody. I just wanted them to hear what I was saying. When Bishop Alder talks to me now, I can hear some of that language—nice parts of it, like "right on" or "later" or "I'll catch up with you."

Many times at first I would leave church with an empty feeling. I really felt like I didn't belong there, and I didn't know why I kept getting this instruction: "You go back up there. These people are your family, and I am your Father. Go back, go back." I realized that the reason I was not feeling the Spirit in church was not because it wasn't there. What was wrong was wrong with me. The missionaries placed my salvation right back in my own hands and let me know that if someone is acting ugly or being unfriendly, that's their problem, not mine. I had to learn that not all Latter-day Saints were all ready to go to heaven except for me.

At first I was disappointed, but later, after I was called to leadership positions, I began to understand. When you become a good member of the family, you begin to hear all these family secrets and then you know that nobody is perfect. The gospel is perfect, but we are imperfect people trying to live a perfect gospel. In Relief Society I learned that I was a daughter of God, that I belonged to a large family of women who came in all shapes, colors, and sizes.

Once I got established in the ward, I was always telling people to be grateful for their history. I didn't know who I was. I didn't know I had a culture. And I found that I had a lot of things in common with this Latter-day Saint culture I was trying to assimilate myself into. Mormons had suffered persecutions and prejudice. They had had to band together to survive. My people—black Americans—had suffered some of the worst injustices there ever were. When the persecution was worst, they worked together, shared the little they had, and took pride in their work. There was no welfare then. I wanted to immerse myself in Mormon culture, to do things the way Mormon women do them. You may laugh, but I was almost traumatized trying to get a loaf of bread to come out right so I could feel like I was a real Mormon sister. I have appreciated the push to find out where I came from, even though when I first realized genealogy was a commandment, I became real upset. I remember going to the Lord and saying, "I can't stand my kindred living and now you want me to worry about my kindred dead!" So, I had to go back and mend some bridges. I can't go back even a generation yet. I have been looking, though. I finally got my dad to give me a copy of his birth certificate, after I promised him that we weren't doing anything with dead bodies in the temple, and now I am almost ready to do my mom's work for her. She had not been baptized in the Church when she died, but she had a testimony about those young men and those kind people who came into my life and encouraged me when I didn't feel like going any further.

As I added a Mormonness to my blackness, I began to find myself. I discovered new ambitions. First of all, I wanted to work in the Church public relations department. I wanted to correct some wrongs, to show that blacks have always been involved somewhere in the building of Zion. Then I was going to teach all others about the gospel of Jesus Christ. My health did not allow me to do that. But I didn't allow health problems to stop the work that I promised God I was going to do. I served as a Relief Society president in the Oakland Ninth Branch. I opened my home to six foster children ranging in age from three to twenty-one years. Mario came at four days old, addicted to crack cocaine. I brought him home, got him a priesthood blessing, and in a couple of months the effects were gone. This little boy prays and folds his arms and is a good example in the nursery. I also have girls at home ranging in age from nine to fifteen. They have all been abandoned or abused. The parents are dead or on drugs or just not capable of caring for a child, but I know and believe in the help and strength to be gained from Church programs — from the nursery, the Primary, all the way to Young Women and camp programs.

Let me tell you about the Oakland Ninth Branch. In 1981 when I first came into the Church, I was in the Oakland Fourth Ward. The Oakland Fourth was combined with the Oakland First Ward in about 1983. The Oakland First Ward was composed of wealthy members. I consider them to be wealthy, although many of them tell me no, they are not. But I say they live in heaven, and if they have any doubt, I can take them on a tour down in the flatlands of Oakland. Coming out of the conditions I was in there, it was very difficult for me to relate in this ward, even as determined as I was to go up that hill where they lived and bring the gospel down to where I could handle it.

As I began to speak out in meetings, I knew some people were offended by my street language. There were others who were discouraged by my speaking out. But there were also changes made because of it. The ugly people I was used to. I felt real comfortable in a hostile environment. The people who were kind were the ones that affected my life. The ones who were kind to me for no reason, who went out of their way to say or do things that were encouraging, touched my heart. God blessed me with a few angels like those two missionaries and Phil and Emma Tadje. I would never have met these people had it not been for the Church because we have nothing in common. The Tadjes were not afraid to come right into the barrio where I lived — among the winos and drug addicts — and sit down on the floor with my children and sing. Those songs were so foreign to us we couldn't even sing them. I thought, I've got to work on some songs for this environment because these songs are going to kill me. I love the Tadjes dearly. When they left Oakland and went back to Utah, I was lost. I remember wanting so badly to hear Sister T's voice that I called her up just to ask her how to sauté vegetables. She got on one phone, and Brother Tadje got on the other, and I cried and cried.

So I stayed in there, trying to find a way, and I began to pray a very personal prayer, asking the Lord that I would be able to be in a congregation that would relate to me. I went to talk to the mission president, Wayne Peterson, about my feelings and found him to be very receptive. In his wisdom, he gathered together this little rag-tag group of people that were coming from the flatlands of Oakland, knowing that the missionaries had told them the truth and hoping to find a place they could fit in. He organized us as a missionary group. We met in the Relief

Society room, and the missionaries brought in investigators to visit. We had single sisters, many of whom had children by numerous men. The teachers were challenged by trying to figure out who belonged to who. As our group multiplied and baptisms began to happen, I began to believe that indeed there was a place for us.

After about three years, in November 1986, we were moved out of the Oakland First Ward to a building on Virginia Avenue. From that nucleus, the Oakland Ninth Branch was born. Little did I know that I would be called to be the Relief Society president. I was the most unlikely candidate of all. I did not consider myself to be a proper LDS woman at that point. As I said, I didn't know how to bake bread, I couldn't sew, and I had no family history. I didn't know who I was. Before the branch was organized, as I found out later from my new friend Patty Malan, the stake Relief Society president, many were concerned that this change would be looked upon as segregation, as the white members' pushing us out. But it did not feel like that to me. When the branch was organized and we began holding our own Relief Society and had our own presidency, I was ecstatic! I thought, "All right! This is where I belong." It wasn't separation that I was looking for. It was identification. To do that, we had to be nurtured in separation, like the olive branch in Jacob 5 that was dissected out and transplanted and then grafted back into the true vine. That is what happened to us. We were given opportunities to work in callings we would never have had on the hill. We took root.

I still had to work on my attitude. You know in some churches, people only come to church and sit and listen and go home. So we had to learn in our Virginia Avenue branch that when you gave somebody your word that you were going to do something, you did it. But when I first got my calling as Relief Society president, I was too militant. My approach was, "Sister, if you sign up for cookies, you better bring cookies! And if you ain't there with them cookies, you better get somebody else to take your place, but I want cookies!" That was my attitude. I had to change.

After a year or two, we were moved to Temple Hill, where we now meet. In the ten years that I have been in the Church, I have changed and I also have seen great change in the attitudes of other people, especially in the Church leadership. I am so grateful for those who were sensitive to me and who helped me find my family history and see that the gospel is for us all. For the past five years, we have put on a black Latter-day Saint history program in Oakland. We had maybe three or four people the first year. The next year more came, and then the year after that so many came we didn't fit in the room. So now we have the interstake center with its big gym and kitchen. Last year we cooked blackeyed peas for days. We made fried chicken, cornbread, sweet potato pie, and peach cobbler. We put that together with some talks and some good gospel music. Seven hundred and fifty people came to this event, most of them white members from all over the Bay area.

There was no logical reason for me to believe what the missionaries taught me, but I know that I do. I know that there is something greater than I am. I am thrilled to know that I have a Mother in Heaven and that I can talk about her and don't have to be ashamed. I was so worried when all I heard about was a Father in Heaven. When I found out that there was a Mother in Heaven, I knew that things would get done and it was going to work out all right. I believe with all my heart that God lives and that Jesus Christ is his Son and that this church has a part of scripture that is important because it makes the gospel plain, puts it on a level that I can grab hold of.

When I made my commitment, I made it to Heavenly Father. When I am down and things don't work out right, I remember that. Inevitably something happens, someone calls, I get a letter, or I hear a voice in my head saying, Betty, continue, you are going the right way. I have to go on. Sometimes when I don't feel well, sometimes when I don't want to, sometimes when I have to serve people that I don't agree with and I don't like, the voice tells me to keep going because I am going the right way, no matter how high the climb or rough the mountains. And my journey is filled with beautiful resting places along the way. I do not profess to be perfect, but I am determined to progress in the righteous direction I've found. If I continue to correct myself, the fruits of my labors will someday speak for themselves. In the meantime, I struggle.

Diversity in Zion

KATE L. KIRKHAM

As members of The Church of Jesus Christ of Latter-day Saints, we are, as of April 1992, well over eight million strong worldwide. If someone you know is going on a Spanish-, Russian-, Greek-, Cambodian-, or Mandarin-speaking mission, that person may never leave the United States. Within the boundaries of this country, the gospel is taught in sixteen languages. There are other differences among us besides language. The 1981 United States and Canadian demographic survey of Latter-day Saint families reveals that 68 percent of Latter-day Saints are married. Less than half that number are married to members. Of those married to members, only 19 percent—or about one-fifth—have a temple marriage and young children at home. So if you have been married in the temple and have children at home, you are part of less than 10 percent of the total Church population. Obviously, diversity in Zion is not the future of the Church. It is already here. Our diversity also includes differences in the identity we acquired at birth—ethnicity, age, gender, race, and culture—plus differences we acquire throughout our lives—educational, geographical, marital, and so on.

Across our diversity, we share similar resources as Church members. Though not all Church materials are available in all 137 countries where the Church has established roots, the Church does a remarkable job of translating materials. What's more important, the blessings of the Spirit are abundantly available to all who seek, no matter where we are.

In the Doctrine and Covenants 59:3 we read, "Yea, blessed are they whose feet shall stand upon the land of Zion." This scripture raises an interesting question. Whose feet will stand in Zion? People only from

Kate L. Kirkham is an associate professor of organizational behavior in the Marriott School of Management at Brigham Young University. Her primary research interest has been race and gender dynamics in the workplace. She serves on the Relief Society General Board.

the Western Hemisphere? People thirty-nine and under? People with incomes over fifty thousand dollars a year? Men only? The scripture goes on to specify the Zion community as those "who have obeyed my gospel; for they shall receive for their reward the good things of the earth, and it shall bring forth its strength. And they shall also be crowned with blessings from above, yea, and with commandments not a few, and with revelations, in their time—they that are faithful and diligent before me." (Vv. 3–4.)

So whose feet? Each of us who has been faithful and diligent. No matter who we are or where we are, each may follow the two central commandments to love and serve God "in the name of Jesus Christ" and to love our neighbor as ourselves. (D&C 59:5–6.) Zion has more to do with the condition of our heart than the circumstances of our surroundings.

Zion is the pure in heart. President Gordon B. Hinckley, in a 1985 conference address, stated, "I have looked into the faces of tens of thousands of LDS saints. Their skins are of varying colors and hues. But their hearts beat as one with testimony and conviction concerning the truth of this great restored work of God. . . . Their languages have been many, but they have spoken as with one voice in testimony of divine and eternal truth restored to the earth."[1] In Moses 7:18, we find an additional description: "And the Lord called his people Zion, because they were of one heart and one mind, and dwelt in righteousness; and there was no poor among them." My intent here is to nurture our desire to learn from and better manage our diversity as we seek to become one people pure in heart and in God's service.

Focusing on our diversity is both a means and an end. It is an end in the sense that focusing on it helps us to value difference. It is a means in the sense that it moves us toward something greater—a fully integrated community. Those who focus on diversity just for diversity's sake often miss the opportunity to connect us back as a part of the community and thus tend to experience diversity as fragmentation and segregation. Actually, the focus on differences can ensure that all of us are both unique as individuals and a part of the community. We might think of a mosaic, with each piece of tile contributing to the whole design. Each of us is a very distinct and important piece of that mosaic. In our contribution to the overall design, we should be distinct as well as attached to one another.

Some of our differences in that mosaic we cannot change. We were born with them. Other differences do change. Most of my examples will focus on the fundamental differences of race and gender. Sometimes I hear, "I don't see any race or gender differences. I just see human beings." The person who says to me, "I don't think of you as a woman, Kate," probably means that he is not stereotyping me because I am a woman. I hope he doesn't mean that there isn't anything about me that indicates I am one. Yes, we are all human. It is good to get beyond the negative view of differences that result in stereotyping, but it is even better to see the positive value in *both* our differences and our similarities as human beings. We need to appreciate both the means and the ends we are seeking: to acknowledge the positive aspects of diversity and to build a Zion community. We also need to know that the mosaic of our congregations requires the very important grouting cement of the Savior's love for each of us and our love for each other.

So what do we do about difference? Some want only to focus on the positive aspects by promoting cultural awareness, for example. Some want to focus only on the negative aspects, such as racism and sexism, that result from how we are treated because of our differences. Both approaches are important. Three tasks will help us do both as we manage diversity in our wards, organizations, and communities: demonstrating the value of diversity, learning how to integrate, and seeking to be a community of faith.

DEMONSTRATING THE
VALUE OF DIVERSITY

First, we each need to demonstrate that we value those who are different from us, even in their absence. In my class at Brigham Young University on diversity and discrimination, we invite several guests over the course of the semester to share with us their experiences. This year we invited guests with differences from the majority of us in sight, in hearing, in race, and in physical movement. One common thread emerged: each felt compelled to learn about the majority world. The blind person felt compelled to learn about the seeing world, the deaf student to learn about the hearing world, the African American student to learn about those who were white. At the end of the class, I asked the students who were majority group members, "Do you feel compelled to learn about worlds of experience other than your own? What motivates those of us who are comfortably in the majority? What might compel us to learn about someone whose life experience is different from our own because of race, gender, or physical abilities?" In the Church, we could answer charity. We should expect Church magazines to carry photographs of members of different nationalities, races, and gender, even if most subscribers are of one race. We should expect a building to have access for everyone, even if no one in the congregation currently needs a wheelchair.

Are racial jokes okay if no one racially different is present? Are put-downs of women or sexual jokes okay in all male groups because no women are there to be offended? No. Neither are jokes about men in women's groups okay. We need to honor the value of difference, even if no one is present who represents that difference. The value of diversity depends upon what we believe and where our heart is and what we attend to. When we value diversity, we seek out and learn those things that prepare us to be a better member of a worldwide community. We confront each other. We coach each other. A student visitor who came in a wheelchair said that he often goes to restaurants with friends. If there are four of them to be seated, the server or hostess will say, "I have three people and a wheelchair." He would prefer they said, "I have four people, one of whom is in a wheelchair." That taught me a lesson about the little insensitivities we can all contribute to unknowingly.

We would learn not just because it is the *correct* thing to do, but because we *value* others in our worldwide Latter-day Saint community as much as we value ourselves. In 1887, when Sarah Kimball, president of the Salt Lake Fifteenth Ward Relief Society and a founding member of the Nauvoo Relief Society, sensed that conversations and comments made in Relief Society work meetings were alienating some members, she urged the sisters to recognize that "when we get older we get very sensitive." She asked them to take care not to offend but also not to take offense where none was intended. "We must govern our sensitiveness with judgment," she pleaded. She felt that the sisters had "wounded each other's feelings" unknowingly. Her encouragement "to cultivate good feelings toward each other" must have met with some success. Recorded in the ward Relief Society minutes that year is this note of praise: "The wool was picked without the merits or demerits of neighbors being discussed."[2] If diversity were valued, we would all, like Sarah Kimball, be coaching each other, constantly exchanging information about how to include everyone and make each one feel welcome.

There are reasons other than our own interests to value diversity. We have been asked to do so. In Alma 5:30–31 we read: "And again I say unto you, is there one among you that doth make a mock of his brother, or that heapeth upon him persecutions? Wo unto such an one, for he is not prepared, and the time is at hand that he must repent or he cannot be saved!" We must learn to listen to the needs of others.

So what do "others" want? (And let us remember that each of us is someone else's "other.") The authors of *Workforce America!* compiled a list of what a diverse group of employees said contributes to comfortable, supportive workplace relationships. They had asked respondents, "What would increase the level of comfort and decrease the tension between people of diverse background when they interact?" Here are a few of the answers:

Both older and younger employees wanted "more respect for their life experiences" and "to be taken seriously." Women wanted to be recognized as equal partners and supported by their male colleagues. Men wanted women to perceive them as allies and not as the enemy. People of color wanted to be valued both as individuals and "as members of ethnically diverse groups." They hoped to establish more open relationships with people of other races while they also hoped to have support in the fight against racism and colorism. White people wanted to have their ethnicity valued and to build relationships with people of color. "Differently abled people" sought greater focus on their abilities rather than on their disabilities.[3] If we listen to the needs of others, we are likely to find we have more feelings in common than we had supposed.

Part of the task of valuing difference falls on those of us who *are* in the minority: we need to claim the right to be different and be present. For example, after my first two semesters here in Utah, I felt very discouraged. I was a minority—a single woman employed as a BYU faculty member. People were focusing on my difference with stereotypic comments, and I contemplated not coming back. When I spoke about my feelings and intentions with a non-Latter-day Saint friend in Washington, D.C., he was appalled. His response puzzled me.

"Why are you so surprised that I'm thinking about not going back?" I asked.

"Just a minute. Aren't you LDS?"

"Yes."

"Don't you believe in the doctrines?" He knew a lot about the Church and enumerated a number of tenets central of our faith, to which I replied, "Yes, all those things are true."

"Well, you have to go back then," he said, "because your very presence calls forth an opportunity for others to be more Christian."

My first response was sarcastic, "Thanks for sharing!" But as I thought about it, I realized he was right. What he was saying to me was, "You have the right to be present. You are a member of the community you value. Be present and enable others to learn from your experience — and you from theirs." So even though at times being in the minority may be painful, I believe in the right to be present and to contribute to the community.

Rosabeth Kanter documented an interesting social phenomenon: when someone in a group is markedly different, the differences among the similars are less noticeable.[4] The group focuses on the dissimilarities between the dominant group and the contrasting member. For instance, a married woman has many similarities with single women, but in a gathering of singles, the lone married woman's differences will be more noticed. This *contrast effect* can block community building because it prevents the group from seeing the diversity among majority members. The first task of creating community is to value the diversity of our members.

LEARNING HOW TO INTEGRATE

The second task is to achieve real integration. Though the term *integration* has become linked primarily with race relations, its dictionary meaning is to bring all parts together into a whole. Integration is achieved when all people are fully contributing in their communities and wards — not just being present but being unified. Let me outline two basic requirements that can help our congregations achieve fuller integration: build a common framework (road map) for discussions, and know what to look for in behavior.

Building a common framework requires that we realize and pay attention to what happens to people at three different levels of experience: as individuals, as members of a group, and as part of an organization. This basic framework can function as a guide. Each level must be considered in arriving at integration. The individual level concerns our one-to-one relationships, our daily associations, the quality of our conversation as we interact in our congregations. To focus on this level, ask yourselves: Am I careful about language? Am I comfortable with someone who is very different from me? Can I speak about my own experience rather than just interview others about theirs? Can I listen to others' experiences rather than just telling my own?

At the group level, we look for patterns in our interactions. What happens to people who are alike by group membership even if they are different as individuals? Being aware at this level means paying attention to effects we may not intend. For instance, in a meeting where there are many more men than women, the course and style of the meeting can be determined by more than just the individual differences in manner or personality of those present. In groups, men and women converse very differently. Gender differences affect such particulars as who selects the topic and who interrupts whom. Even the type of questions asked vary based on the patterns of interaction we have learned as men and women. This does not mean that all women—or all men—are alike. But we are concerned about the norms that tend to surface in group interactions. When we watch the contributions of men and women to a group task, we can observe pronounced differences and learn how to communicate more effectively.

I was once the only woman in a meeting. Each time I commented, no one in this particular group responded to my suggestions or added comments, and I began to feel invisible. Finally one man restated something I had said earlier; his restatement of my idea met with immediate acceptance. Another man then spoke up to note that I had made the same suggestion much earlier. After the meeting, he told me that he had been watching the interaction patterns: at the individual level, some of the members' ideas had been accepted and some had not; some ideas that lacked clarity had been restated by another person. He saw, however, when he watched the dynamics between women and men in this group, that the first requisite to being heard was not clarity of presentation but gender. Although I would not have known this, my ideas were clearly stated. He wanted me to know that he was willing to discuss the pattern he had observed with his male colleagues. One-on-one interactions are not the same as the patterns that emerge in groups. That is why we need to be aware of what happens at both levels.

At the institutional level, seeking integration means evaluating ways of doing things—policies, programs, and practices—which may be more traditional than helpful as ward populations change. The questions relevant to this level focus on how members are asked to be involved in their ward organizations. How are men involved in Primary? How are women's business talents utilized? What callings do singles hold?

Negative interactions and inadvertent exclusion at any of these three levels will block integration. At the individual level, the negative expression of difference is prejudice, literally "to prejudge without sufficient data." Many of us think that if we don't feel prejudice, that is enough. If I am not prejudiced, then I am not causing the problem. This is true in part, but it also helps to know what to aim for beyond the mere absence of prejudice. A bishop might say, "I am not prejudiced against women. I am equally concerned about both the young women and young men in my ward. I love them both." And yet, every time he speaks of the youth, his stories are invariably about Young Men activities only. As he claims, this behavior may have no connection to any feeling which would be regarded as a prejudice toward the young women. Or a Relief Society president may say that she isn't prejudiced against Mexican Americans. And yet, no Spanish-speaking person in her stake or ward has been called to a position because she believes there is not a large enough Hispanic community in the area to warrant it. So an individual may not be prejudiced but still act in a way that contributes to someone's feeling excluded.

At the group level, we need to be especially careful. External identifiers such as race, gender, and marital status are focal points around which a lot of experience can accrue. For instance, when I first came to Brigham Young University in 1978, there were few women in faculty positions in my college. People often assumed I was from the word processing center, the office support area staffed only by women. The first time someone asked me to "photocopy this," I was polite. I introduced myself. I said I was a faculty member and told the person how to contact the word processing center. The second time it happened, I was again pleasant. I think I was pleasant about five times. But, after the fifteenth time of having someone ask me to run some paper to the copy center or request, "Would you help me get this copied?" I began to lose patience. One day I needed to talk to the department chair. His office door was open so I stepped in. The man standing in conversation with him turned to me and said, "Here, dear, would you photocopy this?" Well, I lost it. "Not now, not ever!" was the gist of what I said. To this day I can remember the surprise on his face as he backed up, looking askance at the department chair, probably wondering why he was hiring such surly women.

So who was wrong? The collective effect of others' behavior rebounded all on him. Was that fair? No—but we were both in the right. I was right in having lost patience with the continuing assumption that because I am a woman, I must be the photocopy person. That was the sixteenth time in two weeks! He was right in assuming that I was a little oversensitive for what he saw as *one* mistaken assumption. This cumulative effect happens a lot. Members of our congregations who belong to racial minorities tell numerous stories of unknowing assumptions the majority race make. An African American male watches white Church members extend a hand to shake hands with others and yet walk by him—smiling but not reaching out to shake his hand. These minor slights add up, and add up, and soon someone gets "touchy." We don't know each person's intent—which is often good—but we should watch for behavioral patterns that result in exclusion.

We also experience this cumulative effect as women in the Church. A Relief Society sister told me, "You know, it is one thing not to have your announcement put in the bulletin, it's another to have a scheduling problem, it is another not to be notified of a weekly meeting, it is another to be in the meeting and not be allowed to speak, it is another to speak and have no one hear." Over time these unintended slights and her frustration accumulated. When she was finally released, she felt that she had earned the reputation of being "hard to get along with." But to her mind, she had changed because her ward priesthood leaders were so "hard to get along with."

Third-party observers who intervene and clarify such situations can be peacemakers. My department chair, for instance, immediately said, "You don't realize how many times she gets asked to photocopy." Someone who sees the pattern affecting the disgruntled Relief Society sister might say, "You don't understand how many times she has not been included in decision making that affects her calling." Blessed are the peacemakers. Whenever we can, we need to help the dialogue happen. We need to converse about our differences and about patterns of behavior we observe that may or may not match intentions.

Valuing diversity does not mean adopting a particular political viewpoint. I've seen both liberal and conservative members of a congregation ask about the experience of those who are different. How do the Korean members feel here? Are the ward party activities fun for singles as well as families? I've heard a newly married elders quorum president ask, "What should I know about the sisters in the ward who are over sixty?

What should I be aware of?" People inquire, not out of a political agenda but out of a community of caring. This concern is the first step toward achieving a fully integrated community.

The second requirement is to avoid behavioral traps that undermine our effort at integration. Examples will vary from ward to ward, but let me provide a few from my own experience. When I lived in the East, I worked with Girl Scouting. Leaders in the regional Girl Scout program became aware of the racial and ethnic diversity of young girls of membership age. They talked about inviting more minority girls into the Girl Scout program. Unintentionally, they spoke and acted as if the organization belonged to the white girls who were already members and that through "out-reach" efforts they hoped to invite others into the organization. Discussion focused on the minority girls' behavior: Why weren't they more interested in the organization? If they do join, what changes would have to be made to accommodate them?

Gradually the thinking of the leaders progressed. A major shift occurred as they began to ask themselves, "Who really owns Girl Scouting anyway?" The answer is all girls. The program actually belongs to all girls and not just those who are currently members. Girl Scout activities, pictures in program materials, leaders—every aspect of the organization should provide evidence that all racial and ethnic groups jointly "own" the organization. With this change, the discussion focused more on the behavior of those currently in the organization. What were current members doing that might be barriers to all girls feeling that this was their organization? When perceptions of ownership changed, so did the membership.

Sometimes I overhear conversations that make me wonder, "Whose ward *is* this? Does your ward belong to a particular social set or economic class or gender? Do we focus only on changing the behavior of those not there? A ward belongs to all those in the boundaries (or visiting)—not just the active. Those who are the current leaders do not "own" a ward. When a ward's priesthood and auxiliary leadership or activities reflect only the interest of one racial or ethnic group of members, we send a message. When current leaders talk most comfortably with others of the same social class, marital status, ethnic group, gender, or activity level—even though they are polite to all—we send a message. They establish an in-group and may also communicate a false image of ownership.

The gospel principles belong to all. The ward is a place of worship and nurturing to all. If we currently hold leadership positions, we must ask as often about what we are doing that prevents others from being there as we ask about what others are doing that prevents them from coming to "our" ward. We must see this difference to better see the whole.

We make a mistake if we think about diversity as an agenda rather than as continuous learning. Knowing of my concern, some people will say to me, "I did diversity." And then they'll tell me about having included single women in a Relief Society lesson, or scheduling an event for the widowed women in the ward. These efforts are worthwhile, but the "I did diversity" mindset can also be a behavioral trap. Instead, we need to conceive of diversity as a continuous dialogue about who we are and who others are and about all that we have to learn from one another. This means continuous awareness at all levels, not just the short-term activity.

Doctrine and Covenants 58:15 speaks of "unbelief and blindness of heart" as sins. These are compelling descriptions of another trap that can prevent us from reaching a Zion community. Unbelief and blindness of heart affect not only our faith but also our relationships. If we disbelieve someone's experience, or if our hearts are blind to what another has been experiencing, we will be unable to reach that wholeness that is the community of Zion. We need to look past our own experience. Let me give you an example. Minority group members report over and over again that when they describe something offensive that happened to them as a result of an ethnic, gender, or other difference, the response will be, "Are you *sure* that happened?" or "I've never seen that." Depending on their mood, the person disclosing feelings will either give up — "Oh, come to think about it, maybe it didn't" — or else feel doubly irritated — "Of course it happened!" Dialogue will not occur when our first words are disbelief or when our hearts are blind to how others have been hurt.

Another trap that shows up in our behavior is to confuse intent and outcome. Although it is helpful to state your intent — I didn't mean to be offensive, I didn't mean to be racist, I didn't mean to be sexist, I didn't mean to be insensitive — we also need to hear what others experience and not keep repeating our intent. As one manager put it to me, "Well, Kate, a statement about intent is probably good only once, right? Because if I listen to a complaint and then keep doing what offends, I can no longer claim I have good intent." Good point.

We are also in a trap when we think that the way to achieve unity is to avoid airing any differences. We need to be willing to talk about our intent and evaluate outcomes in conversation – and not just privately with those who are like-minded. The elders quorum president might ask the single person who didn't show up because he felt uninvited, "I don't want to send a message again that the ward party is for young marrieds only. Please tell me what part of my announcement gave that impression." We need to have places where all can come to talk about their reactions, feelings, and life experiences. Ideally, our wards should be one of those places. Despite our different identities and circumstances, our common task is to grow spiritually. What better context to share our frustrations and hopes and to appreciate who we are.

CONTRIBUTING TO
A COMMUNITY OF FAITH

Once we understand the value of diversity and learn how to acknowledge differences and integrate, the third essential task is to contribute to a community of faith. To do so, we need to know what we're looking toward, what a Zion community looks like. To find that out, we need to do a couple of things. Not only must we look past our differences and find our similarities but sometimes we must also look past our similarities and acknowledge our differences. Consider, for instance, a Relief Society presidency discussing homemaking meeting. Suppose this presidency has many similar interests, ideas, and values; they have known each other quite a while. The education counselor hesitates to bring up a different idea about homemaking that she heard from some of the employed women in the ward. She doesn't want to spoil their sense of unity or infringe on the homemaking counselor's stewardship. She doesn't want to be the different one in the group. She herself is not sure how to relate to the employed sisters and approves of the status quo. And yet if she looked past their similarities in thinking and brought out a different viewpoint, the exchange might better serve all women in the ward.

On the other hand, it's also important not to assume differences that set up unnecessary barriers. For instance, I have been really blessed because my sister and her wonderful Spanish Fork neighbors don't think of me as a category: "Oh, here comes Diane's sister, the Ph.D person we can't talk to." Instead, when I visit, we share wonderful stories. They've even complimented me on my cooking – a once-a-year event.

I share with them a wonderful sense of finding the similar but recognizing our differences without putting down or distancing each other.

In our communities of faith, women have many ways to help each other as women. Our experiences, our circumstances, and our opinions differ, but the language of charity can be a common ground. I have a very good friend whom I treasure. She's extroverted; I'm shy. She's dramatic; I'm quiet. She's provocative; I'm more analytical. She'd take on the whole Church and change everything about it, including who had the priesthood. I'm going to take on a couple of things in my ward if I can. We're very different sisters. But one thing we have never said to each other is, "I'm right, you're wrong." Or, "I don't want to hear what you have to say." We have shared our disagreements. We have shared our differences over strategies. We have faced off in a room and said, "I don't believe that's the way to go about it." But we have never said, "I'm right, you're wrong" or "I don't care about you." Whenever we part, we have said what is in our hearts, which is, "I love you." I could not feel more treasured than I do in that relationship. And yes, some days I could not feel more different from anyone than I do from that friend. But I treasure our relationship.

We have an enormous opportunity now as women in the Church to say, "I love you, and how you think about things and how you care about things are important to me." In doing so, we bridge over all of our different opinions, all of our struggles, all of our challenges, all of our different circumstances and choices. We need to hold in common our standards and hear differences of opinion. I have asked that we value differences, learn to integrate, and contribute to a Zion community.

But what do we do when our difference is not being celebrated? Certainly, ego can play a part in that. Let me explain. I can hear Latter-day Saint Metropolitan Opera star Ariel Bybee sing and be astonished at her phenomenal ability, her vocal range. I can celebrate that wholeheartedly, because I'm nowhere close to it. But when somebody that's almost like me gets something that I want but don't get, it is a little harder to celebrate difference and value her gifts. It takes work, but we need to develop the capacity to watch others excel and rejoice in their excellence without feeling diminished by their accomplishments. Our salvation from such envying may be to know that all have the same challenge, namely to consecrate who we are and all that we have in service to God and to building a community of Zion.

We are *all* to be true disciples of Christ. As much as we are a part of worldwide diversity, we are also one — not one in speech, or dress, or custom, but of one heart and one in his service. As Nephi assures us, "He inviteth them all to come unto him and partake of his goodness; and he denieth none that come unto him, black and white, bond and free, male and female; and he remembereth the heathen; and all are alike unto God, both Jew and Gentile." (2 Nephi 26:33.) Paul summarized, "Ye are all one in Christ Jesus." (Galatians 3:28.) My experience, personally, professionally, and organizationally, is that each of us can do wonderful things that will encourage others to be and feel more a part of our community. We ourselves will learn in the process. When we demonstrate the value of difference, really work for integration, and seek to achieve the community of faith that we will call the Zion community, we will find resources and opportunities beyond what we currently think possible to bless the lives of others, and in return, we will know life more abundantly.

NOTES

1. Quoted in "A Thought from the Scriptures," *Church News,* 28 Sept. 1991, p. 16.

2. Jill C. Mulvay [Derr], "The Liberal Shall Be Blessed: Sarah M. Kimball," *Utah Historical Quarterly,* 44 (Summer 1976): 220.

3. Marilyn Loden and Judy B. Rosener, *Workforce America!* (Homewood, Ill.: Business One Irwin, 1991), pp. 76–77.

4. Rosabeth Kanter, *A Tale of "O": On Being Different in an Organization* (New York: Harper & Row, Publishers, 1980).

Women and the Law:
A Matter of Perspective

CHERYL B. PRESTON

Last week my children came home from school with a story you may have heard: the wolf's version of *The Three Little Pigs*. According to the wolf, it isn't his fault that wolves happen to eat little animals; wolves were made that way. If candy bars were cute, cuddly, had warm brown eyes, and were named Wilbur, humans would be labeled "big, bad" too. He has a point. Also, the wolf didn't go out looking for trouble; he only wanted to borrow a cup of sugar from one of his neighbors for his sweet old granny's birthday cake. The neighbor pig was too busy shaving to come to the door right away. And then the wolf's terrible cold got the best of him – poor, sickly wolf – and he finally let go with a mighty sneeze. Now, he points out, it would be an insult to all the starving wolves in China to let a perfectly good ham dinner go to waste just because the pig's demise was caused by his own terrible sneeze in the direction of a clump of straw where this pig (obviously not the brains of the litter) had decided to set up housekeeping. You can imagine how the rest goes. To the arresting officer, the wolf's guilt was so apparent that no judge or jury was necessary, and the wolf was thrown in the slammer.

This is a silly story, but it is also very true. Differences in perspective do change the facts, and if we assume the law is the process of applying just results to the particular facts of each case, changing the facts changes the law.

I came to Brigham Young University to teach banking and finance law. Academics have the rare luxury of doing scholarly and philosophical

Cheryl B. Preston, an associate professor of law at the J. Reuben Clark Law School at Brigham Young University, teaches banking and finance and women's issues in law. She and her husband, Stan Preston, are the parents of three children. She serves as a Compassionate Service/Social Relations teacher in Relief Society.

research. One day as I opened the legal literature indexes to "Banking," I found myself drawn to the last alphabetical topic heading—"Women." I was amazed to find so many entries on this subject, especially on how understanding and attending to the perceptions of women might change the law. Of course, I began to read. I was enthralled.

I entered the legal profession at a time when, and at a place where, there were almost no women. For many years I worked as the only woman attorney in a Salt Lake City firm. I then went into banking—which is worse. I read on those pages in the library so much that explained and validated my experience, my questions, and my sense of fundamental difference. And then as I read on, I began to see how much I had longed during those years for women, for my sisters, for what we can give and share together.

My research suggests that the life experiences of many women are different from those of men. In fact, the reality of women's lives is sufficiently different in many court cases to largely reconfigure the dispute.[1] For instance, does the fact that women are significantly more likely to be the victims of sexual violence cause women to read into unwelcome romantic advances an element of fear not experienced by most men? What does this mean for Title VII,[2] hostile workplace environment, cases?

Last year, the influential Ninth Circuit Court considered whether the offense taken by a woman working for the IRS was reasonable. The woman had repeatedly received unwanted attention, requests for lunch dates and after-work activities, and love letters laced with sexual implications from a male co-worker. One three-page, single-spaced letter included language such as: "I have enjoyed you so much over these past few months. Watching you. Experiencing you from O so far away. Admiring your style and elan."[3]

Courts faced with such questions have looked at evidence of perceptions, including one study in a similar workplace environment where 75 percent of the men indicated that they would find such attention and love letters flattering and innocuous. With nearly exactly reverse numbers, 75 percent of the women stated that it would be offensive and dangerous.[4]

The standard for more than 150 years used in determining the reasonableness of offense taken in tort-based cases has been the proverbial "reasonable man," described by an English judge in 1933[5] as "the man on the Clapham Omnibus"[6] or "the man who takes the magazines at home and in the evening pushes the lawn mower in his shirt sleeves."[7] I learned this standard. Since I came back to teach law school, responsible textbooks no longer teach the "reasonable man" standard; they now use the "reasonable person" standard.[8] The Ninth Circuit concluded, however, in the love-letter IRS case mentioned above, that the standard in a case with a woman victim must now be the "reasonable woman standard."[9]

Other courts have not been as enlightened. Many current court decisions have been disturbing for me and my students in the gender and law class. These cases tell me that the legal system in many ways denies women full participation in the abundant life. Read the following facts and see what you think.

The first case involves a rape. The court's opinion was brought to me by a student who believed he had, after considerable research, finally come across a case in which a man was unjustly convicted of rape. We had read about several cases in which the jury refused to find rape, suggesting that the women had "asked for it."[10] He believed he had found the reverse injustice. Sensing a game was afoot, I sat down to read his case.

The dissenting judge believed the woman must have consented because she was almost as tall and almost as heavy as the man. Though the man was armed, the judge dismissed the man's weapon by saying, "To anyone observing the fragile, delicate and meager size of the 'knife,' it is glaringly apparent that the 'knife' was inadequate to be used as a weapon of force or as a threat for rape."[11] For support, the judge cited trial testimony that the knife, although sharp, was only two inches long. Surely this woman, he concluded, could have escaped had she wanted to.

I wasn't the complaining witness in this case. I like to think I wouldn't have gone with this man to his car. But my life experiences are not so far different that I cannot imagine what it must feel like to be far from anyone who can hear my screams and looking down the glimmering blade of a two-inch knife. Was "escaping" such a reasonable option?

Several other cases deal with women who tried to escape. One woman seeking a divorce in Utah in 1987 was found by the district judge (at the time there were no women district judges in Utah) to be unworthy of the custody of her children or of alimony.[12] The judge stated, "I have difficulty finding where this [husband has] done anything wrong, other than slapping her. Maybe that was justified. . . . [H]e struck her on the one occasion when he was what appeared to be highly provoked."[13] The undisputed facts at the trial were that the husband's physical attack on that occasion was sufficient for her to "crumple and pass out."[14] As a side issue, not deemed worthy of mention by the judge, on the night she returned home from the hospital after surgery to correct infertility, the husband had insisted on physical relations against her will.[15] Fortunately, on appeal the Utah Court of Appeals reversed the judgment and ordered a new trial.

Since that case, almost six years ago, one hopes there has been a great deal of enlightenment on women's issues, especially domestic violence. In an opinion released 23 March 1992, the Utah Court of Appeals again had to reverse a male district judge's decision on a domestic violence issue.[16] A Tooele woman who had been beaten often during her eight-year marriage had some seven months before her court appearance received injuries so serious she had to seek medical care and reside in a protective shelter. She finally advised her husband that she intended to seek a divorce. He threatened to kill her if she served him with divorce papers. She sought a protective order prior to serving him.

The judge denied her request, saying, "I understand that you may be in fear, but this is an improper use of the protective order." This isn't, he specified, what "we call imminent fear."[17] Essentially, the judge advised her to file for divorce and then seek a restraining order in the divorce proceedings, if there was a problem. So much for a stitch in time. Fortunately, she tried another judge who granted her request so she didn't have to gamble her life on her ability to get protection after serving divorce papers. Several other women in Utah have not been as lucky, including Nadalie Noble, who was shot in front of the Park City Albertsons after serving her husband with divorce papers accompanied by a protective order.[18]

These cases were particularly disturbing to me because they came out of Utah courts. It would be easier for me if I could dismiss much of the law I read as being generated by inner-city situations, far removed from the Wasatch Front, and decided by judges with no understanding of family values. But that is not true. Utah is not exempt from domestic violence nor free from gender-biased courts. It is important to understand that this happens in Latter-day Saint communities.

Domestic violence cuts across all social, religious, and educational lines.[19] Women are more likely to be injured by their husbands or boyfriends and more likely to be killed at home than in any other single risk of accident.[20] The Utah Task Force on Gender and Justice chaired by Aileen Clyde[21] determined from interviews with women that domestic violence continues to thrive because women so fear the economic consequences of leaving a husband that they convey unwittingly the message of captivity—they are bought and purchased, unwilling to escape, and unable to fight back. They are selling their physical well-being for room and board for themselves and their children. Unfortunately, their fears are not unfounded.

On 18 September 1991, the Utah Supreme Court considered the divorce of Dr. and Mrs. Martinez.[22] They were married after high school. During the next fourteen years, he attended college and medical school and completed his internship. She had three children. On the very threshold of his new career, the couple divorced. The trial court divided the couple's minimal property roughly equally, awarded her three hundred dollars per month child support and limited alimony for five years—unless she remarried. On appeal, the Utah Court of Appeals attempted to fashion a remedy that would, in addition, give Mrs. Martinez some of the benefit of his medical degree and career. The Utah Supreme Court reversed.

Although at one point the highest Utah court indicated that some other method might be found to be more equitable, note this court language: "Mrs. Martinez did not contribute financially to her husband's medical education.... Mrs. Martinez ... earned a very minor amount of income for a short period which was used for family expenses.... The recipient of an advanced degree obtains that degree on the basis of his or her innate personal talents, capabilities and acquired skills and knowledge. Such a degree is highly personal to the recipient.... In short, we do not recognize a property interest in personal characteristics of another person, such as intelligence, skill, judgment, and temperament."[23]

The one woman on the court dissented, stating that the court's opinion does not adequately address the "termination of a marriage in which one or both spouses have sacrificed in tangible and intangible ways, foregoing income, accumulation of property, an enhanced standard of living, and the educational and career-development opportunities of one so that the other might acquire a valuable and prestigious professional degree."[24]

The students in my class struggle with how they as lawyers can use law to protect their traditional sisters' choices. Although they have chosen to pursue professional studies, they want a legal system that will put our money, as a culture, where our mouth is: they want a legal system that will protect the high percentage of women who may someday be displaced homemakers.

A displaced homemaker is a women whose primary career for a substantial period has been the care of children and home and who is then basically fired from her career because of widowhood or, much more likely, divorce. In 1989 Utah had more than seventy-seven thousand displaced homemakers.[25] Many, if not most of them, are not well suited to enter a competitive workplace where women, whatever their reason for working, are disadvantaged.

This situation affects children as well as women.[26] A study conducted out of Utah State University in a rural Utah community found that on the average, divorced women and the minor children in their households experience a 32 percent decline in their standard of living in the first year after divorce. Their former husbands, in contrast, experience a 73 percent rise in their standard of living.[27]

Although no statistics for LDS Church members are available, in Utah almost half of the children living in female-headed families fall below the poverty line, which means that 82 percent of all the families in Utah living in poverty are single mothers with children.[28] This same group makes up 95 percent of the families in Utah receiving public assistance.[29]

I was fascinated by a March 1992 report in the BYU *Daily Universe* of a speech given by Bryce Christensen, director of the Rockford Institute Center on the Family in America.[30] He suggested that families are breaking down because many women are offended by two ideas: one, that women might be economically dependent on men, and two, that men and women have different roles. The response that came to my mind was a statement made by Helen Keller in a 1915 *New York Call* article entitled "Why Men Need Woman Suffrage": "Please do not misunderstand me. I am not disparaging chivalry. It is a very fine thing—what there is of it. The trouble is, there is not enough to go around."[31]

Wouldn't it be a wonderful world where every woman who chose to devote herself full time to children, family, and home could safely assume that the bare economic necessities would be provided for her and her children, at least to the extent that they are available to her children's father? I know many women who are willing to be economically dependent on a man while they pursue a career in motherhood, but the statistics on child support delinquency suggest there are significantly fewer men willing to commit that support for a lifetime.

Reality tells us that many women are working because they absolutely must work and that many of our next generation must depend on the wages of these women for survival. Unfortunately, the work force is not very supportive of women, whether or not they are the sole support of children.[32] These domestic violence and support cases and the feminization of poverty don't directly involve me; my circumstances are different. But when I read them, I am struck by the fact that these are my sisters, and I can't help but see myself as I imagine their faces. My life tells me what it is like to look up at a man on an elevated bench, with a flag at each hand, and the seal of state behind his head, as he is telling me that I should wait and see if a man—who had beaten me severely for eight years—would actually carry out a threat to hurt me again, or telling me that I had "provoked" being knocked unconscious.[33] I hear the message in the Martinez case: he got a medical degree because he had the "innate personal talents, capabilities, . . . intelligence, skill, judgment and temperament" to acquire one; while you were a wife, a homemaker, and a mother, no matter that you had every capacity to earn a medical degree as well but chose instead to support him and raise children. He should be rich; you should be poor.

People ask me why I spend so much of my time reading and studying the social ills represented by rape and poverty and discrimination against women. Doesn't it just make me angry? Doesn't it take me away from achievements in the traditional fields of law, the kind that the established power system is more likely to reward? Sometimes I wonder. But then I think, if, when I teach law, if, when I write about law and legal theory, I can help increase understanding or do a tiny part to shape the law or the future lawyers in my classes so that even one of my sisters, one of my daughters, is spared the humiliation and pain of confronting an unjust legal system, then I will be well rewarded.

I see great hope in that direction. Our daughters will assume equal justice before the law in a way our mothers have never known.

Other women like me who study law believe that enlarging our understanding of the facts is not enough. Isn't it possible that women derive knowledge, approach problem solving, and, in many respects, rank relative conceptual values differently from men? If so, then isn't it possible, if not likely, that the very core foundations of legal theory rely on only part of the truth of experience, that part known by men? Women were entirely absent in legal decision-making during the centuries when the foundations of our law were being laid.

While it is easy to see the potential for a gender issue in rape and divorce, isn't it possible that the very rules that decide what is an appropriate issue for the legal system to consider, what procedures are necessary to bring it to a resolution, and what evidence is admitted may have gendered implications? Legal rules frequently require difficult policy balancing between competing values. If women define values and balance them in even slightly different ways, women law-makers may reach different ultimate solutions. In dealing with the complex legal issues of our time, don't we want all the input, all the ideas, all the contributions we can get to reach the most fair, the most workable answers?

Imagine a pile of blocks on the floor. Here come two preschool children, Sam and Louise. Studies suggest that one of them will likely build a tall tower with the blocks. He will see how many of them he can stack singly on top of each other. The other, meanwhile, will be constructing a lower profile creation, maybe one that is long, like the Great Wall of China or a row of dominoes, but more likely, two or three blocks tall with each block balanced on two others. We will assume that most Sams are male, but not all; some females may share the characteristics of Sam. We will also assume Louise represents most females, although many men may be Louises.[34]

Now imagine that Sam and Louise have grown up, completed law school, and wear the robes of judges. The blocks are no longer square and oblong, blue and green; they are concepts. Let's put names on them. For instance, one block is CERTAINTY. Certainty is an important value in the legal system. People subject to laws want to be able to predict whether their actions will comply. The competing block might be FLEX-IBILITY. Two other blocks are labeled RIGHTS and RESPONSIBILITIES. Two others are INTERPERSONAL RELATIONSHIPS and ECONOMIC VALUE.

Sam may approach these blocks by stacking them in a linear, hierarchical order, where one is clearly more important than another. He may put CERTAINTY right on top. He is likely to give a higher position to RIGHTS and ECONOMIC VALUE. Louise, meanwhile, might be busily making a multilevel, interdependent structure where FLEXIBILITY, RE-SPONSIBILITY, and INTERPERSONAL RELATIONSHIPS are more prominent. In fact, Louise is much less likely even to identify abstract principles such as FLEXIBILITY or CERTAINTY in problem-solving. Sam may compartmentalize principles, identifying them as separate blocks that can be objectified and evaluated apart from the particular individuals involved in a legal dispute. Louise may identify more closely to the unique context of the legal dispute, claiming to see pain and people rather than principles and abstractions.[35]

Which building is better, Sam's or Louise's? Both are strong, both are beautiful, and both are necessary to solve the difficult problems confronting the law — and life. Each has something to teach the other. We have been relying on only one approach for far too long. While, I believe, the price for this oversight has been paid primarily by women, men too have suffered from the limitations of that single approach.[36]

One of my sisters, one who knows much about the silence of women, left for me her words to describe my thoughts: "Today women are demanding rights that tomorrow nobody will be foolhardy enough to question. . . .

"The dullest can see that a good many things are wrong with the world. . . . [N]ew tools are needed for the work. Perhaps one of the chief reasons for the present chaotic condition of things is that the world has been trying to get along with only half of itself. Everywhere we see running to waste [a] woman-force that should be utilized in making the world a more decent home for humanity. . . .

"It is indisputably true that woman is constituted for the purposes of maternity. So is man constituted for the purposes of paternity. But no one seems to think that incapacitates him for [full participation in] citizenship. If there is a fundamental difference between man and woman, far be it from me to deny that it exists. It is all the more reason why her side should be heard."[37] So concludes Helen Keller in her 1915 suffrage article. We now have the vote and a million other doors open to us; what are we doing to tell about our experience as women? Are we using what leverage we have to say that traditional male definitions of success are no more valuable than other definitions? That success in relationships is as important, maybe more so, than a fat paycheck, a mobile phone, or a key to the executive washroom? That we need not be the same to be as valuable in society and as valuable to our Heavenly Father? Women have demonstrated that they can play the games men play in the workplace, the market, and the halls of power. Now we need to teach of another way.[38]

"The dullest can see that there are a good many things wrong with the world [and] new tools are needed for the work." We, as women, owe to the world what we have learned and what we know—things only we can contribute. We can no longer afford to be silent.

NOTES

1. See, generally, Katharine T. Bartlett, "Feminist Legal Methods," 103 *Harvard Law Review* (1990): 829; Nadine Taub, "Thoughts on Living and Moving with a Recurring Divide," 24 *Georgia Law Review* (1990): 965.

2. 42 U.S.C. §§ 2000e et seq. (1988 & Supp. 1992).

3. Ellison v. Brady, 924 F.2d 872, 874 (9th Cir. 1991).

4. Arthur S. Hayes, "Courts Concede the Sexes Think in Unlike Ways," *Wall Street Journal*, 28 May 1991, B1, B5.

5. Hall v. Brooklands Auto Racing Club, [1933] 1 K.B. 205, 224. See discussion in Guido Calabresi, *Ideals, Beliefs, and Attitudes in the Law* (Syracuse, N.Y.: Syracuse University, 1985), p. 23 n. 94.

6. Clapham is apparently a small town in England where the average citizen rides the bus to and from work. Nancy S. Ehrenreich, "Pluralist Myths and Powerless Men: The Ideology of Reasonableness in Sexual Harassment Law," 99 *Yale Law Journal* (1990): 1177, 1210 n. 125.

7. Hall, 1 K.B., 224. Obviously, the "reasonable man" is not just male, "he is also a property owner (owns a home); he is not wealthy (mows the lawn, rides the omnibus); he is well-informed (reads periodicals); he knows how practical problems are solved (can roll up his shirtsleeves); and he has the responsibility for maintaining a household on a small budget (mows his own lawn)." William J. Wagner, "Book Review," 35 *Catholic University Law Review* (1985): 335, 341 n. 21, reviewing Guido Calabresi, *Ideals, Beliefs, Attitudes, and the Law* (Syracuse, N.Y.: Syracuse University Press, 1985). This fellow in shirtsleeves seems likeable and inoffensive, but "[b]y ignoring the existence of people who have no lawn to mow and cannot read or afford to buy magazines—as well as the existence of those who hire someone else to mow the lawn for them— this image promotes the illusion that we are all the same, rendering invisible those who differ from the 'average' person it creates. Similarly, by gendering its central figure, the symbol also excludes those whose role has never been defined in terms of lawn-mowing and magazine-reading [or riding the bus to work], but rather in terms of cooking, nurturing, and cleaning." Ehrenreich, "Pluralist Myths and Powerless Men," pp. 1212–13.

8. See, e.g., W. Page Keeton, et al., *Prosser and Keeton on the Law of Torts*, 5th ed., 1985, §§ 32 at 174 n. 5.

9. "We realize that there is a broad range of viewpoints among women as a group, but we believe that many women share common concerns which men do not necessarily share. For example, because women are disproportionately victims of rape and sexual assault, women have a stronger incentive to be concerned with sexual behavior.... Men, who are rarely victims of sexual assault, may view sexual conduct in a vacuum without

a full appreciation of the social setting or the underlying threat of violence that a woman may perceive." Ellison v. Brady, 924 F.2d 872, 879 (9th Cir. 1991).

10. I have always been curious why those who rip off luxury cars, burglarize ostentatious homes, and snatch designer-label purses don't get excused from criminal charges by alleging that the rich "asked for it" by flaunting what they have. A particularly unfortunate example of the tendency to assume rape victims "asked for it" arose in an October, 1989 Florida rape trial. When interviewed after returning a "not-guilty" verdict, jurors expressed disapproval of the victim's attire. The foreman was quoted as saying, "We all feel she asked for it." During the trial, a Georgia woman testified that the same man had kidnapped and raped her in September. In the Georgia incident, the man had reportedly told the victim, "It's your fault. You're wearing a skirt." Ironically, after being acquitted in Florida, the same man pleaded guilty to a third rape and was sentenced to life in prison. "Rape Guilty Plea, After Acquittal," *New York Times*, 7 Dec. 1989, B21, col. 6. After he began serving his sentence, he was convicted of attacking a fourth woman in Georgia and received an additional fifty years' prison sentence. "Florida Rapist Convicted in Separate Attack," *Washington Times*, 2 Apr. 1990, A7.

11. People v. Phillips, 536 N.E.2d 1242, 1261 (Ill. App. Dist. 1989) (Pincham, J. dissenting). Judge Pincham begins his dissenting opinion by quoting a seventeenth-century English judge: "[Rape] is an accusation easily to be made and hard to be proved, and harder to be defended by the party accused though never so innocent." And why do women bring these false rape accusations that Judge Pincham believes "victimize unwary males and plague the criminal justice system?" They are supposedly "instigated because of embarrassment, humiliation, remorse, fear, anger, disgrace and revenge." Id. at 1247.

12. Marchant v. Marchant, 743 P.2d 199 (Utah App. 1987), quoting the district judge's findings and the trial transcript.

13. Id. at 207.

14. Id. at 203.

15. Id. The 1991 Utah legislature finally repealed language in the Utah code that excluded from the crime of rape an act against a spouse, even if the persons involved were only technically married. Utah Code Ann. §76–5–402 (1990), amended (1992 Supp.). The wisdom of the existing statutory exclusion was raised in vivid terms just before the 1991 legislative session when David Coon escaped from a Salt Lake correctional center to attend a hearing in which his estranged wife was seeking a divorce. Brian T. West, "Was Suspect Husband or Ex? Rape Charges Hang in Balance," *Deseret News*, 11 Nov. 1990, B1. After the court orally granted the divorce but before an order was signed, Mr. Coon abducted her from the courthouse parking lot, threatened her, beat her, kicked her, and raped her repeatedly. Although the question of rape charges at first seemed hung up on the "tricky legal question" (id.) of whether the couple were still married, the district attorney eventually relied on the oral divorce order to prosecute Mr. Coon for rape. Brian T. West, "S.L. County Says Divorce Was Final, Files Charges in Kidnapping," *Deseret News*, 29 Dec. 1991, A8. What if the abduction had happened on her way into the hearing, rather than after it?

16. Strollo v. Strollo, 828 P.2d 532 (Utah App. 1992).

17. Id. at 533.

18. See "Kamas Woman Shot, Killed Outside Park City Market," *Deseret News*, 28 Feb. 1990, B1; "Summit Man Charged in Death of Wife," *Deseret News*, 2 Mar. 1990, B5;

"Summit Man Faces Trial in Slaying," *Deseret News,* 7 Mar. 1990, E2. The husband, who was later convicted of murder, said he was "distraught because his wife's divorce complaint demanded child support, the family home and custody of their four children." Ellen Fagg, "Kamas Man Convicted for the Murder of His Wife outside Grocery Store," *Deseret News,* 16 June 1990, B1. Mrs. Noble's friends reported the failure of the legal system to prevent her death. A Salt Lake police officer did note that his records reflected a call to the police from Mrs. Noble on 11 February 1990; however, the responding officer reported "the incident as 'no case.' " Mrs. Noble apparently did not see it as "no case;" she fled to the YMCA Women in Jeopardy shelter. Dave Condie, domestic violence program specialist at the Utah Department of Social Services, responded to Mrs. Noble's death with regret and hope: "In the past month, we've had four female deaths in Utah [resulting from domestic disputes]. Nadalie's death may be a way of giving the message to everybody: We've got to take this seriously." Ellen Fagg, "Foreboding Chain of Events Preceded Woman's Slaying," *Deseret News,* 18 Mar. 1990, B1.

19. "Love One Another: The Prevention of Abuse," in *Come unto Me: Relief Society Personal Study Guide 3* (Salt Lake City: The Church of Jesus Christ of Latter-day Saints, 1991), p. 132.

20. Steve Gerstel, "Violence Remains Leading Cause of Injuries to Women," *United Press Int'l,* 2 Oct. 1992, A19, citing report of the Senate Judiciary Committee, "Violence against Women: A Week in the Life of America."

21. "The Utah Task Force on Gender and Justice was established in November of 1986 . . . to inquire into the nature, extent, and consequences of gender bias as it might exist within the Utah court system." Utah Task Force on Gender and Justice, *Report to the Utah Judicial Council* (March 1990): S-1.

22. Martinez v. Martinez, 818 P.2d 538 (Utah 1991).

23. Id. at 539, 541, 542.

24. Id. at 544 (Durham, J. dissenting).

25. Joel Campbell, "Homemaking Isn't Secure Job, Report Shows," *Deseret News,* 3 Nov. 1989, A2.

26. Recent estimates are that two-thirds of children born in the 1980s will experience their parents' divorce. Larry L. Bumpass, "What's Happening to the Family? Interactions between Demographic and Institutional Change," 27 *Demography* (1990): 483, 485. Approximately 90 percent of children will remain with their mothers following a divorce. James A. Sweet and Larry L. Bumpass, *American Families and Households* (1987), 269. In Utah, one in twelve children live in families headed by a single mother. *Utah Children: Key Facts about Children in Utah* (1991), p. 2. Fewer than 60 percent of divorced mothers with children are awarded child support payments; and only half of those receive the full amount. Sara McLanahan and Karen Booth, "Mother-Only Families: Problems, Prospects, and Politics," 51 *Journal of Marriage and the Family* (1989): 557, 560. Only rarely are such payments enough to support a child, and in addition, a quarter of award recipients never receive any payments at all. Greg J. Duncan and Saul D. Hoffman, "A Reconsideration of the Economic Consequences of Marital Dissolution," 22 *Demography* (1985): 485, 488.

27. Barbara R. Rowe and Jean M. Lown, "The Economics of Divorce and Remarriage for Rural Utah Families," 16 *Journal of Contemporary Law* (1990): 301, 324; see also Martha Minnow, "Consider the Consequences," 84 *Michigan Law Review* (1986): 902.

28. Joel Campbell, "Children among Utah's Poorest," *Deseret News,* 3 Nov. 1989, A2.

29. Joel Campbell, "Women in Poverty," *Deseret News,* 3 Nov. 1989, A2.

30. Bryce Christensen, as quoted in Kathleen O'Leary, "Utopian Ideals Weaken Family Ties," *Daily Universe,* 26 Mar. 1992, p. 3.

31. Reprinted in *Between Ourselves: Letters between Mothers and Daughters,* ed. Karen Payne (Boston: Houghton Mifflin Co., 1983), pp. 152–53.

32. Sexual harassment, discrimination in hiring and promotion, refusal to accommodate caregiving demands are only part of what women face in the workplace. For the children they support, pay disparity may be the biggest issue. Nationwide, 75 percent of all workers paid less than the minimum wage are female. *Statistical Abstract of the U.S. Bureau of the Census* (1989). In Utah, the wage gap means a woman earns fifty-four cents to the dollar earned by a Utah male, compared to the national average of seventy-four cents to the dollar. Sen. Karen Shepherd, D-Salt Lake City, as quoted in Cheryl Smith, "Women as Legislators, Women as Employers Striving for Balance in Public Policy," *Utah Business,* Aug. 1991, p. 13. According to a 1989 report from the Utah Department of Employment Security, the median income of Utah women with three years of college is less than the median income of Utah men with a seventh-grade education. According to the U.S. Department of Education, Utah ranks last in the percentage of women enrolled in its colleges and universities. At 41 percent, Utah is at the bottom again when it comes to women university graduates—ten points below the national average. Elaine Jarvik, "Ranking: Utah Trails in Number of Women Enrolling, Graduating from State's Colleges and Universities," *Deseret News,* 28 Dec. 1990, C2.

33. What does *provoke* mean, anyway? The *Deseret News* reported a case in Salt Lake City where the man was "provoked" because tin foil was put over the Thanksgiving turkey. "Turkey Sparks a Battle in S.L.," *Deseret News,* 1 Dec. 1991, B4.

34. See Carol M. Rose, "Women and Property: Gaining and Losing Ground," 78 *Virginia Law Review* (1992): 421. Preliminary studies verify that moral reasoning may follow gender-linked patterns. See Rand Jack and Dana Crowley Jack, "Women Lawyers: Archetype and Alternatives," 57 *Fordham Law Review* (1989): 933; Nona Lyons, "Two Perspectives: On Self, Relationships, and Morality," in *Mapping the Moral Domain: A Contribution of Women's Thinking to Psychological Theory and Education,* ed. Carol Gilligan, et al. (Cambridge, Mass.: Harvard Univ. Press, 1988), 3; Carol Gilligan, *In a Different Voice: Psychological Theory and Women's Development* (Cambridge, Mass.: Harvard Univ. Press, 1982); cf. Lloyd Burton, et al., "Feminist Theory, Professional Ethics, and Gender-Related Distinctions in Attorney Negotiating Styles," *1991 Journal of Dispute Resolution,* p. 2.

35. Professor Carrie Menkel-Meadow draws similar comparisons between the reasoning patterns of men and women as applied to legal analysis in her article, "Portia in a Different Voice: Speculating on a Women's Lawyering Process," 1 *Berkeley Women's Law Journal* (1985): 39, 46–58. She draws primarily on the work of Carol Gilligan; see note 34, above.

36. Legal scholars are exploring ways in which legal principles in a wide variety of fields may be enriched by the increased involvement of women. The jurisprudential perspective contributed by women is called in much of the literature the "ethic of care." See, e.g., Leslie Bender, "Changing the Values in Tort Law," 25 *Tulsa Law Journal* (1990): 759; Suzanna Sherry, "Civic Virtue and the Feminine Voice in Constitutional Adjudication," 72 *Virginia Law Review* (1986): 543; Eric T. Freyfogle, "Vagueness and

the Rule of Law: Reconsidering Installment Land Contract Forfeitures," 1988 *Duke Law Journal* (1988): 609, 645.

37. *Between Ourselves,* 152.

38. I was struck in my most recent reading of the New Testament that the Jews just could not understand why the Savior did not come trailing the traditional symbols of power and glory they had learned to expect of rulers.

Men and Women
in Conversation

CHERYL BROWN

Information about differences between the conversational styles of
men and women comes out of two areas of linguistic study—conversational analysis and cross-cultural communication. In conversational
analysis, linguists look at how conversations work or, in the case of
many of us, how they don't work. In studying cross-cultural communication, we look at problems that sometimes result when people from
different cultures try to communicate with each other.

Let's start with some fundamental principles. One of these has to
do with basic human needs. Students of human behavior and development have long recognized that all people have two very basic needs.
One is the need for independence. Babies learn to sit alone, then walk
alone, then cross the street alone, then drive alone. Teenagers push for
freedom; and parents pull back, not quite ready.

Paradoxically, our other great need is for intimacy. We need to feel
closeness to others, the nearness of other human beings. This need has
been clearly and tragically demonstrated, as we have all heard, by the
infants in orphanages who wasted away and died, not because they
weren't fed and clothed adequately, but because they weren't held and
loved. The need for intimacy is real. So is the need for independence.

Sometimes we have a greater need for independence, and other
times we have a greater need to be intimate. At times the two needs
conflict: independence separates us from others, pushes others away;
intimacy pulls others close. We all must somehow balance these two
needs. Linguist Deborah Tannen compares the conflict to being like

*Cheryl Brown teaches at Brigham Young University as an associate professor in the
Linguistics Department and serves as associate dean of the College of Humanities. She
has been a ward Relief Society president.*

porcupines in winter. They try to get next to each other to get warm. But when they get close enough to be warm, their quills start pricking each other, so they move apart. Then they get cold again. Similarly, we try to get close enough to each other to get "emotionally warm," or intimate. But when we get close, our independence is "pricked." To feel comfortable again, we have to move farther apart. That is how intimacy and independence work within all of us.

Each individual has a different balance between the need for intimacy and the need for independence. Generally speaking, however, men seem to have a stronger need for independence and women a little stronger need for intimacy. These slight differences between men and women make a difference, as we shall see, in how men and women use language and how they converse.

Another general principle that clarifies differences between how men and women converse is that our culture influences the way we interpret things. By *culture*, I mean our individual family cultures as well as our societal group culture and our national culture. To illustrate how culture influences interpretation, let me talk about how national culture influences how far apart we generally stand when we are conversing casually. This distance will vary somewhat according to the size of the individuals in the conversation, but it will vary significantly according to the culture in which they were raised. Casual conversation in "mainstream" United States culture takes place with participants about eighteen to twenty-four inches apart. Our culture interprets this eighteen- to twenty-four-inch distance as "appropriate" for casual conversation. Closer distances are reserved for "intimate" conversations. Latin American culture, however, interprets an eighteen- to twenty-four-inch distance as "cold," a distance to be maintained with strangers, persons we don't know very well or don't trust. In Latin America, the appropriate distance for a casual conversation is twelve to eighteen inches. Because this same shorter distance is interpreted in the United States as being "intimate," North Americans would feel uncomfortable standing that close for a casual conversation. In various Latter-day Saint chapels in Latin America where there are North American missionaries, I have seen Latin American members or investigators move into appropriate distance (twelve to eighteen inches for him or her) to have a casual conversation with a North American missionary. The missionary doesn't feel comfortable in this "intimate" (for the North American) distance, and so steps back. Because this missionary is someone the member or investigator wants to talk to as a friend, the Latin American steps closer. The North American steps back. This conversational waltz goes on all over Latin America in our chapel foyers.

If I were twenty-four inches away from a Latin American, he or she would at some point wonder why I was being distant or cold. Because of culture, a Latin American would interpret that distance as cold; because of culture, I would interpret the same distance as friendly. How we interpret how far apart we stand from each other in conversation is only one of many culturally defined differences in interpretation. We are not even aware of what we are doing, what it is that is triggering our interpretation. Then we try to have conversations across these differences and don't understand why things don't seem to turn out as we hope or expect.

Now that we have established that cultures influence how we interpret things, let me propose that men and women grow up in different cultures and that language – conversation – comes to be used very differently by the two groups. Let me illustrate the differences in culture by showing how we are acculturated differently, how men and women grow up differently. Let's start with little boys.

Little boys usually play outside more, and the games they play are generally competitive, with winners and losers – cops and robbers, cowboys and Indians, Ninja turtles and "bad guys," baseball, and football. Boys' friends are the people they do things with. They like games that require teams and aggression. They also use language competitively and aggressively. For example, we have all heard the expression, "My dad is bigger than your dad." Though little girls may say this, it is usually male talk, little-boy talk. Boys establish friendships by joking competitively about who can do or say the "best" (often interpreted as most outrageous) thing. They also establish their social hierarchy – their status as independent individuals – in this way. Rap music, for instance, is an example of a male way to use language – to see who can be the most clever or who can deliver the most outrageous put-down.

I heard a wonderful true story about the way little boys often use language. Two four- or five-year-old boys were outside playing on some stairs. Two other boys about the same age came along, and the boys on the stairs said something rude like, "Go home!" Frightened, one little boy left, but the other boy stayed, saying, "Make me!" The three argued back and forth, and finally one of the boys on the stairs said,

"I'm going to get a gun and shoot you." The new arrival answered, "Well, I'm going to get a gun and shoot *you*."

At that point, a little girl wearing a cape came out of the door at the top of the stairs and said, "I'm Bat Girl, and I'm looking for Robin." One of the boys said, "I'm Robin." The little girl looked him over and said, "I'm looking for *another* Robin," and then went back into the house. The boys, still in the middle of their "I'm going to get a gun and shoot you" exchange, were nonplussed for a moment, and then the newcomer thought up something totally outrageous: "I'm going to get a gun and shoot you with poop." All three boys laughed hysterically and then went into the house as friends.

Boys typically use language and actions aggressively to establish vertical relationships, to figure out where they each belong in relation to the group and to each other on the "status" ladder. Language helps them demonstrate their independence and stature in handling themselves with regard to the social hierarchy. That is what boys do. The deacons that run in hordes through the cultural hall and terrorize the ward are another good example of this. They are simply acting like typical little boys.

Typical little girls also have groups of friends, but they usually have one best friend. They will be more likely to play indoor games without winners or losers—house, school, dolls, etc. Whereas boys are acculturated to use language to establish independence and status, girls are acculturated to use it to establish intimacy. Your best friend is the one to whom you tell your secrets. I once heard the story of a father who was very worried about his daughter because her best friend had hurt her feelings very deeply. The girl cried for two or three days, and the concerned father felt helpless. Then, one night, he found his daughter playing with her unkind friend. After the friend left, the father asked his daughter why she was playing with that friend again, when she had been so hurt by her. The daughter replied, "Don't worry, Dad. I'm not telling her any of my secrets." Women use language to establish and maintain intimacy.

Now, what happens when grown men and women, who have been acculturated differently, try to talk to each other? What happens when we come together and use language? We get different uses and different interpretations. For example, think for a minute about who talks most—men or women? The traditional belief is that women talk more. Studies have shown clearly, however, that it's a matter of where the talk takes place: men speak more in public, and women speak more in private. If you think about what we have been saying, you can understand why. It relates to our different cultures and our different reasons for using language. Men speak up in public because their status, their independence, their self-worth demands it. At group meetings, it is almost always the men who dominate the discussion. (I do have to say here that I don't think that this is necessarily so in Church discussions, such as in Sunday School classes, however. I have watched, and I have seen a pretty good balance of men and women among those speaking out. But at other public meetings, men will speak out much more.)

When men come home, however, they feel safe, unthreatened. With those close to them, those with whom they feel intimacy, they don't have to jockey for position; they don't have to find their place in the hierarchy or prove where they are on the social ladder. Therefore, they figure they don't have to talk. Instead, they come home and shut up. Then the women who live with them go crazy.

By contrast, women in large groups don't talk much because they don't see that as a way to establish intimacy. If you go to a public meeting, you are more likely to see women whispering to someone next to them than you are to see them speaking out. But, when they are home with the person they care about and feel close to, they want to talk. Silence to them is like being pushed away, excluded, kept out of secrets, punished. They don't understand their husband's silence, and their husbands don't understand their need to talk.

A friend of mine shared with me a delightful "Cathy" cartoon that illustrates what happens. Cathy and her boyfriend, Irving, are sitting on the couch. She is thinking about love, and he, of course, is thinking about sports. This is the way the dialogue goes:

Cathy: We need to talk, Irving.

Irving: We've been talking all day, Cathy.

Cathy: But we haven't really *talked* talked.

Irving: What do you want to talk about?

Cathy: I want you to *want* to talk about things.

Irving: I'll talk about anything you want.

Cathy: I want *you* to bring the subject up.

Irving: What subject?

Cathy: *Us!* Irving, the only time we ever talk about us is when *I* bring it up! I want *you* to bring it up!

Irving: What about us?

Cathy: I want you to bring up things between us that we need to talk about!

Irving: What things?

Cathy: AAUGH!!!

As Cathy walks off, disgusted, Irving asks, "Did all that count as talking, or am I still supposed to come up with something?"[1]

What can we learn so that we don't feel like Cathy all the time? First we have to start with some goodwill, our own goodwill. We have to start by trying to accommodate and understand the male point of view, and then later we can work toward the male understanding our point of view. We can learn from each other.

Let me suggest some specific ways to do this. To begin with, let's talk about how we can handle the issue of the quiet man at home. The first thing is to learn not to misinterpret, not to take offense when none is intended. For us, because talk establishes intimacy, we sometimes feel distant when a man is silent with us. We need to remember that for a man, speech is used mainly to compete or to establish his position. Therefore, when he feels safe, loved, intimate, he doesn't always feel the need to talk. The same silence that indicates distance for us may very well be for him the sign of the closeness we desire. We need to learn to adjust — to allow men to be silent and intimate, and then we can find ways to tell men that we need to talk (like Cathy was trying to do) and to teach men to talk to us in the ways we need if *we* are to feel intimate. Both men and women must give in one way or another to meet differing needs. We can learn together.

And what about talk in public? Here, too, we can learn not to misunderstand. Because public talk is for men competitive, a sign of independence, they consider it an individual's responsibility to enter the conversation. If someone has something to say, she or he will say it because, as an independent individual, status depends on it. So, when women in a group don't say anything, men assume they don't have anything to say. Sometimes they assume that the women are dumb — that because they don't speak up, they don't think. That is one way that men view what is happening.

On the other hand, because women believe talk is a way to build connections, to establish more intimacy among individuals, they feel the need to draw everybody in the group in, to give everyone a turn. I attended a meeting not long ago with about ten people that demonstrated this characteristic very clearly. Although there was one male in the group, most were women, and the women who were in charge of the meeting carefully distributed the speaking turns. Even though discussion was lively, I noticed that if somebody had been sitting there silent for quite a while, one of these women would bring that person in by asking, "What do you think?" That is a typically female thing to do. Another typically female thing to do is to view people who don't distribute turns or who continually speak up and take lots of time as domineering or egocentric, as destroyers of opportunities for better relations, greater intimacy among members of the group. Since men generally do not distribute turns, women often resent them for taking over conversations and frequently view them as self-aggrandizing and domineering, especially in public encounters.

So, women see men as domineering, and men see women as dumb. What can we do to change this dynamic? Once again, we have to start with ourselves. As women, we need to learn to speak up in mixed groups when we have something to say, to recognize how important it is that female points of view get heard. We need to understand that we not only have a right to speak but a responsibility. We also need to recognize always the importance of seeking the Spirit to be with us when we speak, so that we will speak in a way that will bless.

Men, when in mixed groups, need to learn to distribute turns and to ask for feedback. They need to be aware of who has spoken and learn not to assume that, if someone doesn't talk, that person has nothing to say. They, too, need to seek the Spirit so that they will not seem nor be domineering in conversation.

Now some men, for whatever reason, are more threatened than others when women do speak out. Maybe their attempts to establish status have not been as successful as they hoped. Maybe they have not had enough good experience with noncompetitive conversations so that they can see anything about conversations except the competitiveness of them. When you encounter someone like that, it's okay to recognize that it is not your fault—he is who he is and you are who you are. It is okay to be who you are.

My family background taught me this. I have six older and strong-willed brothers and three very bright older sisters. I never knew that I was outspoken. I simply did what I had to do to hold my own in my family, and then later I learned through experience outside of my family that I was considered outspoken for a woman. But from experiences in my family and later elsewhere, I can say that it is possible to be firm without being rude.

My experience has also taught me that how well we are listened to makes a great difference in the manner in which we speak out. We may need to learn to be very good listeners ourselves, but we also need to learn to help others learn to listen to us. As women, if we feel we are not being listened to in the way we desire, we individually may need to express that feeling. Then we can ask the person or persons who don't seem to be listening what we can do to change the situation. We can ask how we might express our opinions and feelings without making them uncomfortable. We can work to help men understand that if they don't listen to women, they are cutting off 50 percent of the points of view, 50 percent of the resources available to any group.

There is another area of talk, of conversation, in which men and women have differing interpretations. This has to do with responses to what has been called "troubles talk." All of us, both men and women, have troubles and needs to talk about them. Because women use communication to attain intimacy, we respond to "troubles talk" in ways that work toward intimacy; however, because men use communication to establish status, some of our responses to them appear to them to be put-downs. For example, if I am having trouble, I go to a female friend and say, "I am having the worst day." Because she is female, her response will at some point be something like, "Oh, you poor dear." Her response communicates that she understands my feelings and is my friend.

If a man is having trouble and goes to a friend whom he sees as a good friend and who sees him as a good friend, that friend would never respond, "Oh, you poor dear." Instead he would say something like, "Oh, that's no big deal. You can handle that," and then he would probably start talking about one of his own problems. This immediately allows the first man to think, "Hey, I am no less than this guy. Maybe this isn't a big deal. Yeah, I can handle it." The response has communicated that they are friends, equals on the status hierarchy. If a woman does that to another woman, the first woman feels she hasn't been understood. The appropriate response for a woman to make is one of empathy, sympathy, the "oh, you poor dear" type. Only after the first woman has had a chance to tell *all* she wants about her troubles might the friend say, "Oh, I've had a rough day, too," and then tell her own troubles.

Once we understand this pattern, we can understand what goes wrong when a man comes to a woman and says, "I've had a hard day" and she sympathetically responds, "Oh, you poor dear." That response communicates to him not only that he is incompetent, but that she, from a higher position on the status hierarchy, can judge and see how inferior he is. She is trying to be kind, and he feels put down. On the other hand, when a woman comes to a man and says, "I've had a hard day," and he responds, "Oh, that's no big deal. Let me tell you about my hard day," she feels that he hasn't understood at all, that he has treated her problems as trivial, and that, therefore, she has been put down.

We also differ in what we want from our "troubles talk." Generally, as women, we just want a listening ear attached somehow to a caring and understanding heart. Just talking things through helps us to figure them out. We generally are not seeking advice. If we get advice, especially early advice before we feel as if we have been thoroughly understood, we feel put down and go looking for a more sympathetic ear. Men, however, prefer the problem-solving rather than the listening approach. They offer recommendations and solutions and think matters are then taken care of. They don't understand why women keep talking about the problem. "We already discussed that," they say.

Also, when they bring up a problem, they are much more likely to be seeking advice. But we shouldn't jump in too early with advice either. Because we don't want to upset the status balance, a good response to a problem a man has just revealed is, "That sounds tough. What are you going to do about it?" If he has an idea, he'll tell us and might even ask for an opinion about it. If he doesn't have an idea, he might ask, "What do you think?" At either of those points, we can give advice without putting him down because we have established a relationship of equality. But we need to learn to give appropriate responses to him and teach him carefully to give appropriate responses to us. We also need to learn to be patient when we get an undesired response.

Deborah Tannen tells a good story about this point. She had been giving lectures and writing books for years on the differences in conversational style between men and women and, by living with her, listening, and reading manuscripts for her, her husband knew everything there was to know about the subject. One night she came home after having a particularly hard day, needing to talk, so she started pouring out the problem to her husband. Midway through her story, her husband burst out, "Wait, wait, wait! I know you don't want advice, but I *have* to say this for *me.*" He offered some advice and then, relieved, let her go on detailing more of the problem.

A good way to handle our differences, then, with regard to responses to "troubles talk" may be to set some ground rules, somewhat as Deborah Tannen and her husband did. We can say, "I need to talk about this, but I don't really want any advice. Please hold the advice for fifteen minutes or so, and then you can give advice if you want to." We can begin to work on our differences in this way. We can learn to affirm his capability to handle problems and give advice rather than sympathy. We can also help him learn to listen sympathetically to us as we talk about problems without offering unsolicited advice. We can help him learn that just telling him about troubles does not necessarily constitute a request for advice.

Clearly, men and women use language differently and to meet different needs—his is generally to communicate in such a way that his worth as an independent person is affirmed, ours is generally to communicate in such a way that we draw others close to us and affirm our membership in humanity. He is likely to communicate more in public and be more quiet at home; we are more likely to be quiet in public and to communicate more at home. He is likely to brush off the problems of his perceived equals as being "nothing"; we are more likely to treat them as being worthy of sympathy. In "troubles talk," he is more likely to give—and want—advice; we are more likely to give—and want—comforting murmurs. The same situations, different interpretations.

Understanding our differences is the beginning of making them work together for our good, of learning other interpretations. We can learn to value his ways to establish independence; he can learn to value our ways to produce intimacy. Together we can learn to value conversation and the voice of the Spirit which can help make us one.

NOTES

This chapter draws heavily on the work of Deborah Tannen, *That's Not What I Meant! How Conversational Style Makes or Breaks Relationships* (New York: Ballantine Books, 1986), and *You Just Don't Understand: Men and Women in Conversation* (New York: Ballantine Books, 1990).

1. Cathy Guisewite, "Cathy," syndicated comic strip.

Working as Partners

I attended high school in the San Francisco Bay area. My senior year I was elected student body president because I was the only candidate who figured out that in a half-white and half-black school, the blacks represented a lot of votes. I talked to the blacks in "their" cafeteria and tried to find out who they were, what they needed, and how I could meaningfully be of service to them. I was motivated by ambition; my behavior was calculated. But by the end of the day, I had learned an awful lot, I had made friends, and I had become much more aware. Some of those black students became my friends at school. I remember one day kidding around with them and calling them "brother" and referring to myself as a "brother" too until one of them set me straight. "Wait a minute, let's draw the line here. You're our friend, but you're not a brother," he said. Some lines are meant to be crossed; others are not. In any partnerships some differences can and must be dissolved, but others need to be respected as matters of essential ethnic and gender identity.

If women and men are to work together as partners, we must face and sometimes cross together all kinds of attitudinal, behavioral, and values borders. For me, partnership means working together in an open, honest, respectful, sometimes painful, persevering way. It is being willing to listen, confront issues head on, and learn from our experiences. Partnership is not condescension—treating others as subordinates or telling them only what they want to hear.

One of the most difficult partnerships to manage is the one between

C. Brooklyn Derr, professor of human resource management, chairs the department of management at the University of Utah and also serves as an adjunct professor at the International Institute of Management Development at Lausanne, Switzerland. He and his wife, Jill Mulvay Derr, are the parents of four children. He serves in the Church as a high priests group leader.

men and women, and gender is often only one factor. Other significant differences in any partnership include age, family and career stage, national culture, family-of-origin norms, styles and values, birth order, personality traits, ideas about success, education and occupational socialization, socio-economic status, religion, and more. Although gender is only one difference that must be managed effectively if men and women are to work as partners, it has become a central issue of the 1990s as more women are entering the workforce in traditionally male-dominated careers.

During the summer of 1970 when I was working in the South, I spoke with a single, working mother who was struggling to raise four children. She complained that her mother's generation had it much easier. A woman's life was easier in her mother's day because help then was very cheap. If you were of a certain social class, you could hire black servants for very little who helped raise your children, cooked the meals, and ironed the clothes. She wished for those days. It's easy to understand why this social inequity would appeal to her. But from the servants' point of view, the situation was intolerable. Clearly power is by nature conservative. No one in a position of power finds it easy to give it up.

Men have traditionally had power in the workplace. Women have not. And so we have had in most organizations during the last fifteen years what psychologist Ann Morrison calls the "glass ceiling."[1] Women entering large organizations do very well up to a certain point and then hit the invisible glass ceiling. They can't understand why the men keep going and they don't. Those who do make it through find themselves struggling to function in their new positions. As one woman explained, "We make it through the glass ceiling, and then we hit the brick wall, the male inner sanctum where it is really masculine and difficult." Men, not wanting to share their privileged position in the workplace, do not readily alter patterns to accept women into upper level executive positions.

Culture can also block effective partnership between women and men. Let me relate a shocking story from my own church experience.[2] My wife, Jill, and I have just spent two and a half years with our children in Switzerland, where I've been teaching at a large international business school. Our ward there was small, and everybody had three or four jobs. We felt needed, we jumped in, and we had a wonderful experience. The ward also had incredible cultural diversity. Members were Spanish,

Portuguese, Italian, Norwegian, Chilean, American, and a few were even Swiss.

The bishop was a Sicilian tailor, I was his first counselor, and his second counselor was French. Peter, a young Sudanese Church member, shortly after his baptism married a Swiss woman who was also a recent convert to the Church. He speaks English, and he's just learning French. When the bishop counseled with Peter, I was the translator. The last time we met with him, he had beaten his wife so severely with telephone cords and belts that she ended up in the hospital. The terrified wife had phoned the sister missionaries to come and physically intervene. This was the fourth such incident. The bishop, feeling totally frustrated, told Peter that his Church membership was on the line, that this was the end of the road, his behavior was intolerable. He told Peter through me that the next time anything like this happened, he would automatically be excommunicated. Peter replied, "How could you take this so seriously? All of the men in my tribe beat their wives. My father beat his three wives. My wife asked a certain question. I've been taught from the time I was a boy that when a wife asks that question, a husband should immediately beat her so that she won't ask again." The cultural gap between Peter's background and white Swiss or Sicilian or American Latter-day Saints is incredible.

Social science research almost always points out that culture is an extremely critical variable in differentiating people. I found that to be so in Switzerland. In another instance, when I taught MBA women students in Europe, women who came from a variety of different cultures, about the American woman's experience with the glass ceiling and the brick wall, several of them asked to meet me after class. "You know," they said when we talked, "we're really not so interested in the American woman's experience. It seems to us that American women can't get it together in an integrated way. They're so hung up about equality and not being feminine at work that they can't seem to put all the pieces together. We'd like to explore a different kind of model." Again culture proved to be a more critical variable than I had anticipated.

In Sweden, 85 percent of women work, but very few of them work in business. Almost all of them work in the public sector and in the professions such as law, medicine, teaching, and architecture. In Italy, study after study shows that Italian men will not work for a woman boss. That's where they draw the line. Women can come into the work force if they want, but they can't boss men. In Switzerland, schools make no provision for children during the one-and-a-half- to two-hour lunch period; working women must come home to prepare a big midday meal or hire a mother's helper to do that. In response to this cultural pattern, women work in meaningful part-time jobs in the morning and then come home and prepare the meal, or they prepare the meal and then go to work in the afternoon. In the Ukraine, where we also stayed for a while, women are on the go from five in the morning to eleven at night, because they do it all: work outside the home, cook, clean, and shop. In France, women take pride in being more integrated in the sense of being both professional and feminine in the workplace, but the women's movement there in some ways doesn't take place around career and paid work outside the home. Work for pay simply doesn't hold the same value for either women or men in France as it does in the United States. It's not the only way the French establish their identity. These eye-opening facts about cultural differences show how what we seek in a partnership may be more determined by cultural programming than we imagine.

The fact of cultural differences, however, does not mean American women's concerns are not vital and important to explore, because in this exploration we learn much about working as colleagues. We learn about how women in one cultural context try to change their status from that of wife, mistress, sister, and mother to that of full partner.

When I talk to American women about career patterns, as I do in my work, I find that these very talented careerists come from all sorts of places, from all walks of life. They have been in one place for a while, and then they moved on to something else, and then they went after more education, and now they're vice-president of such and such. Their career patterns depict lots of mobility, flexibility, and an impressive background of learning experiences.

Most men's career tracks are less complicated. To get promoted, you get on an escalator at age twenty-three and ride it up into positions of influence and authority starting at about age forty-two. You are dedicated to the organization and arrange your personal life, including working hours, travel, and geographical displacement, to meet the company's needs. You punch important "tickets," such as accepting and performing in the right jobs and getting what others consider essential job-related and educational experiences, and you develop mentoring relationships along the way. Traditionally, large organizations have built career paths that reflect these male assumptions. Childcare has not been part of the picture, a critical issue that almost all women have had to deal with.

But new demographics and new values in the work force may be changing this traditionally male orientation and opening important and more flexible career opportunities for women. Note what *Fortune* magazine had to say on 9 April 1991: "Japanese women are a relatively untapped labor source, but they must care for their dependent parents. Therefore, 9,000 new day care centers for the elderly are to be built by the year 2000 to encourage women back to work."[3] United States companies also are shifting management styles to survive in a suddenly very competitive global economy. Companies have to maintain quality or they're out of the global market. Corporations must have state-of-the-art technology or they're out of the game. An ethic of "customers first" and good service is absolutely critical to survival. These are the baseline requirements. But the most important variable for being productive and competitive in the nineties is people. Because of the baby bust that followed the baby boom, an incredible scarcity of talented people is on the horizon. Between 1995 and the year 2000, organizations will start to make every possible change to accommodate talent. Companies are already starting to look very, very carefully at underused, talented people. Who do you think pops first into everybody's mind? Women. Women's potential has never been adequately explored or put to use. Women are the single best source of underused talent for the late nineties and the twenty-first century.

Recruiting and retaining talented women requires offering them the option of more flexibility so all those who wish to can actively parent children. For instance, companies can no longer assume that talented women will come with total career dedication; it will be to the organization's advantage to offer flexible career management during childbearing and child-rearing years. It isn't possible to recruit and retain talented women while ignoring "biological clock" factors or childcare needs.

Not all women are interested in developing a career outside of the home, but for those who are interested or who must work, more opportunities will be coming along in certain areas of scarce talent.[4] These opportunities may be more flexible and will not force women or men to sacrifice or short-change family life for meaningful careers. For example, hierarchies, the standard organizational model for companies since World War II, will not predominate in business anymore. The kind of organization that will dominate in the future will be teams of people working close to the customers. Instead of line authority and bureaucratic controls imposed from the head office, local teams will function independently, directed mostly by vision, mission statements, a few control systems, and guidelines springing from corporate culture. The CEO's job will be to set the vision and manage the culture. In this situation, upper-level managers need more skills at working across boundaries and with specialists, and fewer skills working with bosses and subordinates. Command and control skills will be replaced by negotiating, coalition-building, inspiring, and facilitating. Businesses will no longer be hierarchies; they'll be circles.

In the 1990s, then, managers with people skills will be in great demand. Future leaders in these nonhierarchal business corporations need to be comfortable having more responsibility than authority. They must be skilled at building teams and networks, at working in high-performance teams across organizational boundaries, at communicating knowledgeably and persuasively with specialists, and at developing influence with peers, customers, and colleagues from other parts of the organization. Leadership is more likely to come from sources closer to the customer than from remote central hierarchies.

Women may be more adept than men at networking and working in these circular relationship organizations. They may be more naturally inclined towards teamwork and better able to "connect." I was once at a week-long executive training conference in Virginia where I was one of only two men. The workshops and sessions were all very verbal. These were articulate, bright women, and relationships were being built all over the place. At the end of the week, the other man and I got together and just pitched horseshoes. We didn't talk for about forty-five minutes. All of sudden he looked over at me and said, "Whoo! It feels so good to just do something and not have to talk about it!" Perhaps there were two women off somewhere playing ping-pong in silence, but gender studies indicate otherwise.

Women's ease and interest in relationships will serve them well in the future. The new customer-focused management structures of the 1990s are likely to be more circular, verbal, and feminine than linear and masculine. For instance, one of the most important skills for the nineties will be the use of intuition. Already worldwide studies have begun on how to teach men to use their intuition. As a woman professor from Stanford University remarked to me several years ago, "You know,

40 percent of our classes in engineering, business, and medicine, etc. are now women, and they are working effectively in what were traditionally male disciplines. And you know what? They also know how to use intuition." Intuition, networking, and negotiation skills are all advantages women bring to the nineties marketplace; whether those advantages are natural to women or are socialized traits remains to be seen.

Projected labor shortages and style changes are, then, making the recruitment and retention of valuable employees—both men and women—a key concern in the nineties. Another issue that will affect both genders is how they choose to define a career and, especially, career success. Traditionally, high-potential (HIPO) employees have been identified, selected, trained, and developed by the organization from a surplus of applicants. Now, as indicated above, new dynamics require leaders to study whether HIPOs should continue to be groomed from the outset as a small, select group or whether the opportunity to enter this group should be enlarged. How many managers of the traditional mold will organizations need in the future, and how many specialists and internal entrepreneurs will also join the leadership ranks? Should companies continue to "grow" their own top managers internally or concentrate on recruiting them from the outside? And is it even possible, given the projected wealth of opportunities for talented employees, to find and keep an adequate supply of future managers over a long period of time?

Another change that will benefit women who wish to work is a shift in employee values, and specifically a shift in how talented people are starting to define success, a new values orientation with which enterprises must cope. My research has revealed serious discrepancies between the traditional motivation programs of most companies and the actual motivations of most employees. For example, one 1978 study dealt with 150 very high-potential (HIPO) employees, hand-picked for this research by their organization as potential future leaders. Each was well positioned for success and seemed to be well motivated to pay the necessary price. Surprisingly, the research revealed that only 65 percent of these "high flyers" actually wanted top management positions. In other words, although their organizations saw all of them as HIPOs, one-third of them had other success agendas, including being willing to sacrifice movement up the corporate ladder for personal or job autonomy, for instance.[5]

One of the clearest trends in career development research is that, while young talented workers are serious about their work, Americans have begun to define success in broader terms. Definitions now include at least five markedly different career success orientations:

Getting Ahead. Individuals who hold the traditional view of career success want to move up the hierarchical ladder. They define success as more money, more power, and steady promotions—not just as ends in themselves but also as the means whereby they can accomplish their objectives.

Getting Secure. Many people, who constitute an unappreciated, largely unacknowledged but significant segment of the work force, have a "psychological contract" with the company. In exchange for hard work and unswerving loyalty, these workers expect lifelong employment, respect, steady advancement, and eventually a high-level job where their talents are used and appreciated. They are typically found in large, stable corporations, government agencies, and companies with a reputation for lifelong employment. They feel particularly threatened and even betrayed by downsizing and restructuring movements such as those of the 1980s when many middle managers and specialists lost their jobs after years of competent service.

Getting Free. Other people want personal autonomy and "space" at all costs. They willingly meet deadlines, work within budget constraints, and meet specification standards; but they want to solve problems their own way. Many go into the professions (such as doctors, lawyers, professors, scientists, and work-at-home specialists) or start their own businesses.

Getting High. Still other workers thrive on excitement, challenge, and perfecting the techniques of their craft. Money is a secondary motivation to the challenge of the work itself. *Getting high technicals* are driven by the desire to be challenged in their specialty, to perfect their craft over time. *Getting high entrepreneurs* yearn to undertake new ventures and seek the excitement of using their creativity to conceive and launch a new activity. *Getting high ideologues* get their kicks by pursuing a cause, one in which they deeply believe and which they feel will make a contribution. *Getting high careerists* include engineers, computer programmers, test pilots, courtroom lawyers, entrepreneurs, and even environmental activists.

Getting Balanced. People who seek to balance careers, personal relationships, and self-development work hard, pay their organizational "dues" and thrive on steady, predictable demands, not rush jobs and emergencies. They need meaningful work but pull back if work causes them to neglect personal and family matters. Getting balanced is a stronger trend, especially among young couples who assume dual careers and shared child-rearing responsibilities. As we are called upon to be very serious parents, spouses, and Church workers, this option may become an important alternative for LDS careerists.

This diversity of working styles and values will intensify during the 1990s and work to the advantage of both women and men who have strong family and church commitments. In the past workers felt great pressure to conform to a company's prevailing culture—usually the getting ahead value. In the talent shortage of the 1990s, more talented, highly successful workers will come to their careers with well-developed and diverse definitions of success and a new assertiveness about negotiating to meet their personal needs. While a particular company may need more of one type of worker than another, it will almost certainly encounter each type and must learn to recruit, manage, and retain all types effectively. It will be possible for talented men and women in the Church to lead more balanced lives, even though the organizational rewards may not be as great as for those who are devoted to the company's cause.

Organizational changes will also affect the Church. In the Church, three special considerations are important to keep in mind when talking about partnership not only between women and men but across cultural boundaries. First, the fast-growing international Church makes diversity a very real and complex issue. Our small ward in Switzerland reflects the situation in many wards and branches around the globe. In our Swiss ward, the unity that might come almost naturally to more homogenous congregations seemed unobtainable for a long time. Beset with conflict and misunderstandings, Church programs alone could not build unity, nor could priesthood leaders, nor admonitions from the pulpit.

The impetus for turning around this very frustrating ward experience came from two unexpected sources, the Primary and the sister missionaries. First, the ward saw modeled in the Primary children and their teachers unity and love for one another. Only in the sanctity of the children's organization were the words of the Savior amplified: "If ye are not one ye are not mine" and "Love one another; as I have loved you." (D&C 38:27; John 13:34.)

The second key to change was two sister missionaries who arrived in our ward in late 1991. To the consternation of the elders, they did not begin their missionary labors immediately. What they did instead proved far more effective. They fasted and prayed, talked and planned for the better part of a week. Then they emerged, filled with the Spirit and articulating the most simple of all themes, one directly revealed to them from the Lord: that their work should focus on exercising Christlike love, the most transcending of all forces and the one which is central to managing diversity in the Church. As we watched them minister to the less active members, rally the whole ward at Friday night socials, and strengthen and extend the fifteen or so people who made up the active core of the ward, we felt at each juncture their loving spirits. They taught us both directly and by example that love was the great equalizer. Once Sister Hess stood silent at the pulpit for a full five minutes while we all were refreshed in the spirit of love that she had asked us to experience. No other energy force could have moved a ward like ours forward. But as we accepted the atoning sacrifice of the Savior, put ourselves in his hands, and let his love work through us, long-standing feuds and grudges were resolved. Our small ward began to feel like paradise.

So the first key is to acknowledge and appreciate diversity and also to seek unity through love. Second is to recognize that the Church's partnership requirements differ from those of other organizations. Most religious organizations have a special need for authority, and, based on inspiration that comes to those in office, some unilateral decision making. Many European cultures are also quite comfortable with unequal power relationships. But in the United States one of the most constant critical issues for government is how we will implement our core cultural value of equality, not necessarily a high-order value for many other nations. Some LDS Americans, it seems to me, have difficulty believing that the Lord should operate through inspired authorities and hierarchical channels. Their antihierarchical instincts should not be surprising. By virtue of our founding principles, much of American life is democratic—open to dialogue and grass roots movements. Accepting that one's bishop, the Quorum of the Twelve, or one's Relief Society president are fallible human beings who are, nevertheless, guided and inspired spiritual authorities is a fundamental issue of faith for all Latter-day Saints, but especially for United States Saints.

Thus, the Church balances between a democratic and an authoritarian organizational structure. It creates and encourages autonomy and partnership while, at the same time, allowing for some divinely inspired unilateral authority. In practice, who could deny the democracy of a ward unit where members of all ages, persuasions, personalities, cultural backgrounds, and socio-economic classes are pulling together, involved in building the kingdom? Partnership also exists at other levels. Husbands and wives are asked to be complete partners in their earthly stewardship. In the temple, brothers and sisters stand together in the same robes of the priesthood and take similar vows of consecration.

Nonetheless, the third consideration about partnership between men and women in the Church is the special status of men as priesthood holders. Most active LDS Church members accept that all worthy males are ordained to the various priesthood offices and females are not. Most also understand that women through the temple endowment share in the priesthood and that there is a distinction between priesthood offices and priesthood. *Priesthood* commonly means "service" as much as it means "authority." Moreover, both men and women share Church callings that are equally demanding (and call for equal amounts of authority and responsibility).

If one accepts, as I do, that for the moment this administrative division is the way of the Lord, at some future time to be fully understood by us, and perhaps to change, then two aspects of this condition are important to remember. First, there is absolutely no reason for men and women to be anything but equal partners as they work in Church organizations. Nothing in priesthood doctrine in any way sets up superior-subordinate relationships but, rather, only encourages long-term and full collaboration. (See D&C 121:36–37; Ephesians 4:11–13.) All of us are under sacred obligation to fully use our talents to build up the kingdom of God. My own perception is that those Church leaders who use partnership rather than hierarchical models within their wards will reap the benefits of more internal commitment and complete involvement on the part of the members. Second, I believe it is also our sacred duty to accept the richness of our diversity, even when we don't always understand our differences — including gender differences. Jesus Christ is the model for both women and men, in large part because he is a perfectly integrated being who exemplifies both traditionally feminine and masculine characteristics. Nevertheless, "viva la difference" between women and men!

In actuality, we're diverse even as individuals; we have lots of roles.

I recently overheard some people commenting on the absurdity of the wedding of a female vice-president of their acquaintance. They felt the ceremony to be somehow demeaning in its iteration of traditional, marital roles. "We went to her reception, and there she was, this powerful figure, being a wife and standing next to her husband!" And I thought, How absurd! To think that people can't experience multiple roles or shouldn't fully utilize all of their diverse parts. We need to give each other a break. Marcel Proust said that the real voyage of discovery lies not in seeking new landscapes, but in having new eyes. If we want the spirit of partnership in our work and lives, we need sincerity, honesty, openness, and willingness to conflict and problem solve. We need to work together, to see each other with new eyes and value our differences. Through Christ we can welcome the richness of our diversity.

NOTES

1. Ann M. Morrison, Randall P. White, and Ellen Vanvelsor, *Breaking the Glass Ceiling: Can Women Reach the Top of America's Largest Corporations?* (Reading, Mass.: Addison-Wesley Publishers, 1987).

2. I have altered names and details to conceal the identities of the persons involved in this incident.

3. L. S. Richman, "The Coming World Labor Shortage," *Fortune*, 9 Apr. 1990, p. 47.

4. Basically, management specialists project that there will be three kinds of employees: *self-employed* (usually in service industries) who will enjoy, as today, some flexibility with some problems, such as lack of benefits; *scarce talent*, underused men and women, such as women engineers or other kinds of specialists, whom companies will bend over backwards to attract and retain; and lots of *easily expendable workers*, who may be more valued but who will have to work long hours, juggle their lives, and grind it out.

5. C. Brooklyn Derr, *Managing the New Careerists* (San Francisco: Jossey-Bass, 1986).

Index